THE PERE MARQUETTE RAILROAD COMPANY

AN HISTORICAL STUDY OF THE GROWTH AND
DEVELOPMENT OF ONE OF MICHIGAN'S MOST
IMPORTANT RAILWAY SYSTEMS

BY

PAUL WESLEY IVEY, Ph. D.

THE BLACK LETTER PRESS
GRAND RAPIDS, MICHIGAN
1970

Second Reprinting 1978 by Black Letter Press
L.O.C. 75-120135
SBN 0-912382-03-1

Art Work by Robert Nelson

PUBLISHER'S NOTE

Ida Amanda Johnson's THE MICHIGAN FUR TRADE and Paul Wesley Ivey's THE PERE MARQUETTE RAILROAD COMPANY were published by the Michigan Historical Commission in 1919. Both books were printed in the same volume. Ida Johnson's book was printed in the first half of that volume. Dr. Ivey's book occupied the second half. Even though the two books were printed in the same volume, each book did not receive separate pagination. The present reprinting of THE PERE MARQUETTE RAILROAD COMPANY is a photographic reproduction of the first edition. Thus, since Dr. Ivey's book occupied the second half of the 1919 edition, the first page of the present text is numbered 207.

The editors wish to gratefully acknowledge the assistance they have received in the preparation of this edition from Mr. Donald Chaput and the Michigan Historical Commission.

PREFACE TO THE SECOND EDITION

This book by Ivy remains the most detailed study of any single railroad company in the state. However, Frank Elliott's *When the Railroad Was King* (Lansing: Michigan Historical Commission, 1966), and more recently Willis Dunbar's *All Aboard! A History of Railroads in Michigan* (Grand Rapids: Wm. B. Eerdmans Publ. Co., 1969), summarize and in the case of Dunbar expand on most facets of Michigan railroading.

In the past decade articles on the Duluth, South Shore, and Atlantic, and the Saginaw, Tuscola, and Huron have appeared in *Michigan History*. There is a vast literature on state and local railroads, and the best collection of primary and secondary materials is in the Transportation Library at the University of Michigan.

Other outstanding collections include the Engineering Section of the Detroit Public Library, the Michigan State Library, Lansing, and the State Archives at the Michigan Historical Commission, Lansing. The State Archives has rich collections of railroading photographs.

This reprinting of the *Pere Marquette Railroad* will enable many individuals and libraries to obtain a solid railroad history of an important Midwestern line. Hopefully, other valuable studies of individual railroad companies will be published in the near future.

Michigan Historical Commission
Lansing, 1970

CONTENTS

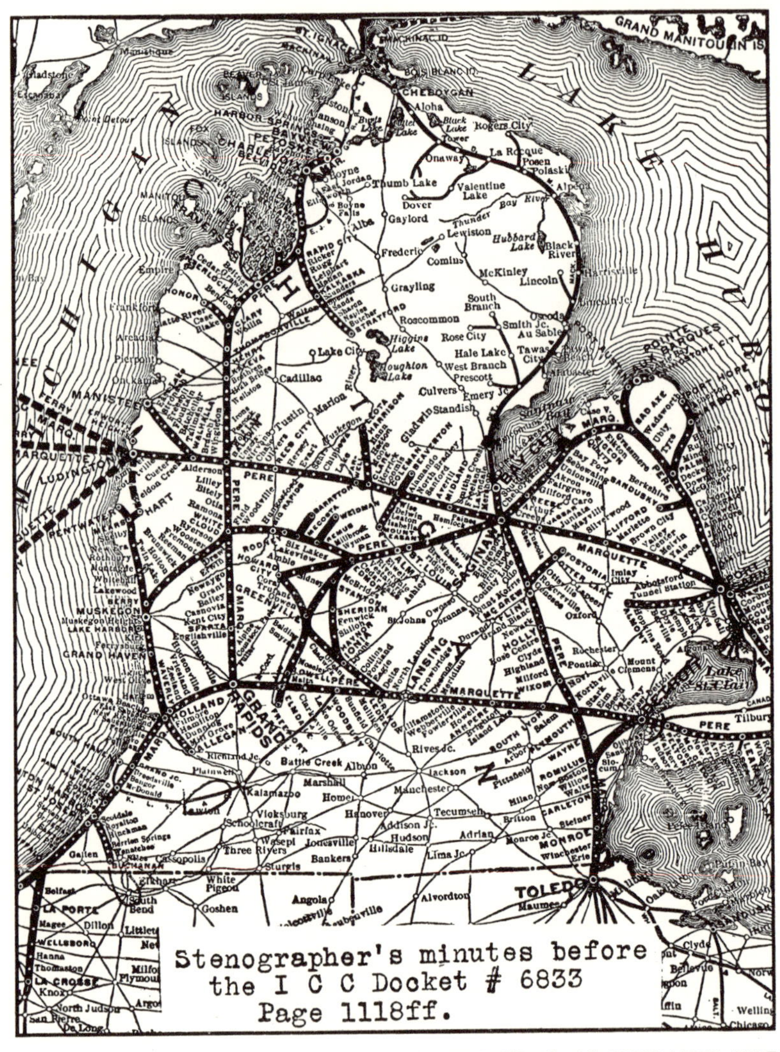

PERE MARQUETTE RAILROAD AND CONNECTIONS, AS OPERATED DURING THE YEAR ENDING JUNE 30, 1915.

PREFACE

EVEN to the most casual student of public affairs it must appear evident that the railroads of the United States present an exceedingly complex and increasingly difficult problem. In recent years the serious nature of this problem has been brought home to the public and the courts by reason of the numerous receiverships even among the larger railroad systems, often caused by financial mismanagement and private exploitation.[1] As a consequence of this fact, capital has shown a reluctance to enter this field of investment and thereby has seriously retarded or entirely prevented the introduction of much needed improvements and extensions.

The public, dissatisfied with inadequate and inefficient service, and the investor, who has seen the value of his securities melt away in numerous reorganization processes, have both attacked the railroad problem through commissions and legislative committees. For the most part, these investigating bodies, as well as most students of the problem, have attempted to comprehend the railroads of the country as a whole, and as a consequence, the results that they have attained have often not been commensurate with their efforts.

This has been true because of the very nature of the railroad system in the United States. It is too large, with too many complex ramifications and local pecu-

---

1. On December 31, 1916, sixty-nine railroads, with a total mileage of 34,559, were in the hands of receivers.

liarities, to lend itself to effective study as a totality. If progress is to be made in understanding the railroad system as a whole, detailed study must be made of the more important constituents of that system. Only in this way can we hope to understand the character of present day developments, and on the basis of this knowledge make intelligent provision for the future treatment of the public carriers. With this view in mind, the present study of a great Michigan railroad system has been undertaken in the hope that it will throw some light on the railroad problem as a whole and perhaps stimulate the study of other individual railroads in the United States.

The Pere Marquette has been chosen from among other railroads as the subject of special study, for several reasons. The first of these may be considered a sentimental one. The Pere Marquette and its constituents have grown up with the State of Michigan, stimulating the development of the State and in turn being beneficially affected by the prosperity developed. Only until recently the lumber industry was the chief business interest in Michigan, and the part played in the development of the lumber industry by the Pere Marquette and its constituent railroads was a very important and intimate one. With the decline of this important industry, the business communities of Michigan have noted a parallel decline in the service and value of the Pere Marquette; and the question arises whether this great public carrier must needs decay because of the passing of the forests, or whether its difficulties are due to other circumstances. The identification of the Pere Marquette with the great industry of the State of Michigan and hence with the State itself, as well as the fact that the Pere Marquette Railroad, unlike other Michigan railroads, is not affiliated with larger systems outside this State, lends to a study of this railroad an especial interest and importance.

But a more fundamental reason for this particular investigation exists in the fact that the history of the Pere Marquette Railroad embodies to an accentuated degree the various evils incident to a policy of *laissez faire* in railroad affairs. Deficits have been capitalized in numerous instances in reorganization processes; dividends have been paid out of capital by under-maintenance of road; stock has been watered; officials have violated their fiduciary positions for personal gain; banking institutions have shown a greedy disregard of the rights of innocent investors; and corporation accounts have been manipulated to misrepresent the facts. The diversity and far-reaching results of these abuses constitute a chapter in railroad history calculated to lend substantial concrete support to the widespread demand for more adequate regulation of public carriers, even though they are doing an intra-state business.

Finally, a number of peculiar characteristics of the Pere Marquette Railroad renders a study of its history and problems of special value. It is cut off to a large extent from through traffic due to the existence of water on three sides of the State. By reason of its undue mileage of branch lines, it has a large portion of its tracks subject to unprofitable operations. Until recently, its practical dependence on a single commodity of traffic made its financial condition fluctuate violently. It has been to a large extent an originating road and hence subject to car shortages. It has been

27

subject to keen water competition from the very beginning of its history because of the bulky commodities like salt and lumber that existed as the chief available tonnage.

It is true that other Michigan railroads have been subject, to some extent, to these peculiar conditions; but it must be said that the situation of the Pere Marquette is different from these other roads in that the latter are constituents of larger systems and as such have received favors and considerations that have not been available for the Pere Marquette.

That such a study as is here attempted has its peculiar difficulties goes without saying. It may be profitable, however, to enumerate a few of them. In the first place, it has been difficult to trace authentically the history of some of the Michigan railroads which have come to constitute the Pere Marquette Railroad System prior to 1871, before which date there was no Railroad Commissioner and hence no official financial reports of the railroads. In some cases this has not been a serious drawback because there are in existence annual reports to the stockholders of the different railroad companies; but in many cases these reports issued to stockholders are not to be found, and as regards certain railroads no reports were ever issued. Besides this, no books of record are to be found for many of these companies, and also for a few of the companies organized after 1871, so that some of the financial transactions and reorganizations are without meaning, except such as can be attributed to them by reason of an understanding of the general conditions existing at the time. This situation is applicable only to a few of the minor lines and does not affect materially the general situation. A third difficulty, and a very serious one, is the unreliable nature of formal entries in the books of the corporations, even in comparatively recent years. A thorough and accurate understanding of the motives and purposes which underlie these entries can only be obtained by access to correspondence files, and even then the investigator is often puzzled to know how far the correspondence represents the true motives of those concerned. This situation appears in numerous cases. Finally, some of the transactions are of such a complicated and designedly muddled character that it has been impossible thus far for the Interstate Commerce Commission and others working with them to determine the true status of affairs.

Nevertheless, in spite of these difficulties, the aim of this study has, for the most part, been accomplished. This aim has been to trace the growth of a large Michigan railroad system, the Pere Marquette Railroad Company, setting forth the causes for its physical existence as it is today, the peculiar difficulties with which it has had to contend, the different forms and consolidations in which it has sought to maintain life and vigor, the various and widely divergent methods employed by its officers and others concerning its operations and relation to other railroads, and finally, and perhaps most important, to present an analysis of its operating and financial condition, with conclusions as to the past and the probable outlook for the future.

The main source of the material which forms the basis for this study is an independent investigation by the Interstate Commerce Commission of the Pere Marquette and Cincinnati, Hamilton and Dayton railroads. Some of the results of this investigation have appeared recently for the benefit of the public, but a large portion of the original evidence which has been used in connection with this investigation has not been published, and probably will not be put into print. This material consists chiefly of stenographic reports of testimony taken in Detroit and Washington in the year 1914.

Other sources of material that have been relied upon extensively may be divided into two classifications: public official reports, and private documents of the railroad companies. Included in the first division are the Annual Reports of the Commissioner of Railroads for the State of Michigan; Orders and Opinions of the Michigan Railroad Commission; Interstate Commerce Commission Reports; statutes; and testimony given before a committee of the Michigan Legislature in 1913. The second classification embraces the annual reports of the different railroad companies to their stockholders, minutes of stockholders meetings, telegrams and letters between officials of the company, books of account, records and reports. And finally, most of the above material has been supplemented by personal interviews with former and present officials of the Pere Marquette Railroad Company and those working under the supervision of the Interstate Commerce Commission.

I desire to thank Professor David Friday of the University of Michigan for suggesting this study and for making available important source material. Thanks are likewise due to Professors Henry C. Adams and I. Leo Sharfman of the same university who have offered invaluable criticisms and materially aided me in organizing the subject matter. I also want gratefully to acknowledge the extensive and important aid given me by Mr. Fred Horton, Accountant for the Interstate Commerce Commission, who has willingly supplied me with material of the Commission at all times and given many valuable suggestions.

Lines acquired or leased since Jan. 1, 1900.
Trackage rights.
The following lines consolidated
into Pere Marquette R.R., Jan., 1900;
Lines owned by Flint & Pere Marquette R.R.
"   "   " Detroit, Grand Rapids & Western R.R.
"   "   " Chicago & West Michigan Ry.
LAKE HURON
LAKE MICHIGAN
Bay View.
Essex
Dix
Elk Rapids
Rapid City
Clary
Williamsburg
Honor
Stratford
Manistee
Leota
Grindstone City
Port Hope
LUDINGTON
Baldwin
Beaverton
Bad Axe
Harbor Bea
Walhalla
Pentwater
Barryton
Coleman
Bay City
Mears
Hart
Weidman
Palms
White Cloud
Big Rapids
Ramus
Mt. Pleasant
Berry
Mecosta
Paines
Sandusky
Edmore
SAGINAW
Fostoria
GRAND RAPIDS
Haynor
Mc Graw
Port Hu
Holland
Grand Ledge
Almont
Freeport
Lansing
Allegan
Oak
West
DETROIT
South Haven
Plymouth
Hartford
Delr
Lawton
Benton Harbor
Steiner
Buchanan
Alexis
New Buffalo
TOLEDO
Port
Wellsboro
B. & O.
dson
dusky
go Je
1. From Appendix I , Inter-
state Commerce Commission
Reports, Docket No. 6833

PERE MARQUETTE RAILWAY COMPANY

CHAPTER I

FLINT AND PERE MARQUETTE RAILROAD COMPANY

THE Pere Marquette Railway Company is the product of a slow and laborious growth. It has been built up piece by piece, often under great difficulties, in every case seeking to serve new communities and making available the great stores of timber and mineral wealth existing in the State of Michigan.

The beginnings of its history go back to the organization of three railroads, viz., the Flint and Pere Marquette, the Chicago and West Michigan, and the Detroit, Grand Rapids and Western. The first of these roads filed its Articles of Association with the Secretary of State at Lansing as early as January 22, 1857, and opened for business the first section of its line extending from East Saginaw to Mt. Morris, a distance of 26.1 miles, on January 20, 1862. The first year the gross revenues amounted to the modest sum of $31,764, $12,510 of which came from freight and $19,254 from passengers.

The following year the road was extended 7.2 miles to Flint, which was then a growing lumbering town having eight very flourishing saw mills capable of sawing sixty million feet of lumber yearly, besides two more large mills nearly completed that could turn out twenty million feet yearly. As a direct result of this extension the gross revenues tripled.

A great need was felt for connections with Detroit in order to form an outlet for traffic originating in Flint and surrounding territory. On November 1, 1864, the Flint and Holly Railroad Company had opened up a line from Flint to Holly, a distance of 17 miles, and there it made connections with Detroit by means of the Detroit and Milwaukee Railroad Company. A month after the opening of this road, the Flint and Pere Marquette trains were running into Detroit pursuant to a trackage arrangement with both of these roads.

The Flint and Holly Railroad Company ran independently for a period of three years, at the end of which time it was purchased by the Flint and Pere Marquette Railway Company. During these three years the Flint and Holly Railroad had been prosperous, paying 4 per cent on its stock the first year and carrying $16.842 to surplus; and the second year paying 8 per cent on its stock, crediting surplus with $31,152. The gross earnings were not so large as they might have been this year due to the destruction of the depot and docks of the Detroit and Milwaukee Railroad Company at Detroit, and the inability of that company to furnish their proportion of flat cars for an outlet to the business forced upon the Flint and Holly Railroad, so that a large portion of the traffic had to seek an outlet via the Flint and Pere Marquette Railway and Lake Huron at an increased freight rate above all-rail rates. What was a loss for the Flint and Holly Railroad was a gain for the Flint and Pere Marquette Railway, as shown by an increase of over $30,000 in the gross earnings of the latter company over the year previous. Taken all in all, the Flint and Holly Railroad was an important road and invaluable to the growing Flint and Pere Marquette Railway System.

The growth of the Flint and Pere Marquette Railroad was stimulated by grants of land by the Federal Government under the Act of 1856. These grants of land were given to the company on condition that the railroad should be constructed to Lake Michigan at the rate of 20 miles per year until completed. In consideration of this yearly construction the railroad was to receive six sections of land for each mile of road built. Twice, the railroad was unable to complete the required yearly construction, but each time· the date of completion was extended.

For the stretch of road from East Saginaw to Flint the company was given 153,600 acres of land which it had the right to dispose of, and which it did sell to settlers for $5.00 to $10.00 per acre according to the location and grade of timber it possessed.

The consensus of opinion was that the road ought to be pushed with all. possible speed toward Lake Michigan, both because of the offer from the government and also because of the rich territory that would be opened up. In the Annual Report to the Stockholders made December 31, 1867, Mr. H. C. Potter, the secretary of the railroad, urged strongly the extension toward the lumber district in the western portion of the State. He says, ''The importance and magnitude of the lumber traffic on the Muskegon and Manistee Rivers urge this company to speedy construction on its road west.''   He then proceeds to give statistics on the production of pine lumber on these rivers, and finishes his statement by quoting Mr. W. B. Sears, the Chief Engineer, as follows: ''It is a region of country inviting to the farmer and lumberman, and in my judgment, the extension of your road to the Tobacco (river) would render the whole line north of Saginaw more valuable, place you in the heart of the lumber region and tend to speedy and rapid settlement of the country, with a corresponding increase of business on the road.''

The year previous to this report had seen construction work started on a line running northwest from East Saginaw for 20 miles into the timber district to Midland City, and this line was opened for traffic December 1, 1867. The traffic increased by leaps and bounds, gross revenues amounting to $381,983 in 1868, compared with $236,958 in 1867, while prospects for the future in the Saginaw Valley were very flattering. The lumber production in this district had increased from 133,500,000 feet in 1863 to 457,396,225 feet in 1868, while salt production had increased from 4,000 barrels in 1860 to 555,690 barrels in 1868. During the same period population in Saginaw County had doubled.

With such prospects in view, extensions were made as soon as the necessary capital was forthcoming. On October 25, 1868, 6.5 miles of line were constructed from Midland to Averill, thus completing 60 miles of road from Flint; and by the construction of the last section of 20 miles, the Flint and Pere Marquette Railway acquired the right to sell 76,300 acres of land.

With this last grant of land the Flint and Pere Marquette Railway had received a total of 307,200 acres, $267,270 being received from the sale of a portion of this acreage. At this time the land department of the railroad indicated that many inquiries were coming in from prospective settlers, and it was optimistic as to the rapid settlement of most of the lands offered for sale.

In October 1870, the fourth division of main line was opened to a point twenty miles west of Averill, and the following month 4.4 miles as far as Clare were. completed in the fifth division. The remaining 15.6 miles in the fifth division were completed in March 1871, and the sixth division of 20 miles was finished in November of the same year, while a month later the road was extended 2 more miles to Reed City with the object of making a junction at that point with the Grand Rapids and Indiana Railway.

Regarding the growth of business interests along the Flint and Pere Marquette Railway, Mr. G. C. Kimball, Superintendent of the road, said in 1870: ''There are in operation at the present time on the line opened the present season, eleven saw mills and shingle mills, that are daily contributing business, and others are being erected as fast as possible, some of them by parties interested in mills on the Saginaw River, while others are being built by parties from Ohio, Indiana and New York, and we are also assured by some of the largest owners of pine lands, that it is their intention to erect large saw, shingle and planing mills for the manufacture of lumber and shingles for the eastern and southern markets. Our facilities for shipping to all eastern and southern points without any transfer make it an inducement for capitalists to invest in the manufacture of lumber as well as in pine lands, and upon the opening of the Holly, Wayne and Monroe Railroad from Holly (our present eastern terminus) to Monroe, 63 miles, now being built by this company, our facilities will be still better and give us the shortest route from Northern Michigan to all eastern and southern points.'"[1]

The new road referred to in the quotation, i. e., the Holly, Wayne and Monroe, was opened for business on June 4, 1872, and was a successful means of connecting up the trade of the northwest part of the State with points south of Detroit.

On the same date was purchased the Bay City and East Saginaw Railroad Company, which had proven to be a profitable investment as a leased road since 1867. It tapped a large lumber center as well as a lake port and formed a ready outlet for lumber when rolling stock was not forthcoming to take care of all-rail traffic toward the east and south.

At the same time three more roads were bought, viz., the Flint River Railroad from Flint to Otter Lake, a distance of 18.9 miles, opening up a valuable timber district on the Cedar River; the Cass River Railroad from East Saginaw to Vassar, 19.4 miles, tapping the great timber resources of the Cass River district and forming the first link in a line from East Saginaw to Port Huron; and the East Saginaw and St. Clair Railroad, a belt line around Saginaw.

It will be remembered that the main line pushing toward Lake Michigan was making progress of about 20 miles per year. Reed City, 48.4 miles from Ludington, had been reached by the first of the year 1872

---

1. Annual Report to Stockholders of December 31, 1870.

and work was commenced on the seventh and eighth divisions soon after this. On the first of December 1874, Flint and Pere Marquette trains ran into Ludington and a continuous line under one management extended from Monroe on Lake Erie to Ludington on Lake Michigan, a distance of 253 miles. Besides this mileage of main line there was 30.7 miles of branches and 62.2 miles of sidings, making a total of about 346 miles of road owned and operated in 1875.

The road had been completed to the Lake and now it was entitled to the sale of more government land. The land was not taken up by settlers so quickly as anticipated, due largely to the competition of fertile lands in Ohio, Indiana and Illinois and lands west of the Mississippi. By the year 1877, the road had received 511,502.20 acres of land under the Land Grant Act of 1857, but of this amount it still had undisposed of, 235,778.51 acres. However, it must be said that the returns from the sale of these lands amounted to $2,369,729.21, which added materially to the construction account funds and without which the road could not have been built so early and the wealth of the State opened up when it was.

Not only did the sale of timber and farm lands not come up to anticipations during the middle seventies, but ·the expected traffic over the main line from Ludington did not materialize. One of the reasons for this is stated by the General Manager, Mr. H. C. Potter, as follows: ''The road was completed to Lake Michigan in the fall of 1874, but rates ruled so low during the following years, that no effort was made to compete for such share of through traffic as this road may fairly claim, until the very close of 1877, when parties interested in the road undertook the construction of a grain elevator at Ludington. This was completed so that through grain traffic was undertaken about the middle of December. Our connections are such that good results may be expected from this business, provided the question of rates can be settled, as to terminate the disastrous competition between roads.''[2]

Another reason was the financial panic of 1873 and the business depression during the years directly following. This period was a hard one for all railroads but especially for those dealing with construction materials, which had felt the effects of business depression much sooner than merchandise and other tonnage. During the ten years, 1862 to 1872, gross revenues had increased from $31,764 to $1,133,612, while net revenues had increased from less than $10,000 to $455,118. From 1873 to 1876 gross revenues had dropped off $133,244 and net revenues $89,044. In 1877 gross revenues continued to fall but not so rapidly as operating expenses, so that the net revenue was larger by $50,605 than during the previous year.

However, it became more evident every month that the bonded indebtedness was too much for the traffic. With bonded interest unpaid amounting to $1,200,000 and accumulating rapidly at the rate of $385,000 per year,[3] it was deemed the wiser course in the interest of the holders of all classes of the Company's securities, that the Flint and Pere Marquette Railway should go into the hands of a receiver on July 1, 1879. The road was operated by the receiver from this date until the

---

2. *Annual Report* to Stockholders of December 31, 1877.
3. *Annual Report* to Stockholders for 1879 and 1880, page 5.

close of September 1880 when the property was sold to a Protective Committee representing the Consolidated Bonds. The Company was reorganized by them as the Flint and Pere Marquette Railroad Company. The reorganization plans provided for the exchange of 4,469 consolidated bonds for preferred stock, as a means of cutting down the fixed charges that had become unmanageable in the previous five years. Preferred stock to the extent of $6,500,000 was issued, but no common stock was to be issued to holders of certificates of old common stock until five consecutive dividends of 7 per cent had been paid on the preferred stock. Not more than 7 per cent could be paid on the common stock in any one year, and any surplus remaining after paying 7 per cent on the preferred and on the common stock was to be divided ratably between the two classes of stock.[4]

During the fifteen months of operation by the receiver from July 1, 1879 to September 30, 1880 gross revenues had begun to increase rapidly once more as business, especially construction work, began anew after the long period of depression, and amounted to $994,375 in 1880 as compared with $868,816 in 1879.

The first construction work since the completion of the main line in 1874 began under the receivership, when a line from Clare to Harrison, a distance of 16.8 miles, was completed, and a narrow gauge line, 14.5 miles in length, was built from Coleman to Mt. Pleasant. This was changed to a standard gauge in 1884.

In 1881 a branch was completed from Walhalla to

---

4   "The annual interest charge on bonded debt of the Company and on past due coupons was about $760,000, and the average annual net earnings for five years prior thereto had been less than $375,000."

Manistee, a distance of 26.4 miles, which opened up valuable salt mines and made further connections with lake shipping.

Between 1875 and 1883 there had been a gradual increase in net earnings from $358,598 in the former year to $807,426 in the latter.   During this period several logging spurs, varying from a fraction of a mile to 9 miles, were constructed by private parties interested in the logging business and with very little expense to the Flint and Pere Marquette Railroad.   These added materially to the gross revenues.

The year 1883 marks a turning point in net earnings which fell to $737,526 in 1884 and to $598,950 in 1885, and not until 1890 did they reach the $800,000 mark again.   There was no change in the physical condition of the road nor were the sources of tonnage dried up, but a business depression had set in all over the country and the chief article of traffic for the Flint and Pere Marquette Railroad, viz., lumber and forest products, felt the slump as did all other building materials.   As is generally the case, it was not possible to meet these losses by prompt and corresponding reductions in expenses.   Substantial and needed improvements had been undertaken, which were well advanced when the road began to feel the effects of the depression, but it was necessary to complete them.

Through traffic by lake and rail from Milwaukee had been started the first part of 1883, but this had to be abandoned in January 1884 until November of the same year because of ''low and unremunerative rates''; and when it was commenced in that latter month, their steamer No. 1 was wrecked near the breakwater at Ludington in a severe storm causing a loss of approximately $35,000. The winter continued with unprecedented severity, holding up their traffic so that only 7,000 tons were moved the first three months of the year 1885.

Business began to increase in 1886 as demand for lumber became more active, and net revenues increased $50,000 over the year previous. But competition with lake traffic for eastern points was growing especially acute. In the four years from 1879 to 1883 the mills in the Saginaw River Valley manufactured over four billion feet of lumber, equal to 500,000 car loads of ten tons each, and of this amount nearly ninety per cent was shipped by water to Tonawanda, Buffalo, Cleveland, Toledo and other lake ports, and distributed from those points by rail, with the exception of shipments through the Erie Canal, which amounted to 326,800,000 feet in 1882, or 75 per cent of the total receipts at Buffalo and Tonawanda. Thus rail traffic east of Buffalo was not benefited to a great extent since a large proportion of the lumber being carried from the Saginaw River Valley was transported by an all-water route.

Of the trifle over ten per cent of rail traffic in lumber, over one half of it was shipped to Michigan and northern Ohio and Indiana points not in competition with water routes, so that only about five per cent of the total production of lumber in the Saginaw Valley for these four years was shipped by all-rail lines to the east, south and west.

Not merely was there great water competition for lumber, but for other commodities as well. Chief of these was salt, nine-tenths of the total production of which, had, up until this time, been shipped by water.

This large amount of water transportation does not indicate that the railroads had not made an effort to increase their bulk of the traffic by a reduction in rates, for there had been a very material reduction in rates for all classes of commodities from 1864 to 1887. From East Saginaw to New York the rates for first, second, third, fourth and fifth class traffic per 100 pounds, had been reduced 50, 43, 46, 30 and 62 per cent respectively. From Detroit to Saginaw there was a reduction of the rate on forest products per car of 65 per cent; on salt, cement and lime per barrel of 75 per cent; on grain per 100 pounds in car-load lots of 68 per cent; on flour per barrel in car-load lots of 71 per cent; and heavy reductions in different classifications of freight. From Saginaw to Chicago there were further reductions on first, second, third and fourth classes of freight, of 16, 20, 25 and 30 per cent respectively.

In April 1887 the Interstate Commerce Law went into effect and competition between the different roads was to become more uniform and less liable to unjust practices. But it was to be several years before the new law made adequate provision for such conditions as existed in 1887 between the railroads of the State of Michigan and water carriers.

The year 1887 was a turning point in the rail transportation of logs, and from that date this sort of traffic began to fall off rapidly. In 1888 it was 193,790 tons ($153,308 of gross earnings) less than the year previous; in 1889, 65,220 tons less than in 1888; in 1890, 87,690 tons less than in 1889; and so on with a loss almost every year.

As an offset to the loss in traffic of logs, the earnings of steamers on Lake Michigan, of which there were now three dealing with through traffic, was $40,556; and a further increase of tonnage was monthly secured from forest products, grain and flour. Total tonnage was increasing, due largely to reduced rates of through traffic, but alongside of the increasing tonnage was a gradual falling off in gross earnings.

Railroading in the so-called "Thumb" district became active in 1879 when the Port Huron and North Western Railway Company began construction work, and two years later opened for operation narrow gauge lines from East Saginaw to Port Huron, 90.3 miles; Port Huron to Harbor Beach, 70.2 miles; Palms to Port Austin, 34.5 miles; Port Huron to Almont, 33.7 miles; together with sidings, making a total mileage of 253.8 miles.[5] With the exception of the East Saginaw-Port Huron Line these lines did not prove so profitable as was expected, due to slowness of growth of industries in this section and because of active water competition. But it was thought they would become valuable lines so they were purchased and consolidated with the Flint and Pere Marquette Railroad in April 1889 and work was immediately commenced to make them standard gauge. The cost of this property to the Flint and Pere Marquette Railway was $2,300,000 in this company's bonds and $1,200,000 was appropriated for widening the gauge.

During the first nine months of operation in 1889 these roads showed gross earnings amounting to $253,859 and a surplus from operations of $37,889. From 1890 to 1897 the gross earnings ranged from

---

5. Began construction in fall of 1878; completed to Harbor Beach September, 1880; to Saginaw February, 1882; Port Huron to Almont as P. H. & S. W. Ry. in October, 1882; to Port Austin December, 1882.

$400,000 to $450,000 and in 1898 reached $478,743. During the period that the Port Huron and Northwestern Railway was in the hands of the Flint and Pere Marquette Railroad it about paid its operating expenses and fixed charges, but at the time it was consolidated with the Flint and Pere Marquette Railroad in 1889 it had accumulated a deficit of about $150,000 during the ten years that it had operated.

In 1890 the Fort Street Union Depot Company, organized and controlled by the Canadian Pacific, the Wabash, the Detroit, Lansing and Northern and the Flint and Pere Marquette railroads, started the construction of a Union Depot at Detroit, which was opened for service in January 1893. In the same year, Flint and Pere Marquette trains entered Detroit via a new route, leaving the main line at Plymouth, using tracks of the Detroit, Lansing and Northern for part of the way and their own tracks for the remainder. This increased the facilities for through traffic, as did also the opening of the tunnel under the St. Clair River at Port Huron the year before, but was unfortunately more than offset by the stoppage of through traffic across Lake Michigan for the first three months of 1893, due to the most severe weather conditions experienced in twenty years.

Together with the adverse weather conditions was the business depression coexistent with the panic, which reduced net revenues $203,877. Strenuous means were taken to lower operating expenses to conform with the reduction in gross revenues, and accordingly on September 1st there was a reduction in wages of 10 per cent for all men getting over $50 per month, and later on a reduction was also made in monthly wages under this amount. The next year the rapidly falling gross revenues[6] was offset, within $10,000, by reduction in operating expenses, so that the net revenue remained about the same as in 1893. $56,289 of this saving in operating expenses was accomplished by decreasing the sum usually spent for maintenance of way and structures.

The Flint and Pere Marquette Railroad had long felt the need of a road into Toledo for an interchange of traffic by direct connection with the Columbus, Hocking Valley and Toledo; Pennsylvania; Wheeling and Lake Erie; Lake Shore and Michigan Southern; Michigan Central; and the Cincinnati, Jackson and Mackinaw railroads. Accordingly, the Monroe and Toledo Railway Company was formed and in 1897 a line was opened for operation from Monroe to Alexis, a distance of 15.2 miles, and in the same year the entry into Toledo from Alexis, 6.6 miles, was obtained by a 99-year lease of road from the Ann Arbor Railroad Company. The immediate increase of traffic from the south and east by means of this extension demonstrated the wisdom of the expenditure.

The classes of freight carried by steamer across Lake Michigan had, previous to 1897, been confined to such articles as could be transferred from car to boat and boat to car. In order to get away from this limitation a new policy regarding this lake service was adopted, and a car-ferry, with capacity for thirty cars, was constructed and began operation. This virtually meant an extension of the Flint and Pere Marquette rails to the great railroad systems of Wisconsin and the procuring of a new and higher class of traffic.

---

6.   Gross revenues fell off $332,906 during this year.

The reaching out for through traffic was the only wise course for the Flint and Pere Marquette Railroad to follow, as the entire dependence on local traffic within the State of Michigan placed the road at the mercy of the lumber business almost entirely; and it was soon discovered in the early days of operation that this was a dangerous traffic on which to depend, since it was the first to feel the widening influences of business depression. Besides, the logging traffic, which was at one time a large per cent of the total traffic, had practically disappeared and thus far agriculture and industry had not produced products of great enough tonnage to fill the gap. Hence it is seen that the growth was a natural one and in fact necessary to the life of the railroad. During most of the lean years of the nineties the falling off in local tonnage and even in passenger traffic was offset, often to a substantial extent, by the increased earnings of lake steamers, with possibly one or two exceptions when the winters were especially severe.[7]

Another factor of great importance in the development of the Flint and Pere Marquette Railroad was the amounts received yearly from the sale of lands given it by the Federal Government through the State of Michigan at the rate of six sections per mile of constructed road. On January 1, 1899, a total of 468,690 acres had been sold (an area approximately two-thirds of the size of the State of Rhode Island) out of 513,000 acres of land granted. This land sold at an average price of $10.34 per acre or a total of $4,847,007. Most of this amount had been put into

7. The passenger traffic fell from $716,528 in 1895 to $660,756 in 1896.

additions and betterments from year to year and was not used up in maintenance of way and structures with a consequent reduction in operation expenses.

SUMMARY OF THE FINANCIAL CONDITION OF THE FLINT AND PERE MARQUETTE RAILROAD AND ITS CONSTITUENTS

The Railroad Commissioner's reports begin in 1872, and from this date figures are given on the income account of the Flint and Pere Marquette Railway, but the first year for figures on the profit and loss account is 1877.

In 1871 the credit balance of $92,854.91 is the accumulated surplus of the company up to that date from the time of its operation, beginning in 1857.

The striking thing to be noted regarding the Flint and Pere Marquette Railway Company from the year 1871 up to the time that it was reorganized into the Flint and Pere Marquette Railroad Company, September 30, 1880, is that it acquired from operations a net deficit of $1,566,275.01, which includes interest on the funded debt. This deficit would have been still larger except for the fact that during the receivership from January 1st to September 30th, 1880, no interest was accrued on the funded debt. Several other items accrued in the profit and loss account, which would make a total deficit of $2,211,147.90 for the Flint and Pere Marquette Railway during the period of operation from 1871 to September 30, 1880.[8]

---

8. *Stenographer's minutes before the I. C. C.*, Docket No. 6833, page **960**.

PORT HURON AND NORTHWESTERN RAILWAY

This road operated independently from 1878 to 1888, and during that time showed a net deficit from operations of $148,411.14, after paying interest charges of nearly $1,000,000. Only one dividend was paid amounting to $65,400, and in the same year that this was paid, viz., 1882, there was a balance of $21,000 in the profit and loss account. From this date until the consolidation of the road with the Flint and Pere Marquette Railroad Company, every year showed a deficit from operation, until at the end of 1888 it amounted to $213,811.14, which is just the amount of loss from operations plus the amount of dividends paid.[9]

FLINT AND PERE MARQUETTE RAILROAD

From October 1, 1880 to December 31, 1899, this company earned $4,891,137.02 and showed a surplus from operation for each year of that period. From 1893 to 1896 there was a large falling off in the surplus, due to the business depression that prostrated not only the railroads but a large portion of other industrial enterprises as well.[10]

The reorganized company showed neither a credit nor debit balance at the beginning of this period, since reorganization had washed out the accrued deficits of the constituent companies.

From 1881 to 1892 inclusive, this company regularly

---

9. *Ibid,* 962.
10. *Ibid.*

paid dividends on preferred stock,[11] and there were also two other dividends, one in 1898 and one in 1899. The former was a regular dividend but the latter was a dividend paid out of assets according to the plan for consolidation of the three roads.[12]

At the time of reorganization into the Pere Marquette Railroad Company, January 1, 1900, the Flint and Pere Marquette Railroad Company had a surplus on its books of $1,668,067.02. This surplus was practically created in 1888 when the major portion of it was derived from the sale of lands which were granted to the Flint and Pere Marquette Railroad by the United States Government.[13]

Taking into consideration the operations of the Flint and Pere Marquette Railroad Company from

---

11. The dividends paid on the preferred stock (none on the common) are as follows: 1881, 5 1-2%; 1882, 6 1-2%; 1883, 7%; 1884, 7%; 1885, 4%; 1886, 5%; 1887, 6 1-2%; 1888, 7%; 1890, 5%; 1891, 4%; 1892, 4%; 1898, 3%.

12. A document headed "Direction from committee to Pere Marquette Railroad Company," dated December 6, 1899, signed William W. Crapo, for the committee of which he was chairman, reads as follows:

"To Pere Marquette Railroad Company:

Referring to our contract of even date herewith, just authorized and executed, I hand you herewith three propositions addressed respectively to Flint and Pere Marquette Railroad Company, the Detroit, Grand Rapids and Western Railway Company, and the Chicago and West Michigan Railroad Company, and direct you to execute and deliver such propositions to said companies."

The sixth paragraph of the proposition to the Flint and Pere Marquette Railroad Company reads: "Flint and Pere Marquette Railroad Company may pay a dividend upon its preferred stock of two per cent for the year 1899, and deduct the amount of such dividend from its assets."

13. *Stenographer's minutes before the I. C. C.*, Docket No. 6833, page 965 ff.

1880, that being the date of reorganization, they show a net credit balance in the profit and loss account on December 31, 1899, of $1,750,000. However, if the entire period from 1857 to 1899 be taken for these three railroads, that is, the Flint and Pere Marquette Railway Company, the Port Huron and Northwestern Railway Company, and the Flint and Pere Marquette Railroad Company, there would be a deficit of $756,-892.02. In other words this deficit would appear if no allowance be made for the washing out or capitalizing at the time of reorganization of a deficit of $2,211,-147.90.[14]

---

14. *Ibid.*

Roads like the Cass River Railway, the Flint River Railway, the Flint and Fentonville (Holly) Railroad, and the Manistee Railroad were organized in the interest of the Flint and Pere Marquette Railway Company, and their operations, for the most part, are carried in the books of the latter company if they operated at all. Some of them did not operate at all, being preliminary construction companies.

CHAPTER II

Chicago and West Michigan Railway Company

THE Chicago and West Michigan Railway Company was the outgrowth of fifteen different railroad companies. The first of these was the Allegan and Holland Railroad, extending about 30 miles between these two terminals, organized on July 29th, 1868. On January 22nd, 1869 a company was organized called the Muskegon and Ferrysburg Railroad, with the intention of building a road between these two towns, a distance of nearly 12 miles. No records exist concerning either of these roads and it is only known that the former was consolidated with the latter on October 13, 1869 to form the Michigan Lake Shore Railroad Company. This road began construction to connect up its two constituents and by 1871 trains were running between Allegan and Muskegon, a distance of 57.5 miles.

The total cost of this line was about $1,330,000 or $23,120 per mile. The gross earnings in 1872 amounted to $110,000, which was nearly evenly divided between passenger and freight. It was essentially a lumber road, four-fifths of the total tonnage consisting of lumber and forest products, and because of that fact it was soon feeling the business depression that preceded the panic of 1873, and which lasted for several years. The road had failed to earn operating expenses, but as soon as the demand for lumber declined, the gross earnings fell off rapidly and toward the latter part of the year 1872 the Michigan Lake Shore Railroad Company was forced into receivership. During the period of its existence it had accumulated a deficit from operations of $466,815.76.

For the next six years, while the road was in receiver's hands, it tended to show a loss each year and by October 1, 1878 revenue had fallen off 40 per cent and a deficit had been accumulated of almost half a million of dollars. On this date it was reorganized under the name of the Grand Haven Railroad Company, the new company purchasing the old property at a receiver's sale. The plans for reorganization did not provide for the assumption by the new company of the funded debt of the old company amounting to $800,000, but merely $160,000 of receiver's certificates. Stock was issued par for par in exchange for all outstanding bonds.

Thus ended in failure the first road that was to form one of the parts of the Chicago and West Michigan Railway and subsequently the Pere Marquette Railroad Company. There was plenty of timber in the great pine forests, but the demand for it was of too fluctuating a character to make assured gross earnings of sufficient magnitude to pay operating expenses and interest on the funded debt. There was no excessive capitalization in this road making fixed charges too high for net earnings. It was a case of having all the eggs of the road in one basket, and the results that followed were the results that usually follow under such circumstances.

The Grand Haven Railroad during its first year of operation in 1879 ran up a deficit of $23,000, although there was no interest on bonded indebtedness but merely on the receiver's certificates. The character of the traffic was changing somewhat, lumber and forest products claiming only 50 per cent of the tonnage, whereas seven years previous this classification comprised 80 per cent of the total tonnage. The tonnage that was increasing rapidly in importance was manufactures and merchandise which together now comprised about 31 per cent of all tonnage. The manufactures consisted to some extent of products of lumber, but this traffic was to be found more reliable than the crude material, since the demand for these manufactured goods was less elastic than the demand for lumber and timber itself, the latter being used largely for construction purposes, and liable to sudden contraction at the first intimation of business sluggishness.

But even with the advantage derived from the greater variety of tonnage the traffic was not heavy enough, and the deficit of 1879, less about $3,000, was carried over to the year 1880. In 1881 this debt was extinguished and was replaced by a small net gain from operation of $541.73. It was in this financial condition when, on September 30, 1881, it was consolidated, with some other railroads described elsewhere, into the Chicago and West Michigan Railway Company.[1]

About the same time in 1869 that railroad activity commenced around Allegan and Muskegon, the Chicago and Michigan Lake Shore Railroad Company was starting the construction of a line from New Buffalo to St. Joseph, a distance of 27 miles, and the beginning of the year 1870 saw construction started on a line

---

1. *Stenographer's minutes before the I. C. C.*, Docket No. 6833, page 993.

running from St. Joseph to Grand Junction, a distance of 34.8 miles. From this point a line was projected for about the same distance to Holland, where connections were made with the Michigan Lake Shore tracks; and finally, from Muskegon at the northern terminus of the Michigan Lake Shore Railroad, a line was being pushed north to Montague, about 15 miles distant. In different months of the year 1871 these four sections of road were completed and opened for traffic, and the Chicago and Michigan Lake Shore Railroad ran its trains over 143 miles of road from New Buffalo to Montague, most of which was its own property, the exception being the stretch of roadway between Holland and Muskegon, a distance of about 35 miles.

The following year the line was extended 26.8 miles further north to Pentwater, opening up a virgin timber country within a day's walk of the point where the Flint and Pere Marquette was slowly forcing its way through the forest for an outlet to the Lake. Within two years and a half, the Chicago and Michigan Lake Shore Railroad Company had built up a line as long as that of the Flint and Pere Marquette, although the latter road had been in process of construction for ten years.

The year 1872 also saw a branch line of 25.3 miles constructed and opened for operation extending from Holland on the main line to Grand Rapids which was then a growing manufacturing city. The following year a line was constructed from Muskegon, then one of the largest lumber centers in the world, to Big Rapids, 51.1 miles distant.

By the construction of these two branches, the

Chicago and Michigan Lake Shore Railroad Company now had about 250 miles of railroad in the State of Michigan. Like the Michigan Lake Shore Railroad, its preponderating tonnage was lumber and forest products, this classification amounting to about two-thirds of the total. The balance was manufactures and merchandise, agricultural products being negligible. The total cost of construction and equipment was $8,658,000 or about $31,000 per mile of road. $6,675,000 of this amount was furnished by first mortgage serial 8 per cent bonds and the balance by capital stock. The road could not command a good market for its bonds and most of them suffered a twenty per cent discount.[2]

The Chicago and Michigan Lake Shore Railroad started out with gross earnings of about half a million of dollars and expenses from operation amounting to $275,000. The interest on bonds alone would have more than eaten up gross earnings, but no interest on bonded indebtedness was paid from the first years net earnings and very little until January 1874, on which date and subsequently large amounts of accrued interest came due for payment. In 1875 accrued interest amounted to over $1,000,000, and in this same year a large deficit was accumulated. Gross earnings had increased, since the opening of the road, by only $150,000, while operating expenses had doubled. In other words, the facts of the case were, that in 1871 to 1873 the road had failed to meet its fixed charges by about a quarter of a million of dollars per year, while from 1874 to 1875 it had failed to meet its fixed charges by one-half million of dollars and it looked as if it would

---

2. Report to Stockholders.

continue to do so. By the end of 1876 a deficit of $1,895,000 had been accumulated and gross earnings had fallen off about $50,000 from the previous year.

It was quite obvious by the end of 1876 that the Chicago and Michigan Lake Shore Railroad could not earn interest on its bonded indebtedness. It was having the same difficulty that all roads were having at this time, whose chief article of tonnage was lumber and forest products. The business depression perhaps was not the cause of the failure of this railroad, as it did not earn its bond interest even prior to 1873; but there is no doubt that indirectly the business depression hastened dissolution, because of its relation to construction materials, chief of which was lumber. A road that did not depend on originating traffic of this nature, but had a through traffic in merchandise and a larger proportion of passenger traffic, would, without doubt, have had a much better chance to survive the business depression.

Accordingly, the road went into the hands of a receiver toward the end of 1876 and was operated in this way until December 28, 1878, when the property was sold at foreclosure sale and reorganized as the Chicago and West Michigan Railroad Company. During the first year of receivership the gross earnings fell off another $50,000 and the deficit jumped to $2,345,000. In 1878 the gross earnings rose slightly, but just covered operating expenses, so that practically all of the bond interest was not being earned. The deficit therefore rose by the amount of the bond interest, or to $2,838,000. Included in this sum are items other than deferred interest, so that if interest on bonds had been paid during receivership, this deficit would have been augmented by about $1,000,000.

The reorganization plan cut down the bonded indebtedness from $6,675,000 to $480,000, and issued more capital stock in exchange for the bonds on which interest had been defaulted, thereby increasing the stock from $1,683,000 to $6,151,000. This was accomplished by exchanging ten shares of $100 each of the capital stock of the new corporation for each $1000 bond with all unpaid coupons thereon. Thus most of the funded debt was extinguished and fixed charges for the new reorganized company materially reduced.

The new corporation, the Chicago and West Michigan Railroad Company, operated from about January 1, 1879 to September 30, 1881, and showed a net credit from operations for that period, of $417,854. Of this amount, $153,572.50 was paid out in dividends on common stock for the year ending September 30, 1881. Miscellaneous debits, regarding which there are no explanatory details, amounted to $127,992.34, thus leaving a balance in surplus of $139,328.64. The dividend referred to was the only one paid on the stock issued in exchange for bonds at time of reorganization. On September 1, 1881 the Chicago and West Michigan Railroad Company, together with some other roads described elsewhere, were consolidated into the Chicago and West Michigan Railway Company.[3]

To go back a few years to the beginning of railroad operations in western Michigan. Trains had been running only a few months over the rails of the Chicago and Michigan Lake Shore Railroad when construction

---

3. *Stenographer's Minutes Before the I. C. C.*, Docket No. 6833, page 994.

31

work was commenced by the Grand Rapids, Newaygo and Lake Shore Railroad Company on a line extending north from Grand Rapids.   May 19, 1872 saw the first section opened for operation, from Grand Rapids to Sparta, a distance of 14.7 miles.   Later in the year the line was extended to Casnovia, 7.7 miles from Sparta, and toward the close of the year a section was completed between Casnovia and Newaygo, a distance of 13.6 miles.   Three years later the line was extended 11.6 miles to White Cloud to make connections with the Chicago and Michigan Lake Shore Railroad.

The cost of these first three sections, thirty-six miles in length, exclusive of equipment, was $1,143,000, or $32,000 per mile.   The equipment would add about $6,115 per mile of the road to this cost.   This sum was secured by the issue of $532,150 of capital stock and $576,000 of bonds.   Part of the bonds sold at a premium which was just about offset by the discount suffered on the other portion of them.

The gross earnings for the first year of operation over the whole road (1873), amounted to $132,771, while operating expenses were about $69,523.   From the net earnings from operation, amounting to $63,247, there was due for bond interest, $46,000, leaving a small surplus for the first year of operation.   Like most of the other roads under consideration, the Grand Rapids, Newaygo and Lake Shore was essentially a lumber road, 80 per cent of its tonnage consisting of lumber and forest products.   This preponderance of lumber traffic was reduced to 50 per cent by 1881 when the road changed management.

The result of operations from 1871 to 1881 was a loss of $36,554.28, although this road had received donations amounting to $24,470.55 to aid in its building. On September 30, 1881 it was consolidated into the Chicago and West Michigan Railway Company, together with some other roads. On the books of the new company the loss suffered by the Grand Rapids, Newaygo and Lake Shore was charged to construction account. In short, this transaction was the capitalization of a deficit by the new organization.[4]

Besides the seven roads that we have considered which actually operated prior to the consolidation into the Chicago and West Michigan Railway Company on October 1, 1881, there were four companies that did construction work for some of these seven roads but did not operate themselves.

The first of these was the Lake Shore Railroad of Western Michigan, organized July 3, 1869. No available records exist regarding its affairs, it only being known that it was consolidated with the Chicago and Michigan Lake Shore Railroad on July 19, 1869.

The next was the Grand Rapids and Holland Railroad Company, organized in 1870 to build a railroad between these two points. There are no available records regarding the affairs of the road. It was consolidated with the Chicago and Michigan Lake Shore Railroad Company on December 19, 1871.

The third of these roads was the Montague, Pentwater and Manistee Railroad Company, organized July 11, 1871 for the purpose of building a line from Montague to Pentwater and perhaps to Manistee. No books of record can be found concerning it. It was consolidated with the Chicago and Michigan Lake Shore Railroad Company in 1872.

---

4. *Ibid*, 992.

The last of these roads was the Muskegon and Big Rapids Railroad Company, organized December 7, 1871 for the purpose of constructing a railroad between these two terminals. There are no records concerning the company's transactions, and when the line was completed this company was consolidated with the Chicago and Michigan Lake Shore Railroad Company on October 24, 1872.

As has already been intimated, the Chicago and West Michigan Railway Company was organized on October 1, 1881, as a consolidation of the Grand Haven; the Grand Rapids, Newaygo and Lake Shore; the Chicago and West Michigan; and the Indiana and Michigan railroad companies. The latter company was organized about the time of this consolidation with the purpose of building a road from New Buffalo to La Crosse, Indiana, a distance of 37 miles. This branch was opened for operation in November 1882.

The new corporation started with a clean sheet, the deficits of the consolidating companies being washed out in the plan of reorganization. The most logical direction for expansion seemed to be the north, where connections could be made with the Flint and Pere Marquette Railroad and a district rich in timber, even further north than this line, could be exploited. It will be remembered that White Cloud was the most northern point on the consolidated lines in 1881, but work had been started on a line from this station to Baldwin, on the Flint and Pere Marquette line, 26.4 miles distant, by a construction company, the White River Railroad Company organized in November 1879. By December 1, 1881 this line was partially completed and open for operation for a distance of 13 miles to Crooked

Lake and by the latter part of the next year 4 miles further to New Troy. In 1883 the entire distance to Baldwin was opened for operation and the next year this railroad, whose officers were the same as the officers of the Chicago and West Michigan Railway, and whose stock was owned by this latter company, was formally taken over by them and made a part of the Chicago and West Michigan Railway Company. The White River Railroad had proven a success, opening up a valuable timber country, and because of the large net revenues resulting was enabled to pay a dividend in 1882 of 4 per cent on its capital stock which had a par value of $124,500. No bonds had been issued.

No new lines were opened up for the next seven years but construction work was soon started on a further extension north, from Baldwin to Traverse City, a distance of 74 miles. In 1890 this line was finished and the following year the Chicago and North Michigan Railroad Company was organized to extend the road from Traverse City for a distance of 78.5 miles to Bay View, and a branch line from Williamsburg to Elk Rapids, 9.8 miles. These extensions were accomplished by 1894 and a new competitive line had now to be reckoned with by the Grand Rapids and Indiana and the Michigan Central railroads, which were north and south lines further east in the State.

The Chicago and North Michigan Railroad Company was practically one with the Chicago and West Michigan Railway Company, as they had common officers and the accounts of the former company were not kept separate from the accounts of the latter. In November 1899 this company was formally taken over by the Chicago and West Michigan Railway Company.

Also in 1899 the Chicago and West Michigan Railway Company leased a line running from Rapid City to Stratford, 32.6 miles, from the Grand Rapids, Kalkaska and South Eastern Railroad Company, for a term of ten years. All this northern district through which the Chicago and West Michigan had been threading its way was heavily timbered and an immediately profitable enterprise it proved to be; but it was short lived, and hence there should have been an amortization of the cost of construction based on the estimated life of the timber. This was not done, and in a few years this road found itself running through a country stripped of timber and without products for traffic, with a funded debt still alive and requiring a portion of the income, when that income was barely large enough to meet operating expenses.

For most of its lifetime the Chicago and West Michigan Railway was essentially a lumber road. In 1882, 69 per cent of the total freight traffic of 875,166 tons was lumber and forest products; in 1885, 65 per cent of a total of 855,068 tons; in 1890, 67 per cent of a total of 1,161,214 tons; and in 1895, 46 per cent out of a total tonnage of 1,205,263. During this period grain had increased from zero per cent to 11 per cent of the total tonnage, while merchandise had maintained about an average of 10 per cent. From 1882 to 1895 total tonnage had increased by 50 per cent and lumber and forest products tonnage had fallen off about 25 per cent. But this is hardly a fair comparison, since the mileage was increased by over 150 after 1890. If we consider the character of the traffic from 1882 to 1890, before the northern extension, we find that the total tonnage was about stationary or even declining, while lumber and forest products had decreased about 10 per cent. In 1890, after the Baldwin-Bay View line had been constructed, the total tonnage of the Chicago and West Michigan Railway had increased by about 300,000 tons over the average of former years, but this total tonnage remained stationary for the next nine years while lumber and forest products dropped off 25 per cent.

This would indicate that the falling off in net revenues during the nineties was partially due, at least, to the using up of the lumber supply and the slowness with which other products came to fill the gap. Total tonnage should have been increasing during this decade, instead of standing still, and no doubt this would have been the case if the land had been of such a character that it could have attracted settlers immediately after the timber had been cut.

Lake competition was also an important factor that tended to prevent a rapid increase in total tonnage of bulky products like salt, lumber and building stone. It seemed that tonnage could be increased only by increasing the through traffic and this meant outside connections. The consolidation with two other Michigan roads in 1900 was the culmination of this feeling of necessity that local roads were at a growing disadvantage compared with so-called through lines.

SUMMARY OF THE FINANCIAL CONDITIONS OF THE CHICAGO AND WEST MICHIGAN RAILWAY AND ITS CONSTITUENTS

The income account for the reorganized company, the Chicago and West Michigan Railway Company, from the date of reorganization, October 1, 1881, until its consolidation with the Pere Marquette Railroad

Company on December 31, 1899, showed that $1,954,-
055.17 was earned from operations, after deducting
interest on funded debt which accrued properly all
through this period. There existed a net surplus each
year until 1892 inclusive,[5] and then operating deficits
through the panic period from 1893 to 1897 inclusive,
during which time a receivership was avoided only by
an agreement with the bondholders which enabled the
company to pay a considerable portion of its bond interest with coupon scrip due in ten years, instead of
with cash. After this date surpluses were earned
again.

From 1882 to 1893 inclusive dividends were paid
regularly, and with one or two exceptions the dividends
were earned during the current year.[6] All together,
during the whole period of operation of the reorganized
company, there was paid out in dividends, $2,031,279.
In 1899 there was a net surplus of $48,528.43, when the
road was consolidated with the Pere Marquette Railroad Company.[7]

However, if we consolidate the income and profit and
loss statements of the Chicago and West Michigan
Railway Company and its constituents, so that all the
deficits that had been dropped at different periods of
reorganization from 1870 to 1899, would be taken into
consideration and not dropped on the books of the new
reorganized companies as has been shown, instead of

---

5. Also a very small surplus of $2,174.29 in 1893.
6. Dividends were paid on common stock (there being no
    preferred) as follows: 1882, 2 1-2%; 1883, 3%; 1884,
    4%; 1885, 1 1-2%; 1886, 3%; 1887, 2 1-2%; 1888, 2%;
    1889, 2%; 1890, 3%; 1891, 3 1-2%; 1892, 3 1-2%; 1893,
    1 1-2%.
7. *Stenographer's Minutes Before the I. C. C.*, Docket No. 6833,
    page 996.

there being a net surplus for this period of $48,528.43, there would have been a net deficit of $3,226,008.79.[8]

While in many cases of reorganization deficits were dropped on the books of the new corporation, it is also likewise true that deficits in some cases were written into the books of the reorganized company as an asset, that is, as cost of road. From available records it is exceedingly difficult to ascertain what became of the deficit items that were dropped at time of reorganization. In nearly all cases of reorganization no attempt has been made to show the cost of the physical property of the consolidated companies but simply a corresponding asset set up opposite the total of the capital stock and funded debt of the consolidated companies, so that profit and loss accounts lose their identity.[8]

8. *Stenographer's Minutes Before the I. C. C.*, Docket No. 6833. pp. 1000-2.

CHAPTER III

DETROIT, GRAND RAPIDS AND WESTERN RAILROAD
COMPANY

THE origin of the Detroit, Grand Rapids and
Western Railroad Company goes back to the
incorporation, September 21, 1864, of the Detroit and
Howell Railroad Company which shortly thereafter
began construction on a line between Detroit and
Howell, a distance of 52 miles. This was to be the
first link in a road from Detroit to Lansing and points
west and north of there, for which there had been an
incessant demand by local interests along the proposed
roadway for some time previous to this date.

The construction of the second section between
Howell and Lansing, a distance of 33 miles, was undertaken by the Howell and Lansing Railroad Company
soon after its incorporation June 23, 1868. After some
grading and extensive construction work had been done
by these two companies they were consolidated to
form the Detroit, Howell and Lansing Railroad Company in 1870. Due to financial difficulties work pro-
gressed slowly and it was not until the next year that
rails were laid and the road was ready for actual
operation.

Five years prior to the finishing of the line between
Detroit and Lansing, construction work had been
started by the Ionia and Lansing Railroad Company
on a line running between Lansing and Howard City.
This road was completed in sections, but as a totality

was ready for operation by the latter part of 1871. The Ionia and Lansing Railroad had difficulty in getting sufficient money to finish its construction and its credit was so bad that it received only $770,000 of cash out of a bond issue with a par value of $1,820,000. Later on, in order to complete the line, it had to take a second mortgage on its property from Lansing to Greenville. The $300,000 of bonds issued under this mortgage were not sold readily and finally suffered a discount of 50 per cent or $150,000. This apparently was not inducement enough to investors, so a stock bonus was given with each bond purchased.

Whatever may have been the difficulties the different roads had to contend with, there now existed a continuous stretch of track between Detroit and Howard City, a distance of 164 miles, owned by two different companies, viz., the Ionia and Lansing, and the Detroit, Howell and Lansing. The consolidation of these two roads to form the Detroit, Lansing and Lake Michigan Railroad Company took place early in 1871, and in this year trains ran for the first time between Detroit and Howard City, connections being made at the latter place with the Grand Rapids and Indiana Railway.

In 1873 a branch line was built from Ionia to Stanton, a distance of 24.3 miles, by the Ionia and Stanton Railroad Company, which company was consolidated with the Detroit, Lansing and Lake Michigan Railroad Company the following year. It was also in 1873 that a branch was extended from Kiddville to Belding, a distance of 1.7 miles. The total mileage of main track and branches was now about 189 miles, and no more was created by this company. Sidings and spurs for the different lumber camps were, however, built from time to time during later years as the need demanded.

The Detroit, Lansing and Lake Michigan Railroad was financed by the issue of $6,060,000 of first and second 8 per cent first mortgage bonds, and an issue of $1,644,000 of common stock given as a bonus to purchasers of these bonds. This stock was wrongly charged into the cost of road account and therefore the credit side of the balance sheet showed a more prosperous condition than in reality existed. The bonds suffered a discount of 20 and 30 per cent, amounting to a total of $1,122,700. No information is available that would give the cost of the property at the time of reorganization.

From the very beginning it was evident that the bonded indebtedness was too great for the earning capacity of the road, and earnings did not materially increase, due to the business depression following the panic of 1873. Like most of the roads that we have been considering, a large portion of the traffic (about 60 per cent) was lumber and forest products which felt the business depression before other tonnage. On July 31, 1876 it became necessary to place the road into the hands of a receiver, and from this date until December 31st of the same year the road was operated by the trustees under the mortgage for the benefit of the bondholders. It was then sold and reorganized by the purchasers under the name of the Detroit, Lansing and Northern Railroad Company; all property, rights and franchises of the Detroit, Lansing and Lake Michigan Railroad Company being taken over by the new company.

During its life the Detroit, Lansing and Lake Michigan Railroad showed a net loss from operation of $1,039,723.97, and this operating deficit was augmented to $2,117,555.18, largely by the addition of $1,122,700 in 1873 on account of debt discount extinguished through surplus.[1]

In the same year (1871) that the Detroit, Lansing and Lake Michigan Railroad began running its trains between Detroit and Howard City, a railroad was being projected by independent parties in the district west of Saginaw. This road was the Saginaw Valley and St. Louis Railroad, incorporated May 18, 1871, with the intention of constructing a road extending between Saginaw and St. Louis, a distance of 34 miles. On the first of the year 1873, 28.7 miles of road from St. Louis to Paines Junction was completed and opened for operation and the balance of the distance between Paines Junction and Saginaw was reached by running over the rails of the Jackson, Lansing and Saginaw Railroad Company.

The road was bonded with first mortgage 8 per cent bonds to the amount of $446,000, and the capital stock authorization was $300,000, one-third of which was given as a bonus to the purchasers of the bonds. The total issue of bonds suffered on the average about 25 per cent discount, or $113,225.

As might be surmised, the Saginaw Valley and St. Louis Railroad carried lumber and forest products for the most part, this traffic amounting to 96 per cent of the total tonnage in 1874 and well above 80 per cent in 1875.

This railroad started out with a surplus of about $27,000 the second year of operation, which was in-

1. *Ibid.*, 972.

creased to $91,000 in 1875, $103,000 in 1876, $135,000 in 1877 and about the same for 1878. From this it can be seen that the Saginaw Valley and St. Louis Railroad was an exceptional road in that it went through the business depression following 1873 without going into the hands of receivers, as so many of the roads in Michigan at this time were forced to do.

In 1879 practically all of the stock of this road was purchased by parties in the interest of the Detroit, Lansing and Northern Railroad Company, and was later taken over by that line, although the road retained its title and separate existence.

In this latter year the Saginaw Valley and St. Louis Railroad was extended 3.7 miles to Alma, the construction work being done under the name of the Saginaw and Grand Rapids Railroad Company. At this point connections were made with roads running north and west and from which it was expected a good deal of traffic would be transferred for the Saginaw River Valley.

The road that it made connections with on the west was the Chicago, Saginaw and Canada Railroad Company, which had completed a road from Alma to Cedar Lake, a distance of 20 miles, in the year 1875. It was essentially a lumber road, 83 per cent of its freight being lumber and forest products. Capital stock to the amount of $4,200,000 was authorized, $14,500 of which was paid in; while the bonded debt was $185,000, consisting of first mortgage 7 per cent bonds.

It was obvious after the first year of operation that the Chicago, Saginaw and Canada Railroad Company could not pay fixed charges amounting to $12,950, and $1,130 of operating expenses, out of a total gross income of $2,163.   Accordingly, it was thought advisable to place the road in the hands of a receiver, which was done on November 20, 1876.   The receiver, Mr. D. D. Erwin, in turn leased the road to one of the officers of the company, Mr. J. A. Elwell, who operated it under the lease for five years and in 1879 extended the road to Lake View, a distance of 15.3 miles.[2]

By 1881 the gross revenues were well over $100,000, with operating expenses and taxes about $60,000, but the unfunded debt had increased to about the size of the funded debt and there was unpaid interest on the former amounting to $223,600.   There was also an operating deficit of $143,936.06.[3]   It was evident that something had to be done to benefit the situation and receivership seemed the only step to take.   So in 1881 the road was sold at foreclosure sale and purchased by parties in the interests of the Detroit, Lansing and Northern Railroad Company, who operated it under

---

2.   For the receiver to turn over the road to one of its own officers, is one of those peculiar situations that one finds in early railroad affairs, regarding which, explanatory material seems to be nonexistent.

3.   There is unsupported evidence to show that the deficit for this period might have been as great as $500,000. The accountants for the Interstate Commerce Commission explain this as follows: "We could not check the income account into the general balance sheet, and the general balance sheet showed other debits at the end of each period than the income account would show, which would lead one to believe that there were items debited and credited to the profit and loss account which were not shown upon the income account, but we ignored the general balance sheet, taking into consideration the figures that went to make up their income account, so that there were items of probably two or three hundred thousand dollars more than show up in the profit and loss statement that are not included in our figures at all...." *Stenographer's Minutes Before the I. C. C.* Docket 6833, page 974.

the name of the Chicago and Western Railroad Company.

Having briefly described all of the roads that were incorporated prior to the Detroit, Lansing and Northern Railroad, which had been taken over by that road, or had their control turned over to it, we will now take up for consideration the main features regarding this road, which, it will be remembered, was the successor of the Detroit, Lansing and Lake Michigan Railroad, having purchased its property at foreclosure sale on January 1, 1877.

The plan of reorganization provided that $901,000 of first mortgage bonds should remain untouched. Holders of $3,794,000 of Detroit, Lansing and Lake Michigan first mortgage 8 per cent bonds, with a total annual interest of $303,520, received one-half of the amount of the principal in new thirty year first mortgage bonds, dated January 1, 1877, bearing interest at the rate of 7 per cent and secured by mortgage upon the entire property. The other half of the principal, $1,189,000, was exchanged at par for preferred stock of the new organization. Also, the unpaid half of first mortgage bond coupons of 1874 and 1875, amounting to $303,520, and coupons on first mortgage bonds of the Detroit, Lansing and Lake Michigan Railroad due in 1876, amounting to $303,520, were exchanged par for par for preferred stock. The total amount of preferred stock in the new organization was $2,504,040. This preferred stock was 7 per cent non-cumulative, and in case on any one year there was a surplus after paying 7 per cent on both common and preferred, this surplus should be divided equally between both classes of stock.

All second mortgage bonds, amounting to $1,358,000, and coupons, amounting to $326,160, together with all floating debts to the amount of $189,458.70, or a grand total of $1,874,613.70 was exchanged for common stock at par.   This made a total of $7,176,653.70 for both stock and bonds.

It has already been shown that the Detroit, Lansing and Lake Michigan Railroad had a deficit of over $2,000,000 at the time of consolidation in 1877 with the Detroit, Lansing and Northern Railroad, but such balance was not carried to the books of the new re-organized company so that the latter started with a clean sheet.   The following year, in 1878, it had a surplus of $206,163.71, and from then on for the next ten years dividends were paid regularly, as the balance remaining to surplus was yearly· more than the dividends paid.

The reorganized company began immediately to expand north and east again, completing a line from Stanton to Edmore in 1878 and extending this to Big Rapids in 1880 where connections were made with the Grand Rapids and Indiana Railway for north and south traffic and with the Chicago and West Michigan Railroad for traffic going east and west.   This added about 65 miles to the road's mileage, making a total of approximately 220 miles of main track.

In 1886 the Saginaw and Western Railroad, which was being operated by the Detroit, Lansing and Northern Railroad, was extended 10.8 miles from Lake View to meet the Detroit, Lansing and Northern tracks at Howard City, and also to make further connections with the Grand Rapids and Indiana Railway.

At this time the Detroit, Lansing and Northern

and the Chicago and West Michigan railroads were in close relationship since they had common directors, and there was a feeling that it would be for their mutual benefit if the tracks of the two roads were connected from east to west. Accordingly, on May 17, 1887 the Grand Rapids, Lansing and Detroit Railroad was incorporated with the purpose of constructing a line between Grand Ledge (near Lansing) and Grand Rapids. This line was completed and opened for operation the following year when it was taken over by the Detroit, Lansing and Northern Railroad. There was now a through line from Detroit to New Buffalo and an outlet for business originating on both lines making the connection.

About 70 per cent of the total tonnage continued to be lumber and forest products until 1885, approximately 60 per cent between 1885 and 1890, 52 per cent in 1890, 41 per cent in 1891 and 37 per cent on the average until the consolidation of the Detroit, Lansing and Northern into the Detroit, Grand Rapids and Western in 1896. Together with this falling off of 20 per cent in lumber and forest products tonnage from 1881 to 1890, there was also a falling off in total tonnage. In 1882 total tonnage was 746,998 but had gradually dropped to 486,624 in 1889. The tonnage rose from 1890 to 1893, but the panic of the latter year and the industrial depression following it lowered it again for several years.

During this period freight earnings had fallen from $1,136,868 in 1882 to $618,602 in 1895, but passenger earnings had increased in the same time from $445,821 to $508,841. The year of 1888 marks the turning point in the road's affairs. Up until this date dividends had been paid regularly for ten years and a surplus had accrued yearly; after 1888 until 1896 net revenues fell off yearly and were $200,000 less in 1896 than in 1877.

One of the chief causes for a decrease in net revenues was the decline of the lumber industry which was not checked soon enough by the rise of agricultural and industrial products tonnage to maintain former earnings. Through connections with western Michigan had helped to some extent in 1888, especially in the passenger earnings, but the freight earnings were not materially altered. What was left of the lumber traffic in 1893 and the few years directly following, was hard hit by the immediate decreased demand for building materials, especially lumber, and there seemed no alternative but receivership.

In view of these conditions the railroad went into the hands of a receiver on April 1, 1896 and was operated in this way until the end of the year when it was sold to representatives of the bondholders and reorganized under the name of the Detroit, Grand Rapids and Western Railroad Company, the new company taking possession on January 1, 1897.

Looking at the period of operation of the Detroit, Lansing and Northern as a whole, it shows a net gain from operations of $2,062,934.71. From this, however, should be deducted about $232,000 of interest charges on funded debt that were not set up during the period of receivership. From 1888 to 1896 the road showed a net loss from operations of $103,004.79.[4]

Included in the reorganization of the Detroit, Lansing and Northern Railroad were the Grand Rapids,

---

4. *Ibid*, 975.

Lansing and Northern, the Saginaw Valley and St. Louis, the Saginaw and Western, and the Saginaw and Grand Rapids railroads. These were all practically owned and operated by the Detroit, Lansing and Northern Railroad.

The new reorganized company started out with $3,442,000 of funded debt that had been outstanding against the Detroit, Lansing and Northern. No balance was carried over to the new company from the old, so that the reorganized company started out with a clean sheet.

SUMMARY OF THE FINANCIAL CONDITION OF THE DETROIT, GRAND RAPIDS AND WESTERN RAILROAD AND ITS CONSTITUENTS

Detroit, Grand Rapids and Western Railroad.

From January 1, 1897 to December 31, 1899, during which time the Detroit, Grand Rapids and Western operated, it showed net earnings from operation of $393,616.70, that is, after paying interest on funded debt. The new company earned no dividends during its existence, but just before it was taken into the consolidation in 1900 it declared a dividend of 6 per cent on its preferred stock, which was taken out of assets by order of the reorganization committee. Nothing was ever paid on the common stock. After the payment of this dividend there remained a balance in surplus of $202,882.70.[5]

The Saginaw Valley and St. Louis Railway.

This road operated for a period of 25 years from 1872 to 1896 and showed a net deficit from operations of

---

5. *Ibid*, 981.

$56,203.23.   Miscellaneous items in the profit and loss account brings this deficit up to $196,190.87.   However, in 1879 this company appropriated $137,652.42 from its surplus for investment in physical property, and since this was a betterment paid for out of earnings in lieu of cash dividends the actual deficit in 1896 would be only $60,000.[6]

The Detroit, Lansing and Lake Michigan Railroad.

This road operated three years from 1873 to 1876 and had a net loss from operations of $1,039,723.97, which would be augmented to $2,117,555.18, if we take into account the amount of debt extinguished through surplus.[7]

The Chicago, Saginaw and Canada Railroad Company operated from 1875 to 1882, for the most of this time under receivership.

The Detroit, Lansing and Northern Railroad.

This railroad succeeded the Detroit, Lansing and Lake Michigan Railroad without assuming the deficit. It operated from 1877 to 1896 and showed a net gain from operations of $2,062,934.71, from which should be subtracted $232,000 of interest charges on funded debt that was not set up during the period of receivership.[8]

---

6.   *Ibid*, 971.
7.   *Ibid*, 972.
8.   *Ibid*, 975.

The Lowell and Hastings Railroad.

This company was incorporated in May 1877 and began operations in 1888 over 12 miles of road between Lowell and Freeport. It operated from this date until 1899 when it was taken into the consolidation with the Pere Marquette Railroad Company and for this period showed a net gain from operations of $17,031.63.[9]

Taking the Detroit, Grand Rapids and Western Railroad and all its constituents for the entire period from 1872 to 1900, it is found that they earned from operation $1,218,219.78. In spite of this net earnings from operation, there was a deficit on December 31, 1899 of $2,356,877.41, which is accounted for chiefly by the fact that there was $1,122,700 of discount charged to surplus, and also by the fact that there was $2,053,173.50 paid in dividends. In other words, the actual net earnings up to December 31, 1899 from operations of the road just about balanced the discount leaving the dividends as a loss. That is, the dividends were responsible for the net loss on the date of consolidation with the Pere Marquette Railroad.[11]

It must be remembered that this net loss is not shown on the books of the different corporations, but is the cumulative loss made up by carrying into this compilation the actual figures of all the companies and dropping nothing incidental to reorganization.

9. *Ibid*, 977.
11. *Ibid*, 981.

CHAPTER IV

Crapo-Heald Administration (Jan. 1, 1900 to Jan. 1, 1903)

THE Pere Marquette Railroad Company came into being on January 1, 1900 as a consolidation of three railroad systems, viz., the Chicago and West Michigan, the Flint and Pere Marquette, and the Detroit, Grand Rapids and Western. The mileage of these roads totaled about 1700, all of which, with the exception of 41 miles and the car-ferry lines, was in the State of Michigan.

The properties were taken over subject to the existing liens against them, such liens for the most part consisting of mortgage bonds and a small amount of equipment trust bonds. The total indebtedness against the different roads taken into the consolidation amounted to $28,860,000[1] and for the most part was divided among the roads as follows: Bonds covering the old Flint and Pere Marquette Railroad, $11,465,000; bonds covering the Chicago and West Michigan Railway, $8,440,000, exclusive of $663,000 of script which had been issued in former years by that company to cover interest charges which it had been unable to pay; and finally, the bonds of the Detroit, Grand Rapids and Western Railroad, $5,380.000. There were also miscellaneous equipment bonds issued by the different

---

1. This figure differs from the bonded liability given in appendix A, in that the latter statement does not give miscellaneous equipment bonds that were liquidated a short time later.

companies, aggregating $575,000. All these bonds referred to are called underlying bonds, constituting first liens upon the different divisions of the reorganized company, for which, bonds of the new company for an equal amount were exchanged.

The Pere Marquette Railroad Company was capitalized at $28,000,000 which consisted of $12,000,000 four per cent non-cumulative preferred stock and $16,000,000 of common stock. This capital stock was exchanged for the stock of the different corporations that entered into the consolidation, in the following manner: In exchange for the $6,342,000, 7 per cent preferred stock of the Flint and Pere Marquette Railroad, the latter company received an equal amount of the preferred stock of the new company. For $3,298,000 of common stock, the Flint and Pere Marquette Railroad received $4,122,750 of the new common stock, or an excess of $824,550 over the par value of its stock.   The Chicago and West Michigan Railway had outstanding $7,512,800 of common stock (no preferred) and received in exchange for this stock an equal amount of new common stock.   The Detroit, Grand Rapids and Western Railroad had $3,183,500 of preferred stock which was exchanged for $3,820,200 of new preferred stock, or an excess of $636,700 over the par value of its own preferred stock.   The Detroit, Grand Rapids and Western Railroad also had $2,510,000 of common stock which was exchanged for an equal amount of common stock of the new company. There remained $1,837,800 of the new preferred stock either to be sold or kept in the treasury for future requirements.   Of the common stock to be sold or to remain in the treasury for future requirements there remained $1,854,450.[2]

From the above it is seen that a total of $1,461,250 consisting of both common and preferred stock was issued to the three combining companies in excess of the stocks of both kinds that were turned over to the new corporation. There is reason to think that the parties interested believed such a procedure justifiable on the grounds that the value of the new corporation, that is, its earning power, would be greater than the totality of earnings of the separate constituent corporations. Whatever their view may have been, it would seem that any increased earnings due to consolidation would have been reflected in a rise in value of the stock of the new corporation if it had been issued par for par for the stock of the constituent companies, thus making it unnecessary to anticipate those increased earnings as though they were an assured element of value on the basis of which extra stock could be issued. If the increased earnings due to consolidation did not materialize then the excessive stock would be worthless and tend to embarrass the corporation, since the same earnings as existed prior to consolidation would now be spread over a larger number of shares of stock, and hence would amount to a lower dividend per share. This would in turn tend to reduce the value of the shares more quickly than if a smaller number of shares of stock were out-

---

2. The difference between the capital stock figures on this page and those in appendix A, is due to the fact that some stockholders did not present their shares for exchange, and thus a portion of the capital stock of the new company was held in reserve for this purpose.

standing, especially if earnings of the consolidated company began to fall off.

The property, physical and non-physical, behind the total issue of $56,860,000 of bonds and stock, had a value of $30,845,588, leaving $26,014,412 as an excess of securities behind which there was no physical or non-physical property.[3] The only value this excess would possess would be derived from the capitalization of any earnings that existed above what would be necessary for fixed charges and operating expenses. At the rate of 5 per cent per annum on this sum, it would be necessary to earn $1,300,720.60 above fixed charges and operating expenses; but from what the three constituent roads had earned prior to consolidation it is quite fair to say that any such extravagant views could not be considered seriously. In fact it would have been doubtful whether half of this amount could have been earned.

From what has been said it would appear that the stock could not be worth $26,014,412 due to the possibility of future earnings or in the light of past earnings of the three roads. Neither can it be said that it was worth this amount because of its purchase price, for much of it had been given as a bonus to purchasers of bonds and to equipment companies and other parties.

---

3. Table I and II.   See next page.

TABLE I.—STATEMENT SHOWING THE AVERAGE EARNINGS AND INCOME AND AVERAGE EXPENDITURES INCIDENT TO OPERATION OF THE THREE CONSOLIDATED PROPERTIES IN THE YEAR 1900.[1]

	Chicago and West Michigan		Detroit, Grand Rapids and Western		Flint and Pere Marquette	
Number of years averaged	9½		9½		10	
Gross earnings	$1,743,654		$1,357,301		$2,415,572	
Operating expenses	1,278,488		1,026,328		1,715,640	
Net income from operation		$465,166		$330,983		$699,932
Net income from investment		6,366		4,846		123,220
Total corporate income		$471,532		$335,829		$823,152
Rents of Michigan property not included in Cooley appraisal	0		0		0	
Interest on interest-bearing current liabilities	1,842		2,138		39,519	
Permanent improvements in Michigan charged to income	0		0		10,724	
Total deductions from corporate income		1,842		2,138		50,243
Surplus from Operation		$469.690		$333,691		$772,909
Deficit from Operation						

[1]From private papers of H. C. Adams.

TABLE II.—STATEMENT SHOWING COMPUTATION OF THE NON-PHYSICAL VALUE OF THE THREE ROADS.[1]

	Chicago and West Michigan		Detroit, Grand Rapids and Western		Flint and Pere Marquette	
Number of years averaged....................	9½		9½		10	
Mean value of physical elements (computed from Cooley appraisal).....................	$8,614,417		$6,270,074		$11,832,989	
Corporate surplus from operation..............		$469,690		$333,691		$772,909
Tax of 1% allowed on mean value of physical elements....................................	86,144		62,701		118,330	
Annuity of 4% allowed on mean value of physical elements....................................	344,577		250,803		473,320	
Sum of tax and annuity.....................		430,721		313,504		591,650
Net corporate surplus.....................		$38,969		$20,187		$181,259
Net corporate deficit........................						
Capitalization of net corporate surplus at 7%, giving value of non-physical elements........	$556,700		$288,386		$2,589,414	
Cooley appraisal of physical elements..........	9,243,105		6,468,854		11,699,129	
Present value of property.................		$9,799,805		$6,757,240		$14,288,543

[1]From private papers of H. C. Adams.

Between 1880 and 1890 it is true that dividends had been paid, for the most part at least, on the stock of the three constituent roads, but during the last ten years of their operation before consolidation the surpluses were wiped away in some cases and dividends suspended; and also, receiverships made unnecessary the payment of interest on bonds while the roads were out of the hands of the owners. In fact if the entire period of operation of all the different roads that enter into the Pere Marquette Railroad be taken into consideration, and no allowance is made for the washing out of deficits incident to reorganizations, and interest is charged for bonded indebtedness during the different receiverships, it will be found that little if any dividends could be paid on stock, thereby making it approach closer to zero value than to par value. Only by being relieved of paying interest on bonds during receiverships, and by dropping deficits at each reorganization, had the stock of these different railroads been able to make a showing as regards the payment of dividends.

Early in 1900 the Pere Marquette Railroad took over the operation of the Grand Rapids, Kalkaska and Southeastern Railroad, 32 miles in length, which was being run under a ten-year lease made to the Chicago and West Michigan Railway in 1898. It also took over under lease the Grand Rapids, Belding and Saginaw Railroad, 28 miles in length, which, at the time of reorganization of the Pere Marquette Railroad, was under lease to the Detroit, Grand Rapids and Western Railroad, the latter having an option to purchase that railroad at $10,000 per mile, less mortgage indebtedness of $260,000.

In March of the same year the Pere Marquette

Railroad took over the Saginaw, Tuscola and Huron Railroad, 65 miles in length, subject to the $1,000,000 of outstanding bonds. Thus, early in 1900 the funded debt of the Pere Marquette Railroad was increased by $1,260,000.

Soon after consolidation, the Marquette Equipment Company, Limited, was organized as a means of purchasing new equipment on time payments. The Pere Marquette Railroad, like a good many other railroads, found it needed to expend large sums on equipment which sums could not be taken out of earnings. Instead of paying for the equipment down through the proceeds of general mortgage bonds, the Pere Marquette Railroad financed the purchase of equipment by placing the title of the equipment purchased, in the Marquette Equipment Company as its trustee, and received an interest in the equipment only to the extent of the payments that it made from time to time. In other words, the Marquette Equipment Company, Limited, became the purchasing agent for the Pere Marquette Railroad Company. The latter company guaranteed the bonds of the equipment company which were secured by a first lien on the equipment, so that the seller of the equipment who held the bonds of the Marquette Equipment Company was secure against any loss, for any general mortgage would be subordinate to the equipment lien. The stock of the Marquette Equipment Company was all owned by the Pere Marquette Railroad Company.

During 1900 and 1901 a total of $921,000 of these equipment bonds of the Marquette Equipment Company were issued, covering the unpaid purchase price of miscellaneous equipment. These bonds matured serially over a period of ten years and the last payment on them was made in 1910.

It might be noted that both the Flint and Pere Marquette and the Chicago and West Michigan railroads had become responsible upon bonds of equipment companies at different times prior to consolidation in 1900. They were included in the $28,860,000 of bonds which the Pere Marquette Railroad became responsible for on taking over the three companies.

The Pere Marquette Railroad issued its first general mortgage known as the Consolidated Mortgage, on January 1, 1901, covering the entire system and subject to the underlying bonds. It was for an authorized issue of $50,000,000, $26,656,000 of which was reserved for the purpose of refunding these underlying bonds as they should mature, and also the equipment bonds outstanding. The remainder of the bond issue was reserved exclusively for the purpose of paying for the cost of additions and betterments, with the restriction that the total, including underlying bonds and those issued previously under the Consolidated Mortgage, should not exceed $20,000 a mile for single mileage, and $25,000 a mile for double track mileage.

During the first year of the Consolidated Mortgage, namely 1901, a total of $2,500,000 of bonds was issued, $1,726,000 of which was expended in additions and betterments and approximately the remainder in refunding. These bonds were sold to Robert Winthrop and Company of New York, $1,500,000 selling for $92\frac{1}{2}$ and $1,000,000 selling for 90. The money secured on the bonds that sold for $92\frac{1}{2}$ cost the railroad company $4\frac{3}{8}$ per cent per annum and the money secured on the bonds selling for 90 cost the company $4\frac{1}{2}$ per cent.

In 1902, $2,105,000 additional Consolidated Mortgage bonds were issued and all excepting $75,000 were sold to the same banking house for 92½. The amount excepted was sold to the trustees of the Nathaniel Thayer Estate. The sum received from these bonds cost the company 4⅜ per cent per annum and was expended for new equipment, changes in grades, real estate and miscellaneous improvements.

The finances of the railroad were vitally affected by a law passed in 1901 and taking effect in 1902, that changed the method of taxing railroads in Michigan. Prior to this, state railroads had been taxed on a specific (gross earnings) basis, but the new law changed this basis to an ad valorem one. The important results of this law can be seen from a statement of the taxes from 1901 to 1910 inclusive, as follows: 1900, $253,000; 1901, $255,000; 1902, $482,000; 1903, $713,000; 1904, $471,000; 1905, $474,000; 1906, $461,000; 1907, $496,000; 1908, $514,000; 1909, $620,000; 1910, $606,000.

In other words, during the nine years of the ad valorem tax the average amount per year paid for taxes was $537,000, while the average amount paid under the specific tax law was $254,000. This tax paid to the State is exclusive of terminal taxes on property in Grand Rapids and Detroit, which is used by the Pere Marquette Railroad but is not owned by it. The Pere Marquette's proportion of these taxes amounts to about $15,000 per year. To sum up the results of the new tax law, the average annual increase in Michigan taxes levied on the Pere Marquette for those nine years was $283,000, a sum equal to nearly one per cent on $30,000,000.

During the latter part of 1902 an important transaction took place which was to have a far-reaching influence on future Pere Marquette Railroad affairs. F. H. Prince who had been a director of the Flint and Pere Marquette Railroad before 1900 and a director of the Pere Marquette Railroad since its organization, together with associates, acquired a large block of the common stock, so that with what they held previously they owned or controlled 110,000 shares of the par value of $11,000,000. This was less than a majority of the stock outstanding but it amounted to virtual control. As a result of this purchase the board of directors was reorganized in December of 1902 to suit the demands of F. H. Prince and associates. Mr. W. W. Crapo who had been with the company or its constituents for over forty years, resigned, as did others who had been connected with the lines referred to.

The Crapo-Heald administration came to an end by reason of the resignation of Mr. W. W. Crapo the president and Mr. Heald an officer of the company. The funded debt had increased by $6,148,000 during this administration, and the total funded debt now amounted to $31,433,000. Of this latter sum, $990,000 consisted of outstanding equipment bonds and the remainder of underlying and general mortgage bonds. Dividends had been paid regularly on preferred stock during the first three years of operation, and apparently the road was in first class condition. There had been some talk by a certain few of the stockholders that the Pere Marquette Railroad ought to be made more of a through line from Chicago to Buffalo, but the Crapo-Heald administration refused to make

35

the purchases that would accomplish this end. It remained for the new administration to further this plan.

CHAPTER V

PRINCE ADMINISTRATION (JAN. 1, 1903 TO MARCH 1, 1905)

THE new administration immediately took up the task of making the Pere Marquette Railroad a through line. It was felt that it was necessary and desirable to do this in order to secure a portion of the heavy through tonnage between Chicago and Buffalo, and also to increase the length of the haul on business originating on its own lines.

As a first step toward this desired goal, the Pere Marquette Railroad Company in January 1903 purchased the capital stock of the Lake Erie and Detroit River Railway Company which owned a line extending from Walkerville, opposite Detroit, to St. Thomas, Ontario; and another line from Sarnia, opposite Port Huron, to Rond Eau, on Lake Erie. The capital stock of this company was paid for in 4 per cent twenty year bonds of the Pere Marquette Railroad, amounting to $2,870,000, which represented the full purchase price. Furthermore, the Pere Marquette Railroad became responsible for $3,000,000 of 5 per cent bonds outstanding and issued prior to this date of purchase. As long as interest was paid on these bonds the Pere Marquette Railroad was to have voting power of the stock, but in case of default on interest the voting power would revert to the former owners.

This purchase added directly to the Pere Marquette Railroad, lines aggregating 199 miles, and indirectly, control of the London and Port Stanley Railroad, 23 miles in length, extending from Port Stanley on Lake Erie to London, Ontario, which had been leased for a term of years expiring January 1, 1914 to the Lake Erie and Detroit River Railway Company. It also added to the fixed charges of the Pere Marquette Railroad 4 per cent on the purchase price and 5 per cent on the underlying bonds of the Canadian lines, the interest charges aggregating $264,000. As an offset to these charges it gave the Pere Marquette Railroad all the earnings of these lines and also the indirect advantage that it would obtain from the additional traffic originating in or destined to points on the Canadian lines.

As evidence of the favorable light in which this purchase was held at the time, it might be noted that three-fourths of the outstanding shares voted at the stockholder's meeting and every share voted for the ratification of the purchase.[1] It has since been demonstrated that this purchase was a profitable line, and during subsequent receiverships of the Pere Marquette Railroad interest was paid on the bonds of the Canadian lines because it was believed that they were paying their way.

Not only were the Canadian lines in a prosperous condition at the time of purchase, but they had been a profitable investment prior to this time. From 1892 to 1903 the net result from operations was a credit balance of $175,204.08. There were no books prior to that date, but on January 1, 1892 a surplus of

---

1. The stock voting was all practically owned or controlled by F. H. Prince, hence all that can be said is that the purchase was favored by the banking house which he represented and of which he was president.

$25,902.75 was brought forward, which had accumulated from the time of organization up to 1892.

The credit balance was cut down by dividends paid in 1902 and 1903 to the Walker sons who owned the road, so that when the Lake Erie road was finally merged into the Pere Marquette Railroad it showed an accumulated surplus of $12,003.51. In 1903, during the months that the Pere Marquette Railroad operated this road, dividends were declared amounting to $86,100, the sole stockholder of the Lake Erie road at that time being the Pere Marquette Railroad.

With the purchase of these Canadian lines only part of the distance to Buffalo was covered, and it now remained to make some arrangements to complete the rest of the distance so that Pere Marquette trains could tap traffic originating in the East and carry it by a short-cut to the Northwest via Sarnia, Ontario, Ludington, Michigan, and car-ferry across Lake Michigan.

Accordingly, negotiations were commenced in December 1903 and an agreement was made with the Canadian Southern Railway and the Michigan Central Railroad, granting the Pere Marquette Railroad the right to run freight trains over their tracks between St. Thomas, Ontario, and the Niagara River, with terminals at Niagara Falls and at Black Rock opposite Buffalo, a distance to the former place of 116 miles and to the latter 118. Even this extension gave the Pere Marquette Railroad only a very roundabout route between Sarnia and Niagara River over the Lake Erie and Detroit River Railway, so a further agreement was entered into with the Canadian Southern Railway giving the Pere Marquette Railroad trackage rights from Courtright, Ontario (nearly opposite Port Huron) to St. Thomas, Ontario. This line was never used as its use would have compelled the Pere Marquette Railroad to pay a portion of the maintenance expenses appertaining to it. Rent, however, was paid for this line for a time even though it was not used, but later on the Pere Marquette was released from this obligation.

The trackage contract with the Canadian Southern and the Michigan Central provided for an annual rental of $165,000, which sum was $2\frac{1}{2}$ per cent of the total value of the property; on the theory that 5 per cent was a normal rate of interest at the time, and that by this contract the Pere Marquette Railroad was virtually made half owner of the property. The contract also provided· for payment of one-half of the taxes, also a car mileage proportion of the expenses of maintaining the track. Likewise, any expense for additions and improvements would be divided equally between the Pere Marquette Railroad and the owners.

As yet the goal, Buffalo, had not been reached, so in the beginning of the year 1904 negotiations were taken up with the New York Central Railroad for trackage rights east of the Niagara River. As a result of these negotiations, extensive trackage rights were secured, both for passenger and for freight trains on the tracks between Niagara Falls and Buffalo and in the terminal facilities at Niagara Falls. By these arrangements the Pere Marquette Railroad, in July, 1904, was able to make direct connections with nearly all the trunk lines east of Niagara River. There was no fixed rental for these privileges and this right to use the tracks but the compensation consisted of so much per car.

About the same time, more direct connections were made with Buffalo by means of an arrangement with the owners of the International Bridge between Black Rock and Buffalo, which enabled the Pere Marquette Railroad to run its trains across the bridge at the rate of a dollar per car for loaded cars and fifty cents for empty ones.

By means of these connections with eastern roads, both at Buffalo and Niagara Falls, the Pere Marquette Railroad was now in a condition to handle a much larger business and increase the length of its haul on its own lines. It was now not so dependent on traffic originating in Michigan and it was hoped that this new connection would counteract to some extent at least the decrease in tonnage over some of the branch lines caused by the decline of the lumber industry. That it succeeded in this respect there is little doubt.

During the early part of 1903 when the Pere Marquette was being pushed east by means of purchase and lease, plans were being made and measures taken to extend the Pere Marquette Railroad westward, ultimately to Chicago. Pursuant to this intention three small roads were purchased on April 1, 1903 from Frederick W. Steele. These roads were the South Haven and Eastern, from South Haven to Lawton, a distance of 33.8 miles; the Milwaukee, Benton Harbor and Columbus, from Benton Harbor to Buchanan, a distance of 26 miles; and the Benton Harbor, Coloma and Paw Paw Lake, from Coloma to Paw Paw, a distance of 2.7 miles. These purchases added an aggregate mileage to the Pere Marquette Railroad of about 63 miles.

These roads were purchased at a cost of $726,000

free of any incumbrance or indebtedness. The purchase price paid for these properties was covered by a cash payment of $26,000 and $700,000 par value in Consolidated Mortgage 4 per cent bonds.

The chief reason for making this purchase, as already intimated, was to secure a shorter route to Chicago from Detroit and points east. This was to be accomplished, it was planned, by extending the South Haven and Eastern Railroad from Lawton (its terminus at time of purchase) to Kalamazoo, a distance of 25 miles; and then by the purchase of the Chicago, Kalamazoo and Saginaw Railroad that extended from Kalamazoo to Woodbury, the last named place being a station on the main line of the Pere Marquette Railroad. By the purchase of the Chicago, Kalamazoo and Saginaw Railroad and the construction of this 25 miles of road between Lawton and Kalamazoo, the Pere Marquette Railroad would cut off a large bend in its main line and be able to compete to a greater extent for through traffic from the eastern points to Chicago. Moreover, it was thought desirable for the Pere Marquette Railroad to get access to the city of Kalamazoo.

A further reason for the purchase of these three properties was the desire for a larger mileage in proportion to the cost, so that a basis could be had for the issue of additional bonds under the mortgage of 1901, thus affording a temporary means of raising additional moneys.

The shortening of the line from Detroit to points west failed to materialize, as the Michigan Central bought the Chicago, Kalamazoo and Saginaw Railroad before the Pere Marquette Railroad could complete its negotiations.

Financially, these three lines had proven unsuccessful prior to purchase by the Pere Marquette, and after purchase by that company continued to live up to their reputation. The most important of these roads, the South Haven and Eastern Railroad, began business in 1877 and operated until 1893 under the name of the Toledo and South Haven Railroad. During the period of operation this road showed a surplus of $44,537.46, but no interest was accrued by the receiver from June 11, 1890 to May 20, 1894 on the $216,000 of first mortgage bonds bearing interest at the rate of 6 per cent, which would have amounted to $12,960 per year or $51,840 for the four years. If this had been paid, instead of the road showing a surplus of $44,537.46 it would have shown a deficit for the entire period of $7,302.54.[2] In 1894 the Toledo and South Haven Railroad was reorganized into the South Haven and Eastern Railroad which operated until 1903 when it was taken ovei by the Pere Marquette Railroad. During the period after 1894 the reorganized company had been losing money and it was believed at the time of purchase by the Pere Marquette that it could only prove successful if it was extended to Kalamazoo, or was used as a cut-off from the main line for through Chicago traffic. Since this scheme failed of realization it seemed that there was no other alternative than to run it in its present condition at a loss. Finally, in 1906, during the receivership of the Pere Marquette Railroad, the South Haven and Eastern Railroad was

---

2. *Stenographer's Minutes Before the I. C. C.*, Docket No. 6833, page 1011.

leased to an electric line known as the Kalamazoo, Lake Shore and Chicago Railroad Company, and it was operated by that company under a lease by which the Pere Marquette received a rental of $20,000 a year.

The line from Benton Harbor to Buchanan had also proven financially unsuccessful prior to purchase in 1903 but it was thought that it might be a paying proposition if it could be extended to South Bend, Indiana. These plans were never carried out and this road continued to run at an actual loss.[3]

Simultaneously with the purchase of the so-called Steele properties and the extension in Canada, plans were being made for an extension of the Pere Marquette Railroad into Chicago. Until 1903 the nearest its tracks approached Chicago was New Buffalo, Michigan, from which point it operated to Chicago by turning its coaches over to the Michigan Central Railroad.

The original plans contemplated the building of a line extending from New Buffalo to Hammond, Indiana, which is close to the line of the city of Chicago. The proposed roadway was surveyed and the Pere Marquette Railroad, through a subsidiary company known as the Pere Marquette Railroad Company of Indiana, "organized for purposes of convenience in acquiring right of way and so forth," began the construction of a line toward Chicago from New Buffalo.[4]

By the latter part of December 1903, when the road had been extended to Porter, Indiana, a distance of 22 miles, an agreement was entered into with the Lake Shore and Michigan Southern Railroad Com-

____

3. Before a Committee of the Michigan Legislature, Testimony
    of Frederick W. Stevens, I, 37.
4. *Ibid*, 35 ff.

pany for trackage rights over their line from Porter, Indiana, to Pine, Indiana, a distance of 18 miles, for a period of 99 years. At the same time an agreement was executed with the Chicago Terminal Transfer Railroad Company for trackage rights over its lines from Pine, Indiana, to the Grand Central Station on Harrison street, Chicago, a distance of about 34 miles, extending for a period of 99 years and including the use of the passenger station at Chicago.

The original cost of these piece-meal attempts to get into Chicago was great while the traffic resulting was disappointing. The first lap on the westward expansion, i. e., the line constructed from New Buffalo to Porter, cost $713,000. The Pere Marquette Railroad Company of Indiana, the subsidiary company, issued its 4 per cent bonds aggregating $675,000, secured by a first mortgage on this 22 miles of road. It also issued stock to the par value of $500,000, so that altogether, $1,175,000 of securities were issued on this stretch of road, or more than $53,000 per mile. This issue also includes a small amount of equipment and some terminal property in Chicago.

The next lap in the extension, that from Porter to Pine which consisted of trackage rights, was rented to the Pere Marquette Railroad for an annual sum of $26,000, the payment of a proportion of the taxes and a proportion of the maintenance expenses on the car-mileage basis. This trackage contract was similar to the one made with the Canadian lines, in which the Pere Marquette Railroad agreed to pay an increased rental equal to $2\frac{1}{2}$ per cent of the additions and improvements. By reason of this stipulation the rental increased to over $30,000 while the Pere Marquette's proportion of the taxes on that line have run over $8,000 a year.[5]

The rent charged by the Chicago Terminal Transfer Railroad Company for its freight and passenger facilities amounted at first to $88,000 a year, but by the terms of the contract that rent increased without reference to additions and improvements until in 1912 it amounted to $159,000 a year. The Pere Marquette Railroad also agreed to pay a proportion of the taxes which, at the start, amounted to about $25,000, and a proportion of the maintenance expenses of the property which it used jointly with other companies, as well as all expenses of maintenance on the property that it used exclusively.[6]

Operation of Pere Marquette trains into Chicago commenced in December 1903, and thereby a new competitive line from Detroit and western Michigan to Chicago was created. But it was soon found that the tracks of the Chicago Terminal Transfer Railroad Company from Pine to Chicago were so congested with freight traffic that the Pere Marquette passenger service would suffer in competition with other lines by reason of the delays in getting into the passenger terminal. In order to get a more direct route and avoid the delays due to crossings and to the use of the tracks for freight purposes, it was considered necessary to make other arrangements for entrance into Chicago. This was accomplished on June 30, 1904 by making an agreement with the Pennsylvania Railroad Company and the Chicago and Alton Railway Company whereby, for a period of ten years, the Pere Marquette

5. *Ibid*, 34.
6. *Ibid*, 35.

passenger trains were given joint use of their tracks from Clark Junction, Indiana, to a connection with the tracks of the Chicago Terminal Transfer Railroad Company at 16th street in Chicago, a distance of 21 miles.

According to the agreement the Pere Marquette Railroad was to pay a yearly rental of $125,000 for five passenger trains per day, or about $68 per train. This rental was to be increased if a greater number of trains were operated and decreased if a smaller number of trains used the tracks.[7]

The Pere Marquette was now running through trains from Michigan to Chicago but the achievement was won at a great cost. The annual fixed charges had greatly increased due to these rentals, taxes and interest which amounted in the beginning to $277,000 and grew later, due to the terms of the contract, to about $339,000 in 1912. In other words, it cost this sum for Pere Marquette trains to travel over 77 miles of track from New Buffalo to Chicago, which amounts to about $4,402 per mile. Up until 1912 the increased traffic due to the Chicago extension was not of sufficient magnitude to cover the additional fixed charges. Since that date plans have been formulated for more favorable financial arrangements at the Chicago terminal.[8]

Since 1900 the Pere Marquette Railroad had been operating the Grand Rapids, Kalkaska and South Eastern Railroad under a ten-year lease made in 1898 with the Chicago and West Michigan Railway Company, which provided that the Chicago and West

7. *Ibid*, 35.
8. *Ibid*, 36.

Michigan Railway Company pay an annual rental of $20,000 in monthly installments, and in addition, pay 15 per cent of the gross receipts from the road on all shipments, except pine, wherever they originated. These features in the lease proved to be more burdensome than anticipated, so the Pere Marquette purchased the Grand Rapids, Kalkaska and South Eastern Railroad in August 1903.

The terms of the purchase provided that the Pere Marquette Railroad should become responsible for the $203,000 of 4 per cent bonds outstanding, and also exchange Consolidated Mortgage bonds of the par value of $107,000 for the $264,000 of stock of this company. This effected a yearly saving, since the annual payment under the purchase for interest on the aggregate of bonds would be $7,600 less than it was under the lease, not taking under consideration the 15 per cent of the gross earnings which it was no longer necessary to pay.[9]

Two other reasons for the purchase might be given. One was the contemplated carrying into execution of a plan to extend this property down to the branch running to Leota, thus forming a through line from the old Flint and Pere Marquette line at Clare to Charlevoix and Petoskey by a much shorter route. Due to financial difficulties and also the fact that the district through which this contemplated line would run was not of such a character that much valuable traffic would be originated, this plan was never carried out.[10]

Another reason for the purchase was the fact that this 32 miles of railroad could be made the basis for an

---

9. *Ibid*, 38.
10. *Ibid*, II, 48.

additional issue of bonds under the 1901 mortgage. About $8,000 per mile was paid for the road, and under the mortgage of 1901 the Pere Marquette Railroad was permitted to issue $20,000 of bonds per mile of single track.

The road had originally been built from the proceeds of about $155,000 of bonds, and $264,000 of stock had been given to the purchasers as a bonus. The stockholders, therefore, were given extraordinary consideration when they received $107,000 of Pere Marquette bonds and the assumption by the Pere Marquette of all indebtedness against the road.

What the value of this stock was at the time of purchase by the Pere Marquette is a matter of doubt. The Grand Rapids, Kalkaska and South Eastern Railroad had moved large amounts of timber from the terminus of the road to Muskegon and other points but its earnings were not kept separate from the earnings of the Chicago and West Michigan Railway, so it is impossible to ascertain whether the Grand Rapids, Kalkaska and South Eastern Railroad operated at a loss or not. But judged from the business done since that date it is reasonable to say that the road was barely earning operating expenses in 1903 with no better prospects for the future, so that the stock for which Pere Marquette bonds were given was practically worthless except for purposes of control. The timber traffic which had been the chief asset of the road was exhausted and there was nothing else to take its place. The policy that the Grand Rapids, Kalkaska and South Eastern Railroad should have followed in its earlier years of operation, was to have written off the assets of the road in a period of years estimated on the life of the timber. If such a policy had been followed this road would not have fallen into the embarrassing situation in which it then found itself, i. e., with no products for transportation, and bonds, still alive, demanding the payment of interest.[11]

To sum up the situation, the purchase of this lumber road by the Pere Marquette Railroad was a transaction of doubtful validity and one that brought loss to the Pere Marquette Railroad.[12] Recently the Michigan Railroad Commission has given permission for the abandonment of part of this branch, extending from Kalkaska to Stratford, thus relieving the Pere Marquette of the expense of operating a portion of the road at a loss.

Besides the extensive expansion of the Pere Marquette Railroad already described, several other important connections and extensions were made in the year 1903 under the Prince administration. The extension of greatest significance resulted from a consideration of the question of providing a larger coal traffic. This matter was seriously discussed with the Bessemer and Lake Erie Railroad Company, which operated a line running from Conneaut, Ohio (on Lake Erie) into the coal fields below that point, with an idea of stimulating through traffic from the coal fields on their line in Pennsylvania to points on the line of the Pere

---

11. *Ibid*, 50.
12. It has been held by some that the chief stockholders of the Grand Rapids, Kalkaska and South Eastern Railroad were intimately and closely associated with the affairs of the Pere Marquette and caused the latter railroad to give its bonds in exchange for their worthless stock. This, however, has not been verified.

Marquette. The outcome was the formation of the Marquette and Bessemer Dock and Navigation Company capitalized at $50,000, each railroad company subscribing to 50 per cent of the stock. This new corporation was to operate a car ferry across Lake Erie from a connection with the Bessemer and Lake Erie Railroad at Conneaut, Ohio, to a connection with the Pere Marquette lines at Port Stanley, Ontario; and to operate a collier from the former place to a connection with the Pere Marquette Railroad at Rond Eau, Ontario. The Bessemer and Lake Erie Railroad and the Pere Marquette Railroad jointly guaranteed the principal and interest on $500,000 of first mortgage 4½ per cent thirty year gold bonds, and on $80,000 of 5 per cent thirty year debenture bonds of the Navigation Company. The result of this traffic connection was a movement of a large amount of tonnage over the lines of the Pere Marquette.[13]

Further expansion took place in August of 1903 when the Pere Marquette Railroad purchased the entire capital stock (10,000 shares) of the Huron and Western Railroad Company, 11 miles in length, which operated and owned a line running from Bay City out to some mines owned by the Wolverine Coal Company; and at the same time it purchased 50 per cent of the stock of this coal company. These two purchases cost the Pere Marquette Railroad $325,000 in cash and the assumption of $106,000 of bonds outstanding against the railroad company.[14]

The Pere Marquette operated these mines with the consent of the Consolidated Coal Company of Bay City

---

13. *Ibid*, I, 31.
14. *Ibid*, 39.

which owned the other half of the stock. The purpose of this purchase was to provide a cheap, permanent fuel supply for the Pere Marquette locomotives, it being agreed that the Wolverine Coal Company was to give the Pere Marquette Railroad all the output of certain of its mines at cost of production plus ten cents per ton. The transaction proved to be a profitable one for the Pere Marquette Railroad and materially reduced the portion of its operating expenses formally allotted for coal.

Other minor extensions were made in 1903 the first of which was one from Harbor Beach to Port Hope, a distance of 8 miles, built as a result of an appeal made to the general manager of the Pere Marquette Railroad by a delegation of citizens from Port Hope. The cost of the extension was $77,000 but it seemed at the time that sufficient traffic would be secured at Port Hope to warrant the building of it. Unfortunately this was not to be true, and almost since the date of commencement of operation the road has been operated at a loss, including the stretch of road from Harbor Beach to Palms.[15]

The Pere Marquette Railroad became the owner of another small piece of property in June 1903, viz., the Sanilac Center branch, extending from Sanilac Center to Portland, about 7 miles. This branch had been built some years previous under a contract stipulating that the Pere Marquette Railroad should pay half the cost and take half the stock. On this date the Pere Marquette purchased the remainder of the stock amounting to $60,000 and thereby became sole owner of the line.

---

15. *Ibid*, 39.

Futher expansion was attempted in 1904, this time in Northern Michigan, which resulted in a loss for the Pere Marquette. The owners of the stock of a railroad known as the Manistique, Marquette and Northern, extending for 47 miles between Shingleton on the Duluth, South Shore and Atlantic Railway, and Manistique on Lake Michigan, were anxious to sell their control and gave the Pere Marquette Railroad the control of this line for a limited time, together with the option for the purchase of the stock for $75,000, subject to the outstanding bonds against the property. The Pere Marquette took over the property under these conditions for a year but the operation of the road proved to be a losing proposition, the Pere Marquette Railroad sustaining a loss during this time of approximately $21,000. The option, therefore, was not exercised, so the property went back to the former owners.[16]

Another matter of importance during 1903 was the organization of the Eastern Equipment Company based on the same lines as the Marquette Equipment Company, through which corporation $5,503,000 of rolling stock, car-ferries and other equipment was purchased. A further important transaction was the issue of more Consolidated Mortgage bonds, the nature of which is taken up in the appendix on the analysis of the bond issues. Also, the payment of the first dividend on the common stock of the Pere Marquette Railroad was made in this year, thereby indicating a condition of financial prosperity that in fact did not exist.

On June 28, 1904 a very peculiar transaction oc-

---

16. *Ibid*, 38.

curred that was to have far reaching consequences for the welfare of the Pere Marquette. The board of directors of the Pere Marquette Railroad authorized the purchase of the capital stock of the Chicago, Cincinnati and Louisville Railroad Company which owned a line extending a distance of about 254 miles between Cincinnati, Ohio, and Griffith, Indiana, a town located about 30 miles from Chicago. This company had 42,060 shares of capital stock, par value $4,206,000, for which the Pere Marquette gave $3,500,000 in new bonds, the only security behind the bonds being the stock. The Pere Marquette also issued $500,000 of bonds to this company for the purpose of providing improvements to its property.[17]

17. *Ibid,* 39.

CHAPTER VI

Syndicate Control of the Pere Marquette Railroad

THE purchase by the Pere Marquette Railroad of the capital stock of the Chicago, Cincinnati and Louisville Railroad, can only be explained by the fact that a syndicate was formed July 7, 1904 in order to acquire 6,500 shares of the stock of the Cincinnati, Hamilton and Dayton Railroad. The syndicate was composed of twenty-nine separate individuals and companies, among which were: F. H. Prince and Company and their associates; A. Fernald and Company, a nominal subscriber for Chicago, Cincinnati and Louisville stock, the interested parties, mostly St. Louis people, remaining in the background; the Commonwealth Trust Company of St. Louis, representatives of the Toledo Railway and Terminal Company; the American Car and Foundry Company; the United States Express Company; and others. It seems that every member of the syndicate had something or other to sell to the Pere Marquette or to the Cincinnati, Hamilton and Dayton railroads, and becoming a member of the syndicate insured a market for their wares and also a favorable price.[1]

The first member of the syndicate to close a contract for the "sale" of its wares, was the representative of the stockholders of the Chicago, Cincinnati and Louis-

---

1. *Stenographer's Minutes Before the I. C. C.*, Docket No. 6833, page 90 ff.

ville Railroad, the purchaser, as already noted, being the Pere Marquette Railroad. Now the stock of this purchased railroad was worthless at this time, except for purposes of control, since the Chicago, Cincinnati and Louisville had not been earning operating expenses for some time previous to 1904; and it did not earn them for a long time after. In fact, the road was on the verge of bankruptcy, which was well known to all the parties interested in getting the stock off their hands; but even under such conditions, the Pere Marquette could be "induced" to make such a purchase because it will be remembered that F. H. Prince and his associates had secured control of the Pere Marquette in December 1902 through the purchase of 110,000 shares of its common stock. By reason of this control, the board of directors of the Pere Marquette had been changed in personnel in order to secure men peculiarly fitted to meet the new demands that were to be made upon officials of the company.

F. H. Prince and Company having relieved the Chicago, Cincinnati and Louisville stockholders of their worthless stock, by forcing the Pere Marquette to agree to purchase it, was to receive its compensation from the syndicate. In return for its "services," the syndicate agreed to pay F. H. Prince and Company the fancy price of $125 per share for its 110,000 shares of common stock of the Pere Marquette Railroad. Of this sum, $75 per share was to be payable in refunding mortgage bonds of the Cincinnati, Hamilton and Dayton, and $50 in non-interest bearing notes of the same road, which were convertible during the two-year period at the option of the company into its common stock. That the Pere Marquette stock was worth

$125 per share, even the most optimistic would have hesitated to allege. But the members of the syndicate were not ordinary railroad people. They saw hidden values in this stock that the stock market was unable to discern. For it can be said positively, that in the light of the financial condition of that year and later years, the value over par at least was a purely fictitious one.

Other members of the syndicate now had to be satisfied. The Toledo Railway and Terminal Company, represented on the syndicate by the Commonwealth Trust Company of St. Louis and Lawrence B. Pearce of the same city, had tracks and terminal facilities to rent. Now both the Cincinnati, Hamilton and Dayton and the Pere Marquette railroads had adequate terminals in Toledo at this time. That is, the Pere Marquette used the Ann Arbor terminals on Cherry Street, and the Cincinnati, Hamilton and Dayton used the Lake Shore and Michigan Southern passenger terminals known as the Union Depot. However, what was necessary from the standpoint of the two railroad systems and what was expedient from the standpoint of the syndicate were two different things. So an agreement was drawn up providing for a fixed annual rental of approximately $88,000, divided equally between the Pere Marquette and the Cincinnati, Hamilton and Dayton; and in addition, these companies were to pay a proportion, on the basis that was stated in the agreement, of maintenance charges, taxes and other expenses attending the handling of such property. Further, the Pere Marquette and the Cincinnati, Hamilton and Dayton railroads jointly agreed to guarantee $3,500,000 of four and one-half per cent first mortgage bonds of the Toledo Railway and Terminal Company.

It would seem that this ought to have satisfied the wealth-hunger of the Toledo Railway and Terminal people but unfortunately for the Pere Marquette this was not to be. Proceedings were soon taken by the syndicate, through the Pere Marquette and the Cincinnati, Hamilton and Dayton, whereby the entire capital stock, amounting to 3,500 shares, of the Toledo Railway and Terminal Company, was purchased; and for that stock there was issued by the Pere Marquette $1,645,000 of Pere Marquette refunding mortgage bonds which were guaranteed by the Cincinnati, Hamilton and Dayton Railroad and sold to the general public. At this time the Toledo Railway and Terminal Company was not paying operating expenses, and the Pere Marquette and the Cincinnati, Hamilton and Dayton railroads had paid the sum of $146,000 to cover interest charges on those bonds. An interesting feature regarding the Pere Marquette refunding mortgage bonds is that they sold at a heavy discount *which was paid by the Pere Marquette.*

The stock of the Toledo Railway and Terminal Company was held partly by individuals in Toledo and partly by individuals in St. Louis in the interest of one of the officials, Lawrence B. Pearce. These parties sold the stock to H. B. Hollins and Company for $41 per share, H. B. Hollins and Company made an easy profit by selling it to the Cincinnati, Hamilton and Dayton Railroad for $42 per share, and the latter company took another and larger slice of profit by selling it to the Pere Marquette Railroad at $47 per share. This amounted to nothing less than the selling of worthless stock by interested parties who received some of the proceeds of the sale from that stock and by reason of their connection with the Pere Marquette and Cincinnati, Hamilton and Dayton railroads, in whose name and with whose notes and securities the stock was purchased, they made themselves liable for the loss.   Nor was this all.   The public was defrauded by reason of the fact that these bonds got into the hands of innocent holders who were unaware of the nature of the underlying security.

The effect of the Toledo Railway and Terminal Company arrangement upon the financial condition of the Pere Marquette, as has been stated, was a large loss.   Now that the Pere Marquette had come into possession of the stock it was enabled to cancel the trackage contract made in June 1904, but it still had on its hands the property of the Terminal Company; and during 1905 and part of 1906, in order to keep it supplied with funds necessary to pay its current expenses, the Pere Marquette Railroad advanced a total of about $70,000.   When the receiver was appointed for the Pere Marquette and the Cincinnati, Hamilton and Dayton railroads in December 1905, the Toledo Railway and Terminal Company was not paying interest on its bonds, amounting to $3,500,000, and the question arose as to the disposition of the property.   In 1906 a receiver was appointed for the Toledo corporation and in January 1907 the trustee of the mortgage securing the bonds began proceedings for foreclosure.   In March 1907 there was a sale of the entire property but the sale resulted in a deficiency of about $1,800,000.   Since the Pere Marquette and the Cincinnati, Hamilton and Dayton railroads were jointly guarantors of those bonds, the trustee of the mortgage advanced a claim against them for this deficiency. How the Pere Marquette finally emerged from this maelstrom of financial difficulties is a matter that will be taken up in connection with the receivership affairs of later years.

Two other members of the syndicate that had to be recompensed for their favorable votes on matters already referred to, were the American Car and Foundry Company and the United States Express Company. The former was favored with car orders from the Pere Marquette and the Cincinnati, Hamilton railroads and the latter was given the privilege of operating over the Pere Marquette lines when the contract with the American Express Company should expire.

The last matter arranged for by the syndicate was the lease of the Pere Marquette Railroad to the Cincinnati, Hamilton and Dayton Railroad for a period of 99 years. The lease provided that, at the option of the Cincinnati, Hamilton and Dayton, the lessee, the business over the Pere Marquette lines might be conducted as before, and in the name of the Pere Marquette Railroad, for account of the Cincinnati, Hamilton and Dayton Railroad; the latter company being responsible for the payment of all fixed charges of the Pere Marquette and for meeting all its liabilities and taking over, as part of the transaction, the current assets to offset current liabilities. Under the terms of the lease the Cincinnati, Hamilton and Dayton also received two lots of Pere Marquette treasury stock approximating some $3,200,000.

Further, the lessee obligated itself to pay a rental of 4 per cent on the Pere Marquette's preferred stock which amounted to $10,500,000, and 5 per cent upon its common stock which aggregated about $3,000,000 over and above the 110,000 shares held by the lessee.

The lease did not go into effect until March 1, 1905 on which date the Prince administration closed and the Zimmerman-Harding administration began. Mr. Zimmerman was the syndicate appointee for president of the Cincinnati, Hamilton and Dayton Railroad, and Mr. Harding for president of the Pere Marquette Railroad.

During the Prince Administration and the period of syndicate control lasting two years and three months, the funded debt had increased by $20,765,000, making a total on March 1st of $52,198,000. Of this sum, $5,412,000 consisted of outstanding equipment obligations, $5,870,000 were Canadian line obligations, $675,000 were Chicago extension bonds, and the remainder consisted of underlying bonds and general mortgage bonds.[2]

A good deal of this increased bonded indebtedness[3] had nothing of value to show for it. F. H. Prince and his associates, chief of whom was Mr. Eugene Zimmerman syndicate appointee for president of the Cincinnati, Hamilton and Dayton, had effectually brought the Pere Marquette and its lessee to the point of receivership. These men had followed a policy of under-maintenance which decreased operating expenses more than was legitimate and thereby increased the net revenue unduly, making it possible to pay dividends on common stock.[4] This was in effect the payment of

---

2. Before a Committee of the Michigan Legislature, Testimony of Frederick W. Stevens, I, 138.
3. Approximately $5,000,000.
4. See appendix D.

dividends out of capital. By these methods interested parties were reducing the Pere Marquette system to a physical and financial condition that was destined to menace its very existence and cause a loss to innocent holders of bonds and stock. But the results of such extraordinary policies did not rest alone on private individuals. The communities that were being served by the Pere Marquette suffered by reason of poor service and the growth and development of the State of Michigan was retarded. Unfortunately, this great commonwealth had not yet come to realize the true relationship existing between the public carriers and itself, and therefore had not made provision for such supervision and regulation as would have made these transactions an impossibility.

ZIMMERMAN-HARDING ADMINISTRATION

(March 1, 1905, to October 20, 1905.)

Exactly speaking, a new administration came into being on the date that the lease went into effect, viz., March 1, 1905, by reason of the fact that Mr. Russel Harding succeeded Mr. F. H. Prince as president of the Pere Marquette. Actually, however, the syndicate was still the real administration since it owned the control of the Cincinnati, Hamilton and Dayton Railroad and the latter owned the control, or 110,000 shares of common stock, of the Pere Marquette. In fact, Mr. Zimmerman had been the chief administrator of the affairs of the syndicate since its formation on July 7, 1904, and therefore, together with F. H. Prince, was the real dictator over the Pere Marquette Railroad. Now that the lease was in effect there was merely a closer relationship between the Pere Marquette and the Cincinnati, Hamilton and Dayton railroads, if such a thing were possible.

As regards the Pere Marquette during the Zimmerman-Harding administration, its funded debt was increased by $2,750,000, not including $2,015,000 which was the excess of current liabilities over current assets. Of the total funded debt at the end of this period, amounting to $54,948,000, equipment obligations claimed $4,975,000 and the balance consisted of underlying and general mortgage bonds.[1] It was also agreed during this period that the Cincinnati, Hamilton and Dayton Railroad purchase refunding mortgage bonds of the Pere Marquette Railroad up to the amount of $4,000,000, at $90 per share and accrued interest. $2,361,000 of bonds of the Pere Marquette were sold pursuant to this agreement but they suffered a discount of 14½ per cent instead of 10 per cent. Contrary to the agreement, this larger discount amounting to $236,100 was all charged against the Pere Marquette, and was later charged into the cost of road account on the Pere Marquette books.

As regards the Cincinnati, Hamilton and Dayton Railroad, Mr. Eugene Zimmerman had been president since the formation of the syndicate on July 7, 1904, when the Woodford-Shoemaker administration came to an end. During the Zimmerman administration a floating debt of approximately $3,650,000 was accumulated, of which $2,650,000 consisted of demand notes given in the spring and summer of 1905, and $1,000,000 consisted of an accumulation of miscellaneous claims for materials and supplies that the Cincinnati,

---

1. Before a Committee of the Michigan Legislature, Testimony of Frederick W. Stevens, I, 138.

Hamilton and Dayton Railroad had been unable to pay. This entire sum remained unpaid at the close of the Zimmerman administration, October 20, 1905, at which time the company had exhausted all its credit and borrowing power.

Strange to say, there had been no publication of the results of the operation and business of the Cincinnati, Hamilton and Dayton Railroad during the preceding fiscal year ending June 30, 1905, during which time the Zimmerman administration was in control with the exception of six days in July 1904.

When the report was subsequently published under Receiver Judson Harmon, it developed that there had been a slight decrease in gross earnings of the Cincinnati, Hamilton and Dayton Railroad; that there had been an increase of about $220,000 in its operating expenses over the preceding fiscal year of the Woodford-Shoemaker administration; that there had been an increase in the interest charges of about $760,000, which would have been more but for the fact that some of these transactions, whereby the interest bearing obligations were created, were not issued until the close of that fiscal year. In other words, the annual interest charges on the new obligations issued were over $1,100,000, but some of them were not issued until well toward the close of the fiscal year ending June 30, 1906. so that the accrued interest during that fiscal year showed only $760,000 interest. Further, as against a surplus of the preceding year of about $793,000, there was a deficit during the Zimmerman administration of $241,000.

From the foregoing statement of the financial condition of the Cincinnati, Hamilton and Dayton

Railroad, it will be seen that the syndicate not only ruined the Pere Marquette and brought it to the verge of receivership but left the Cincinnati, Hamilton and Dayton in a similar position. Both railroads had been fairly prosperous before the control by the syndicate, at least to the extent of meeting their current liabilities, and no doubt would have continued to be moderately successful had not their assets been dissipated by those in whose trust they had been placed.

There was still a great problem before the syndicate, viz., how to get out from under the financial chaos that it had created. Everything of value had been taken that could be taken, so that the stock of the Cincinnati, Hamilton and Dayton Railroad held by the syndicate was practically worthless except for purposes of control, and its value in this respect was rapidly diminishing. Just how the syndicate finally relieved itself of the worthless Cincinnati, Hamilton and Dayton stock at a good profit to itself, has been a matter regarding which there have been widely differing opinions. Two versions of how this coup was effected are taken up in the following chapter.

CHAPTER VII

The Erie Railroad Administration (October 20, 1905 to December 4, 1905)

THE Zimmerman administration ended by reason of the purchase of the Cincinnati, Hamilton and Dayton Railroad by the Erie Railroad on October 20, 1905. The parties to the Erie purchase were the Erie Railroad as buyer of the Cincinnati, Hamilton and Dayton stock, J. P. Morgan and Company as its financial agent in the transaction, and H. E. Hollins and Company as the owners of the stock or as the representatives of the owners. In the first place will be given the version of the sale of the Cincinnati, Hamilton and Dayton stock as testified to by a representative of J. P. Morgan and Company before the Interstate Commerce Commission.

On August 17, 1905 the Erie Railroad entered into negotiations with J. P. Morgan and Company for the purpose of purchasing the Cincinnati, Hamilton and Dayton Railroad. The reasons for desiring this purchase are to be found in a letter from Mr. F. D. Underwood, president of the Erie Railroad, to J. P. Morgan, dated August 17, 1905, as follows:

" . . . . The Erie Railroad has been furnished with a plan of grade reductions, terminal and station improvements that will enable it, upon completion of the work, to handle twenty-five per cent more traffic than it now does, without materially increasing its operating expenses. Putting it broadly, it will be in a position to handle more traffic than is now tributary to it.

"The acquirement by the Erie of the properties should largely increase the volume of traffic tributary to it, for the reason that the traffic that is now billed via other lines from Buffalo and other junction points would legitimately move over the Erie rails.

"It is the duty of the management of the Erie Railroad to acquire for it, additional traffic on as favorable terms as possible. The properties are worth more to the Erie than to any other interests on the map, and, while the price is high, there is no probability that it will ever be less.

"These statements as to the traffic to be developed are not haphazard—they are the result of four year's study of the situation and a research of the traffic relations between these properties and the Erie by several officials of this company, who are competent to pass upon the matter.

"The best paying traffic the Erie has is that derived from the carriage of coal to Buffalo and Chicago by rail. The opening of the territory covered by the two properties will inevitably afford a larger market for the Erie anthracite coal, both in the States transversed by the lines and through their connections across Lake Michigan to the Northwest. It is safe to predict that, in five years' time, the increased revenue from the haulage of the coal on the Erie and the sales in the territory above described will go a long way toward paying the interest on the investment which it is proposed to make.

"It seems to me that the matter will go by default if you do not take a strong hand, and I earnestly hope that you see your way clear to make the purchase. If it is impossible at this moment to vest its ownership in the Erie, I trust that can be accomplished later.

"In conclusion: I have seen no favorable geographical or traffic movements made toward the Erie by its competitors. The things that have been done in the interest of the Erie have been done by J. P. Morgan and Company, and it is to them that I feel we must look for such assistance as we are to have. I have written earnestly because I have a deep conviction that the proposed move is the move to make; the error is that it was not done before."[1]

J. P. Morgan and Company gave its consent, and the terms of the purchase, which are embodied in the resolution agreed upon at the board of directors meeting of the Erie Railroad, September 1905, are as follows:

"Resolved, That the President be and hereby is, authorized and directed in behalf of the Erie Railroad Company to contract with J. P. Morgan and Company, to purchase by or through them approximately 74,000 shares of the common stock of the Cincinnati, Hamilton and Dayton Railroad Company, at a cost thereof to J. P. Morgan and Company, not exceeding $160 per share, with a commission to them of 3½ per cent upon the total amount of such cost; it being understood that at present only Syndicate subscriptions may be obtained; such purchase to include 1,603 shares long since acquired and now held by J. P. Morgan and

---

1. *Stenographer's Minutes Before the I. C. C.*, Docket No. 6833, Vol. II.

Company, at a lower price on their own account, for which this company will pay them $135 a share without commission."[2]

The stock was paid for by money borrowed on notes of the Erie Railroad Company from the First National Bank of New York, the National Bank of Commerce of New York, and the United States Trust Company, and the balance borrowed on notes payable to J. P. Morgan and Company.

The board of directors of the Pere Marquette and the Cincinnati, Hamilton and Dayton railroads were reorganized to include members of the Erie board of directors, several of the Erie officials including Mr. Underwood, and three or four vice-presidents; while several other officers were elected to similar positions on the Pere Marquette and Cincinnati, Hamilton and Dayton railroads.

J. P. Morgan and Company claim that when the contract of purchase and sale was made between themselves and the Erie Railroad on September 27, 1905, the true financial condition of the Cincinnati, Hamilton and Dayton and the Pere Marquette railroads was not known to either party to the contract; and that it was only after investigation subsequent to the execution of the contract that the real financial situation of the purchased roads was disclosed.

From this investigation it appeared that since July 1904 the Cincinnati, Hamilton and Dayton Railroad had been accumulating large numbers of bills for materials and supplies which it was unable to pay because it lacked funds and had reached the end of its borrowing

---

2. *Ibid.*

power. There were over $2,600,000 of demand notes held by banks in New York, Chicago, Cincinnati and elsewhere, but there was no money with which to meet any considerable part of them. Besides $1,000,000 of accumulated bills for supplies already referred to, there was $15,000,000 of notes becoming due three years later. Then there was the liability of the Cincinnati, Hamilton and Dayton on the Pere Marquette lease, which it was perfectly evident it could not perform, and a liability that was practically perpetual. Likewise, the liability on the Chicago, Cincinnati and Louisville transaction, and the Toledo Railway and Terminal Company bonds, with an installment of interest coming due January 1st, both of which liabilities it was evident that the road would be unable to meet. All this and more pointed to receivership.

This so-called "unexpected" bad financial condition of the Cincinnati, Hamilton and Dayton Railroad caused dissatisfaction among the Erie interests, which dissatisfaction became known to J. P. Morgan and Company. At a meeting of the executive committee of the Erie Railroad on November 28, 1905, J. P. Morgan therefore appeared before the committee and because of this dissatisfaction offered to purchase from the Erie the 74,000 shares of common stock of the Cincinnati, Hamilton and Dayton at the price that had been paid for it.

The next day at a meeting of the board of directors the offer of J. P. Morgan was unanimously accepted, and the following resolutions adopted:

"Resolved, that the unanimous sentiment of the

Board of Directors of the Erie Railroad Company is that the thanks of the Company are due and hereby are tendered to J. Pierpont Morgan, Esq., for his extraordinary services and assistance to the company; first, in his quick and efficient compliance with the direct personal appeal of the company through its president to obtain for it a large majority of the common stock of the Cincinnati, Hamilton and Dayton Railway Company; and finally after the development of doubt in this board as to the continuing ability of the Erie Company satisfactorily to maintain and extend that system, in view of the demands of its own railroad, in his magnificent, unparalleled and absolutely voluntary offer himself to assume the entire purchase, and to relieve the Erie Company from all contracts and cost in connection therewith."[3]

This evidence submitted by J. P. Morgan and Company would tend to indicate: first, that the initiative in the purchase of the Cincinnati, Hamilton and Dayton stock came from the Erie Railroad; second, that the Erie Railroad did not know anything about the financial condition of the property that it was anxious to buy; third, that the Erie Railroad believed that the Cincinnati, Hamilton and Dayton was necessary for its own most complete prosperity, and that this judgment was the result of "four year's study of the situation," etc.; fourth, that it was necessary for the Erie to act quickly for fear of purchase by competitors; fifth, that the stock was worth $160 per share; sixth, that J. P. Morgan and Company "in their magnificent, unparalleled and absolutely voluntary offer," sought to bear the loss on the purchase

—————

3. *Ibid.*

of the stock, rather than allow the Erie Railroad to suffer loss, although the latter company requested the purchase of the stock and had opportunities to ascertain its value and the status of the road that had issued it.

Taking these up in the order given, it seems evident in the first place, that the syndicate was anxious to dispose of its holdings since there was nothing more to be gained from association with the Pere Marquette and the Cincinnati, Hamilton and Dayton railroads; and this could only be done by finding a customer. This was a case of the seller seeking the purchaser and not vice versa.   Besides the profit on the sale of this stock that the syndicate members were seeking, there were commissions that would accrue to J. P. Morgan and Company if they acted as broker.   This banking house expected, it is thought by some, to sell this stock to the Erie Railroad at a higher price than they bought it for from the syndicate, and thus make the difference between the buying and the selling prices, as well as gather a commission from both the Erie Railroad and the Cincinnati, Hamilton and Dayton syndicate.   How the Erie Railroad ever came into the position of a buyer of such stock at such a price is not quite clear to all.   That this road must have known of the situation as regards the Cincinnati, Hamilton and Dayton's financial affairs, seems to go without saying; as it appears incredible that a purchase of this nature would be attempted without gathering knowledge regarding the property.   In case this view is true, it means that the board of directors were violating a fiduciary trust imposed in them by the stockholders.   By their action, allowing the railroad of which they were officers, to enter a transaction which would impair its securities and cause a loss to innocent holders, as well as endangering the credit of the corporation and injuring the public by making the railroad incapable of adequately serving them, these officers would have made themselves liable on criminal charges.

On the other hand, in case the board of directors were ignorant of the nature of the property that they declared themselves so anxious to purchase, they can equally be condemned, since the law stipulates that directors of a corporation are liable for loss due to gross negligence and inattention to the duties of their trust.[4] That the purchase of a railroad with one's eyes closed, is adequately and for all purposes exercising the sacred trusteeship granted by the stockholders, can hardly be defended successfully. Which ever, then, was the true situation, the board of directors can be condemned.

That J. P. Morgan and Company knew the true financial condition of the Cincinnati, Hamilton and Dayton, seems certain because of two facts. First, they had been a minority shareholder in this railroad previous to the syndicate formation, and by reason of that holding must have been aware of the developments that directly affected the status of their stock.

In the second place, there was found in the files of J. P. Morgan and Company, a general financial statement of the Pere Marquette Railroad Company.[5] To start with, this statement showed the capitalization of the Pere Marquette and the Cincinnati, Hamilton

----

4. Marshall v. Bank, 85 Va. 676, 8 S. E. 586, 2 L. R. A. 534, Am. St. Rep., 84.

5. By the I. C. C., referred to in their report, Docket No. 6833.

and Dayton railroads. Then it showed the fixed charges, interest on funded debt, taxes estimated on the basis of last year's taxes, and estimated earnings and operating expenses; then a notation at the bottom in reference to the fact that the Cincinnati, Hamilton and Dayton Railroad had taken up and paid for all of its preferred stock excepting 4,000 shares which was then outstanding, and had deposited with the Central Trust Company of New York a sum sufficient to pay for this outstanding stock. The total issued stock of the Pere Marquette was given, then the amount that was held by its lessee. Also, the statement that the Cincinnati, Hamilton and Dayton and the Pere Marquette railroads had agreed to issue joint collateral trust bonds for $3,500,000, with interest at 4 per cent, from July 1, 1905, in payment for the entire capital stock of the Chicago, Cincinnati and Louisville Railroad. It notes certain guaranteed bonds of the Toledo Railway and Terminal Company and other similar items, and, on the whole, would indicate, although it does not state so definitely, that the Chicago, Cincinnati and Louisville Railroad and the Toledo Railway and Terminal Company were not earning their operating expenses.

The third point, viz., that the Erie Railroad believed, after "four years' study of the situation," that the Pere Marquette and the Cincinnati, Hamilton and Dayton railroads ought to be part of the Erie Railroad so that the latter would be able to most fully utilize its own equipment, seems to contradict the second point in the evidence, viz., that the Erie was unaware of the financial condition of these railroads. It is difficult to understand just what was "studied" during the period referred to, if the financial affairs of the roads which they contemplated purchasing were not taken into consideration. All the advantages contemplated from the purchase, as indicated in the letter from Mr. Underwood to Mr. Morgan, would go for naught if these roads were about to fall of their own weight, as was the case. In conclusion it should be said, that according to the Morgan evidence, the Erie officials who investigated the Pere Marquette and the Cincinnati and Hamilton and Dayton railroads must have used an unusually high order of discrimination in order to see all aspects of these roads excepting the most important one, viz., their extremely bad financial condition.

In the fourth place, there was no need of acting quickly since buyers were not crowding each other to get a chance to purchase this stock. Plenty of time existed in which a further investigation could be started in case the former one was not thorough enough, or because other complications had arisen.

In the fifth place, it could not be thought that this stock was worth $160 per share, taking it for granted of course that the real financial situation of both roads was known. Railroads that had to pay interest on bonded indebtedness by means of contracting floating debts would obviously be unable for some time to pay dividends on stock. Yet, apparently, the Erie Railroad was willing to ignore all this and designate a price to J. P. Morgan and Company that compared favorably with the price of stock of other railroads in the country that had always paid dividends, were earning the interest on their funded debt, and, taken all together, were in a sound financial condition.

Again, it seems that not only was the stock not intrinsically worth $160 per share, but that it could not have been *thought* to be worth that price. In other words, a price of this magnitude for stock of the Cincinnati Hamilton and Dayton would imply certain forces acting to keep it up to this point, that is, natural forces like competition among buyers or investors who realized the true value of the stock, or, artificial forces like competition among those who want stock simply because others are demanding the same stock. That competition (either naturally or artificially produced) to buy this stock, and its high price, existed as cause and effect, can not be considered for a moment as a legitimate explanation of the price of this stock. Neither force acted to produce this result. Causes other than these mentioned must have had an influence in raising the price of this security to $160 per share.

Finally, it has been noted that J. P. Morgan and Company made an "absolutely voluntary offer" to assume the purchase of stock, which in reality meant a loss, since the stock could be sold to no one else at the price of $160 per share nor any figure thereabouts. For this kind act of generosity and willingness to suffer a loss in order that others would not be affected by the consequences of their own misdeeds, J. P. Morgan endeared himself to all those connected with the transaction, and received a letter from the Erie Railroad with sentiment to that effect. He likewise endeared himself to the members of the syndicate who were now clear of the transactions with which they had been connected, having emerged from the situation not only with the booty, but also with a fancy price secured from the sale of the tool by means of which the booty was acquired.   Unlike most men of this character, the members of the syndicate were not satisfied with the contents of the safe, but wished to further increase their wealth by forcing an innocent bystander to pay an exorbitant price for the instrument with which the ill-gotten gain was secured.

From what has been given, it is seen that in a matter of this nature one has to delve beneath the correspondence if the entire truth is to be found.   The view held by the Interstate Commerce Commission after an investigation of the affairs of the Pere Marquette Railroad, is, that J. P. Morgan and Company sought to sell the Cincinnati, Hamilton and Dayton stock to the Erie Railroad and temporarily succeeded, but when the true financial condition of the Pere Marquette and its lessee became known to the stockholders of the Erie Railroad such opposition arose that the loss was forced back on J. P. Morgan and Company.

The motive for J. P. Morgan wanting to sell this stock is not even clearly seen by the Commission, or, at least, is not of such a nature that the evidence regarding it could be called conclusive, so the Commission sums up the situation by characterizing the sale, by the Zimmerman-Hollins interests, of the broken-down Cincinnati, Hamilton and Dayton Railroad to J. P. Morgan and Company at $160 per share, as an "astounding coup."

Whatever may have been the reason for the attempted sale, J. P. Morgan found himself on November 28, 1905 with a large block of Cincinnati, Hamilton and Dayton Railroad stock on his hands.   This road, as well as the Pere Marquette, had been "milked" to such an extent that the only way open was receivership, which took place on December 5, 1905, Judson Harmon being appointed receiver.

The property and affairs of the Pere Marquette were so tied up to the Cincinnati, Hamilton and Dayton at this time, due to the lease under which the former road was controlled by the latter, that the receivership of the Cincinnati, Hamilton and Dayton almost necessitated a receivership for the Pere Marquette. Accordingly, on the same date as the Cincinnati, Hamilton and Dayton went into receivership, a receiver was appointed for the Pere Marquette.

CHAPTER VIII

PERIOD OF THE FIRST RECEIVERSHIP (DECEMBER 5, 1905 TO DECEMBER 15, 1907)

AS a result of the Cincinnati, Hamilton and Dayton Railroad going into the hands of a receiver, the trustee of its refunding mortgage (the United States Mortgage and Trust Company of New York) secured the voting power of the 110,000 shares of Pere Marquette stock. This stock, it will be remembered, was paid for in part by bonds issued under the Cincinnati, Hamilton and Dayton refunding mortgage of 1904, the shares being placed as a security for the mortgage, and the certificates of stock going into the possession of the trustee of that mortgage, that is, the Trust Company to which reference has been made. Under the terms of the mortgage, the voting power remained with the Cincinnati, Hamilton and Dayton until such time as it should fail to pay interest on the bonds, or should go into the hands of a receiver. Accordingly, on the date of receivership of the Cincinnati, Hamilton and Dayton, the power to vote these shares passed to the United States Mortgage and Trust Company, and it exercised this right with the advice of a committee of the bondholders until August 1909, nearly four years later.

The Pere Marquette had been allowed to run down during the period of syndicate control, which now made necessary large outlays for equipment by the receiver. Box-cars, to the value of $4,346,000, were contracted for, to be paid in monthly installments of $51,000 per month, including interest. This was an expensive way to buy the equipment but no other method could be employed at the time. Also, thirty-five locomotives were purchased for $486,000 cash payment. In addition, the receiver paid during these two years, $1,095,000 of principal payments on equipment purchased before the receivership and $316,000 for additions and improvements.

In April 1906 the case involving the ad valorem tax law was decided in favor of the State of Michigan by the United States Supreme Court, and the Pere Marquette became a debtor to the State for $1,208,000 of taxes. $475,000 of this amount were current taxes for the year 1905 and the remainder consisted of unpaid portions of the taxes for the years 1902, 1903 and 1904, together with accrued penalties under the law, computed at one per cent per month.[1]

These taxes, expenses for equipment, and $400,000 paid to settle the Chicago, Cincinnati and Louisville case (referred to later), amounting to a total of about $3,617,000, were paid by the receiver in receiver's certificates to the amount of $2,438,000 and the balance in short term notes.

It was during this receivership that the two-cent fare law was passed and it was thought by some that the lower rate would stimulate traffic to such an extent that net income would not be cut down materially. This, unhappily, did not prove to be true, since in 1908, the year following the passage of the law, the increase in passenger receipts amounted to only 6.7

1. Before a Committee of the Michigan Legislature, Testimony of Frederick W. Stevens, I, 84.

per cent, which was less than the normal increase in 1906 over 1905, and less than the normal increase of 1905 over 1904. Taking the average passenger rate from 1900 to 1907 and applying that average rate to the years subsequent to 1907, the loss or decrease in passenger earnings due to the two-cent fare law amounted to: $458,000 in 1908, $632,000 in 1909, $708,000 in 1910, ·$742,000 in 1911 and $692,000 in 1912. This was at a time when equipment and supplies were beginning to feel the stimulus of business activity after the panic of 1907 and prices were on the upward trend. There seems little doubt, that in this case at least, the new law placed the Pere Marquette at a peculiar disadvantage in its attempts to recover from the consequences of its previous transactions.[1]

Early in 1907 the stockholders of the Pere Marquette and other interested parties began the consideration of some plan whereby this road could be taken out of the hands of the receiver. There were good prospects of the Pere Marquette paying all its indebtedness and reorganizing without any foreclosure sale provided it could clear away some special transactions that were weighting it down.

First among these was the Chicago, Cincinnati and Louisville affair. On July 7, 1904 the Cincinnati, Hamilton and Dayton had agreed to take one-half of this purchase and assume one-half of the obligations pertaining thereto. It was thought that it might be profitable for the Cincinnati, Hamilton and Dayton to operate the Chicago, Cincinnati and Louisville Railroad if it could complete its construction to Chicago. The Pere Marquette had advanced about $425,000 to be

1. *Ibid*, 85.

spent in improving it, and to pay the bond interest which was not being earned. However, a short time later, representatives of the preferred stockholders of the Cincinnati, Hamilton and Dayton threatened proceedings to set aside the purchase of the Chicago, Cincinnati and Louisville stock, on the grounds that their securities were sadly impaired by the transactions of the syndicate on July 7, 1904: The Cincinnati, Hamilton and Dayton promptly silenced this protest by arranging with Hollins and Company for the purchase and extinguishment of the preferred stock, which was accomplished by issuing $9,388,000 of one year five per cent obligations or notes and using these to retire the $6,676,925 of preferred stock. Thus the syndicate killed all opposition to its operations.

Since the syndicate controlled the Pere Marquette, it could have made that road live up to its contract and purchase the stock of the Chicago, Cincinnati and Louisville Railroad, but this was never done. The stipulations for the purchase were never carried out by the Pere Marquette, although it had advanced nearly half a million dollars to the Chicago, Cincinnati and Louisville for improvements and interest payments on bonds. For this failure to carry out the terms of the contract of purchase, suit was brought (in 1907) against the Pere Marquette by the owners of the Chicago, Cincinnati and Louisville stock, who, it will be remembered, were effectively represented on the syndicate of the Cincinnati, Hamilton and Dayton Railroad. As a result of this suit, the court ordered the Pere Marquette to pay $400,000 in settlement.

It seems that there was nothing left undone by the syndicate that would further its own interests. Syndicate members interested in the Chicago, Cincinnati and Louisville had forced the Pere Marquette into a bad contract, had relieved it of $425,000 for improvements and advances, and then had sued it for $400,-000 for not living up to its contract. For the expenditure of $825,000 the Pere Marquette had nothing of value to show.[2]

By this court decision, the Cincinnati, Hamilton and Dayton also lost heavily. This loss was in the form of valuable trackage rights in the city of Cincinnati, which the Chicago, Cincinnati and Louisville needed very badly and which rights it received at the time of settlement.

Not long after this suit the Chicago, Cincinnati and Louisville Railroad went into the hands of a receiver and was sold at a foreclosure sale. It was in a bad physical condition, not being able to pay operating expenses much less interest on bonded indebtedness, and the only wonder was that it had kept out of receivership so long as it did. For a time, the Pere Marquette had paid the interest on its bonds, but with this handy source of revenue gone there was no one who could be induced to make such payments and hence the road could follow only one course, viz., receivership.

Another important transaction to be taken care of was the settlement of the Toledo Railway and Terminal Company affair. In 1907 there was a liability on the part of the Pere Marquette for nearly $2,000,000, due to the deficiency arising from the foreclosure sale of the bonds that it had guaranteed as a result of the workings of the syndicate.

2. *Ibid*, 61.

This matter involved the Cincinnati, Hamilton and Dayton Railroad very intimately, and all parties connected with the reorganization agreed that the whole matter of settlement between the Cincinnati, Hamilton and Dayton and the Pere Marquette railroads should be left to W. W. Crapo and Judson Harmon as arbitrators. W. W. Crapo had been with the Pere Marquette or its constituents for nearly forty years and had the confidence of everybody. Judson Harmon represented the Cincinnati, Hamilton and Dayton and was held in high esteem by all who knew him. Testimony was brought to the arbitrators from both roads. Mr. Frederick W. Stevens was in charge of the matter for the Pere Marquette and presented, among other claims of that road, a claim for reimbursement on account of this Toledo Railway and Terminal Company stock purchase. He based the claim upon the fact "that at the time the transaction occurred, the Cincinnati, Hamilton and Dayton was in control of the Pere Marquette's property and also of its board; that the intercorporate relations arising out of that fact and the fact of common directors was such as to create a fiduciary capacity on the part of the Cincinnati, Hamilton and Dayton." He also presented evidence to show "that the stock was practically of no value at the time of purchase; that it would not have been under ordinary conditions; that is, to say, except for the fact of this common directorate and control; that the circumstances, ... showed that the purchase was made as much in the interest of the Cincinnati, Hamilton and Dayton as of the Pere Marquette. . . . ," etc.[3]

---

3. *Ibid*, 71.

In return for the loss that the Pere Marquette had undergone, amounting to $1,645,000 spent on worthless stock and about $70,000 which it had advanced to the Toledo Railway and Terminal Company, the arbitrators gave an award to the Pere Marquette of $1,364,000. This sum was probably approximately reached by subtracting from the total loss the sum of $458,249 expended in betterments on the Pere Marquette by the Cincinnati, Hamilton and Dayton during the period of occupation under the lease.[4]

The $1,364,000 was to be paid[5] in Cincinnati, Hamilton and Dayton general mortgage bonds of the par value of this sum. These bonds had a market value of only about $60 per share at this time so that the total award amounted to $818,000, at which figure the bonds were later written upon the books of the Pere Marquette. They were really income bonds with fixed interest at the rate of 1 per cent and $3\frac{1}{2}$ per cent additional if it was earned. In 1914 it was to become 3 per cent fixed and $1\frac{1}{2}$ per cent additional dependent upon income, while in 1916 the interest was to become for all time $4\frac{1}{2}$ per cent per annum.[6]

The award was made public to all parties concerned, but since there was no complaint within the time of protest it was thereby confirmed by all and made effective.

Now it was necessary to make some arrangements to dispose of the guaranty of the Pere Marquette and the Cincinnati, Hamilton and Dayton on the $3,500,000

---

4. *Ibid*, 72.
5. This award was not actually paid to the Pere Marquette until the reorganization of the Cincinnati, Hamilton and Dayton in 1909.
6. *Ibid*, 78.

of Toledo Railway and Terminal Company bonds.   In order to accomplish this end a reorganization of this latter company was necessary.

This was accomplished by inducing five railroad lines entering Toledo, viz., the Michigan Central, the Lake Shore and Michigan Southern, the Pennsylvania, the Grand Trunk and the Clover Leaf, to take a 12 per cent interest in the Toledo Railway and Terminal Company, with the belief that the property might not be a very valuable one at that time but would be of greater value at some future time.   The Pere Marquette and the Cincinnati, Hamilton and Dayton each took a 20 per cent interest in this Toledo Company.

A new company was organized called the Toledo Terminal Railroad Company which acquired the property from the purchasers at the foreclosure sale by giving its bonds to the amount of $4,000,000.   This sum was approximately the amount of bonds which had been the subject of the foreclosure, including accrued interest and the expense of the foreclosure. In this way the guaranty of the Pere Marquette and the Cincinnati, Hamilton and Dayton on the $3,500,000 of bonds was disposed of, and these bonds were destroyed.   The 20 per cent stock in the new company had a par value of about $800,000 but it had no real value other than for purposes of control.[7]

Another important matter that had to be settled was the question of the lease.   It was quite obvious that the Cincinnati, Hamilton and Dayton in its present financial condition could not fulfill the terms of the lease in guaranteeing dividends on stock and meeting other obligations.   Accordingly the lease was

____

7. *Ibid*, 68 ff; 75.

terminated by the award of the arbitrators, as of the day of receivership, which was the day that the Cincinnati, Hamilton and Dayton passed out of the control of the Pere Marquette. The lease had been a means of loss to both roads and a financial relief was experienced in both directions when it was terminated.

This lease had come into being as a means by which the Cincinnati, Hamilton and Dayton, or rather the syndicate, could more easily and thoroughly control the Pere Marquette Railroad, but there are other reasons as well ascribed for its existence.

One of these indicates the belief that the Cincinnati, Hamilton and Dayton and the Pere Marquette would make a profitable north and south system. The Pere Marquette originated a great deal of traffic destined to points on the Cincinnati, Hamilton and Dayton and beyond, and this could be turned over to this latter railroad instead of turning it over to several roads in Ohio reaching Toledo. In return for this, the Cincinnati, Hamilton and Dayton originated a large amount of traffic destined to Pere Marquette points or beyond, which it could turn over entirely to this latter railroad instead of turning it over to several lines like the Michigan Central, the Ann Arbor and others.[8]

Events did not shape themselves as was expected, for it developed that lines entering Toledo which formerly turned over traffic to the Pere Marquette no longer did this, but gave it to the Michigan Central, the Ann Arbor and the Grand Trunk, so that the Pere Marquette was left entirely dependent upon the Cin-

8. *Ibid,* 101 ff.

cinnati, Hamilton and Dayton for traffic originating beyond Toledo.

Likewise, the Cincinnati, Hamilton and Dayton also met retaliation from other roads to which it had formerly given traffic. These roads no longer gave their traffic to the Cincinnati, Hamilton and Dayton, and this latter road was therefore dependent upon the Pere Marquette for traffic originating north of Toledo. In this manner both the Pere Marquette and the Cincinnati, Hamilton and Dayton lost valuable traffic which was not offset by the business that they could give to each other.

Not only was the union through the lease a failure as regards freight traffic but it also caused a distinct loss in passenger traffic. Formerly, the Cincinnati, Hamilton and Dayton had had an arrangement with the Michigan Central north of Toledo and both companies had done a profitable business. Now, the Pere Marquette took the place of the Michigan Central and that road made a new alliance with the Hocking Valley and the Big Four, put on new trains and vigorously competed with the Pere Marquette and the Cincinnati, Hamilton and Dayton. This resulted in a division of the passenger business and caused a loss on all through trains.

Before reorganization could successfully be effected, there was discovered the necessity of obtaining an extension to the time of payment for car equipment ordered by the receiver. This contracted payment was maturing at the rate of $51,000 per month or the sum of over $600,000 a year, which was more than could be taken care of, with many other debts maturing at the same time. Therefore, an arrangement was made with the Pullman Company, with whom the car contract was made, whereby the Pere Marquette was to deposit $750,000 par value of its refunding mortgage bonds of 1905 as additional security for the remainder of the purchase price; and further, there was to be made, at the same time, an advance payment of five months installments amounting to about $250,000, after which for twenty months no payments would be required.   At the end of this time monthly payments would be resumed at a rate per month large enough to pay the debt within the date of maturity originally set in the contract of sale, or about $67,000 per month.   This plan was adopted because it relieved the tense situation at the time, and it was believed that at the expiration of twenty months the Pere Marquette would be better able to meet these obligations.[9]

Another matter that had to be given attention was the Canada Southern rental which all agreed must be reduced.   The Pere Marquette had contracted for but had not used the line from Courtright to St. Thomas, yet was paying rental for it as if it were being used by them.   The matter was taken up with the New York Central and after lengthy negotiations the Pere Marquette was released from the contract for the use of this branch, and its rental cut down $50,000 per year for five years and $27,000 per year thereafter.

One of the greatest difficulties in bringing about reorganization was to get the consent of the trustee of the 110,000 shares of stock, without which no action looking toward reorganization could be taken.   It will be remembered that the trustee was acting under the

---

9.   *Ibid*, 91-2.

advice of a strong committee representing the holders of $11,500,000 of 50 year 4 per cent Cincinnati, Hamilton and Dayton refunding bonds which were then selling considerably below par, and it was the intention of this committee to better the position of the bondholders before it consented to any plan of reorganization of the Pere Marquette. The Pere Marquette interests argued that since the Pere Marquette stock was part of the security under the mortgage, anything that bettered the Pere Marquette was a good thing for the bondholders. This was agreed to but something more tangible was desired, and plans for reorganization could not be considered until the trustee, which controlled the majority voting power of the Pere Marquette, could be satisfied. The one condition on which they would vote the 110,000 shares favorable to reorganization was that those long time bonds be refunded into short time obligations, five-year notes, par for par, and that such notes should be secured by the deposit of an equal amount of those outstanding bonds. This would not increase the interest charge of the Cincinnati, Hamilton and Dayton, merely expediting the maturity of the bonds by about 46 years; but the effect on the bondholders would be greatly beneficial because it would give them a security worth on the market much more than their 50 year bonds. After delays, negotiations resulted in procuring the result which the holders of the 110,000 shares of common stock demanded, and this stock was subsequently voted in favor of the reorganization.[10]

Finally, there was the problem of raising money to pay the bills of the receiver and if possible make

10. *Ibid*, 92-93.

some provision for the future. After a great deal of effort the latter idea was given up and it was decided to raise only $5,000,000 from the Pere Marquette stockholders. The plan adopted provided for the raising of this sum on a pro rata basis from the preferred stockholders, giving in return for the money received, 6 per cent five year debentures. The preferred stockholders who should contribute their pro rata share of the sum required were to receive in place of their 4 per cent non-cumulative stock, new first preferred 4 per cent cumulative stock, cumulative not only to dividends but also to assets which was not true of the old preferred stock. The pro rata share could be paid in installments over a period of six months. As an inducement to subscribers to these debentures, a bonus of 15 per cent of capital stock was given to the holders of the 95,042.40 shares of preferred stock, and a bonus of 20 per cent of capital stock to the 12,394 shares of common stock, or a par value of $1,074,360.40 of capital stock was given as a bonus. Besides this expense there was about $95,042 spent for underwriting the notes.

The amount received from this plan was to be used to pay $900,000 of debts of the old company which had been in suspense for two years, and the receiver's certificates amounting to over $2,400,000. The balance was to be used in meeting maturing capital payments on equipment and for necessary additions and betterments. The holders of the first preferred stock of the old company who did not contribute to this fund were to receive second preferred stock of the new company, which was preferred over the common to the extent of 4 per cent but was not cumulative nor preferred as to assets. That a large portion of the outstanding preferred stock contributed to this $5,000,000 fund is evidenced by the fact that there was approximately $11,000,000 of first preferred stock outstanding before the reorganization, while after reorganization there was $10,929,000 of first preferred and $923,000 of second preferred.[11]

The plan as briefly described above was submitted to both the Canadian and United States Courts for their approval. Before the courts would authorize the receiver to give up possession they required him to file a statement that all the debts and liabilities of the old company and of the receiver would be paid; since it was recognized that the $5,000,000 could not be secured in advance but depended upon the reliance placed in the new company. But the order of the courts provided that in case any provisions were not complied with this would be sufficient reason for the courts to take possession of the property again.

The final item in the plan of reorganization provided that the Pere Marquette Railroad Company of Indiana should be consolidated with the Pere Marquette Railroad Company in order to effect the exchange of stocks and create new stocks of different grades. The laws of Michigan require that any consolidation of railroads must have the approval of the Michigan Railroad Commission. Accordingly, after action of the stockholders and the courts, petition was made to the Michigan Railroad Commission setting forth the facts of the proposed consolidation, and on December 10, 1907 the plan met the approval of the Commission at a public hearing held at Lansing

______

11. *Ibid*, 96.

and five days later the Pere Marquette was given back to its owners.[12]

It has been held by some that the approval of the plan of consolidation of the Pere Marquette by the Michigan Railroad Commission amounted to a ratification of the indebtedness issued prior to that time, represented by the outstanding bonds and notes, including those that were issued for the Toledo Railway and Terminal Company stock and those that were issued to pay receiver's certificates, $400,000 of which was for settlement of the Chicago, Cincinnati and Louisville suit.[13]

Something, perhaps, can be said in favor of this view, for, even though the Railroad Commission did not know all the facts connected with the various financial transactions of the Pere Marquette previous to the receivership, they were furnished all the facts they asked for; but apparently they were not disposed to investigate the earlier transactions any closer and procure evidence on which the validity of some of the debts that the court ordered paid might be questioned. On the other hand, it must be said that some of the transactions were not obvious to the naked eye, and it is no defence to claim that because they were not found out sooner than they were, these transactions were therefore ratified; because what is not known can hardly be ratified.

There seems to be little doubt that the financial situation of the Pere Marquette was too rapidly passed over and agreed to by those whose consent was necessary to place the road in the possession of its owners.

12. *Ibid*, 97.
13. *Ibid*, 98 ff.

In the first place, $5,000,000 was far too small a sum to meet the rapidly maturing equipment notes, one block of which amounting to $2,612,000 was due on March 1, 1908. Being unable to meet this promptly when ·due, arrangements were made, as in a great many other cases, to postpone it until the future; awaiting some favorable contingency that might happen in the meantime which would better the paying power of the Pere Marquette. This postponement of payment was accomplished by instructing the First Trust and Savings Bank of Chicago to purchase all these notes at maturity, accept them on deposit and keep them alive as collateral for a new issue of notes. The new notes provided that the $2,612,000 was to be distributed over a period of four years, $650,000 to be paid on March 1st of each year. Since the equipment which was security for these notes was already five years old, this bank required as further security for the notes $500,000 par value of Pere Marquette refunding mortgage bonds.[14]

Again, in the face of a falling gross revenue due to the two-cent fare law, and rising operating expenses, the receivership failed to eliminate the evils resulting from the misdeeds and mistakes of previous years. The Pere Marquette was still paying interest on bonds that had been given for the stock of some of its constituents, this stock having originally been given as a bonus to the purchasers of the bonds of the constituent roads; and when exchanged for bonds by the Pere Marquette this stock must have had a very low value since dividends had not been paid on it for some time and there were no prospects that dividends would

____

14. *Ibid*, 100.

ever be paid on it. Such were the so-called Steel roads, the Kalkaska branch and a few other small branches.

Still further, it ought to have been quite evident that there was a good deal of deferred depreciation and maintenance on all parts of the road, and that in the near future this would have to be met, thereby increasing the operating ratio and endangering the equity. Even at this time there is no doubt that, for its earnings, the Pere Marquette was too heavily burdened with fixed charges, even though its funded debt per mile of road was not more than is normally found elsewhere.

On the date that the receivership closed, December 15, 1907, the total funded debt, plus $400,000 of receiver's short term notes outstanding and subsequently funded, was $60,087,000; of which, $7,875,000 was equipment obligations, $2,038,000 receiver's certificates, and the remainder, underlying bonds and general mortgage bonds issued under previous administrations.[15]

From the end of the receivership, December 15, 1907, to August 20, 1909, when the Baltimore and Ohio Railroad came into the situation, the credit of the Pere Marquette was low and its 5 per cent refunding bonds would not bring more than 75 on the market. At this price or slightly above, nearly a million dollars of bonds were disposed of during this period in payment for equipment. By March 1909 it became necessary to borrow at the banks securing these loans, at very disadvantageous rates, with deposits of 1905 refunding mortgage bonds.[16]

---

15. *Ibid*, 139.
16. *Ibid*, 103 ff.

CHAPTER IX

Baltimore and Ohio Railroad Administration (August 20, 1909 to March 1, 1911)

IN August 1909 the reorganization of the Cincinnati, Hamilton and Dayton Railroad was accomplished after four years of continuous effort. The reorganization plan provided: first, for the eventual release from the Cincinnati, Hamilton and Dayton refunding mortgage of 1904, of the 110,000 shares of Pere Marquette common stock (which was accomplished in 1911), thereby making it a free asset in the treasury of the Cincinnati, Hamilton and Dayton Railroad Company; and second, the executing of a contract made between the Baltimore and Ohio Railroad Company and J. P. Morgan and Company, whereby the former agreed to buy the Cincinnati, Hamilton and Dayton common stock from the latter (J. P. Morgan had acquired this stock in 1905) at a price to be determined by arbitration in July 1916.

The Baltimore and Ohio, by means of this stock purchase, took over the Cincinnati, Hamilton and Dayton at the time of reorganization, August 20, 1909, and reorganized the boards of directors of both the Cincinnati, Hamilton and Dayton and the Pere Marquette, so that a majority of each board consisted of the directors and principal officers of the Baltimore and Ohio. For the next year and a half, the boards of directors of the Cincinnati, Hamilton and Dayton and the Pere Marquette were more or less identical.[1]

____

1. *Ibid,* 105 ff.

To the superficial observer, the Pere Marquette appeared quite prosperous in 1909 and 1910, having a surplus of $40,000 in the former year and $469,000 in the latter. The prosperity was imaginary rather than real, however, as indicated by the overwhelming deficit of $1,813,000 appearing in the year 1911, which made everyone hopeless of the situation.[2]

The most immediate occasion of this huge deficit after two years of surpluses, was the wage increases that took place July 1, 1910, the beginning of the fiscal year that showed this large deficit. These increases in wages occurred in all departments of the railroad, ranging from 8 to 21 per cent for different employees and making a total increase for the year of $1,022,000.[3]

These increased payments to employees were largely due to the higher rate of wages paid. Other portions of the increases, however, were due to changes in the basis under which work was done. That is, more men had been required to do the same amount of work than had heretofore been the case, or the same number of men were now required to do a little less work than formerly, in nearly every branch of service, due largely to the requirements of new laws. For these reasons and because of natural growth of the railroad business, there was an increase of 821 men employed over the previous year.

The average rate of wages per month increased as follows: In the passenger train service, the average increase per month for every man employed was $19.89; yard engine men, $13.71; freight train service, $7.81; car department service, $6.03; track department,

2.   *Ibid*, 108 ff.
3.   *Ibid*, 112.

$3.96; station service, $3.65; mechanical department, $3.41. The average increase in amounts paid out in wages per month for the 8,214 men employed, was $10.36.

Since this wage increase in 1910, there have been subsequent substantial increases among the different employees, among which was the engineer's wage increase passed in 1914 but taking effect back to May 1912. Also an increase for the firemen decided by arbitration.

A second factor that was fundamental in bringing on the deficit in 1911 was the increased cost of materials and supplies consumed in daily use. With a little less than the total amount of business done as compared with the previous year, the costs of materials and supplies for 1910 had increased over 1909 by $492,822. It was about this time that railroads were crying in vain to the Interstate Commerce Commission for an increase in freight rates to relieve them from their precarious position—caught between higher operating expenses and stationary or slightly falling gross revenues. But while other roads, or at least a good many of them, had a surplus to fall back upon, or had no enormous deferred maintenance charges like the Sword of Damocles hanging over their heads, the Pere Marquette was coping with the absence of the former and the ominous presence of the latter, as well as poor credit, and fixed charges far too large for past or prospective net earnings.[4]

A third, though minor cause for the change between 1910 and 1911, was the increase in the debit balance of the Hire of Equipment account, amounting to

---

4. *Ibid,* 112.

$427,000. The Hire of Equipment is the payment of 35 cents per day (now 45 cents) for the use by the Pere Marquette of "foreign cars," or cars belonging to some other railroad company. Compared with most railroads, the Pere Marquette is in a peculiar position with respect to the interchange of cars between it and other railroad systems. Carload freight goes to its destination from its point of origin regardless of the distance and the number of railroads to be traversed. Because of this fact there are always a great many "foreign cars" on the Pere Marquette lines and also a great many Pere Marquette cars on foreign lines. But due to the fact that the Pere Marquette is largely an originating line as distinguished from a receiving line, there are always more of its cars on other lines than there are cars from other lines on its line. When these Pere Marquette cars move on other roads, and there is a car shortage in Michigan, the other roads are not always prompt in returning them because it is for their self interest to use them for their own traffic. In other words, when cars are badly needed by all lines there are always more cars leaving the Pere Marquette lines than are coming to it because of the originating character of the road, and hence a car shortage is felt more keenly in Michigan than in most other states.[5]

A final reason for the deficit is found in the fact that the funded indebtedness had been materially increased, thereby increasing interest charges by $149,000 over the previous year. The increase in the funded indebtedness was due partly to the taking up of some deferred maintenance and also to the purchase of

---

5. *Ibid*, 116 ff.

$832,000 worth of equipment, $159,000 of which was paid down and the balance of payments spread over a period of years.[6]

At the beginning of the year 1911 the Pere Marquette had a floating debt of $2,536,000 as a result of loans that were begun in March 1909. There was due on March 1, 1911, $650,000 of the extended Eastern Equipment notes, referred to elsewhere, due originally March 1, 1908; while in April taxes to the amount of $720,000 would become due. Large amounts of money were needed for additions and improvements and for new equipment, estimated by the president, Mr. Cotter, at $2,318,000.[7]

With the deficit growing larger every month and these heavy payments coming due, there was a good deal of lively discussion and many conferences among the stockholders and the officers of the company. It was the opinion of Mr. Cotter that if something over $2,000,000 was spent for equipment and improvements, gross earnings would show a decided increase for the year ending June 30, 1912, which he estimated at $18,000,000; and at the same time this expenditure would reduce the operating ratio to 72 per cent, so that there would be a probable surplus for the year 1912 of $450,000.

But before this amount could be raised for improvements, rapidly maturing debts had to be paid; and how this was to be done constituted a problem that sorely perplexed everyone connected with the company's affairs. The credit of the Pere Marquette was in a pitiable condition. The company had no money to

---

6.   *Ibid*, 112.
7.   *Ibid*, 123 ff.

meet these capital payments; it had exhausted the bonds which had been available as collateral, and hence could not secure a bank loan; but even if these bonds could have been released from the notes which they secured they were not at that time marketable at any price that could be considered. In short, the Pere Marquette had reached the limit of its ordinary borrowing power.

A former source of financial aid besides the banks, was the preferred stockholders who resided largely in New England. These. were advised of the growing deficit and of the needed improvements of the company, but indicated their unwillingness to give any further financial help, feeling that they had done their part in 1907 when they had put the company on its feet after the receivership.[8]

The next source appealed to for help, was the Baltimore and Ohio which had acquired control of the Cincinnati, Hamilton and Dayton Railroad from J. P. Morgan and Company, and, therefore, through that control, had the voting power of the 110,000 shares of common stock of the Pere Marquette which was a free asset in the treasury of the Cincinnati, Hamilton and Dayton. Also, it will be remembered that the Baltimore and Ohio controlled the Pere Marquette by virtue of having nominated a majority of its directors.

After having given due consideration to the subject, the directors of the Baltimore and Ohio decided that the Pere Marquette lines were not a natural part of the Cincinnati, Hamilton and Dayton Railroad, and that the interest of the Baltimore and Ohio in the Pere Mar-

---

8. *Ibid*, 125.

quette traffic was too remote to warrant it assuming the burden of financing this road. At the same time, the Baltimore and Ohio expressed their willingness to turn over the control of the Pere Marquette to others, by having the Cincinnati, Hamilton and Dayton sell the 110,000 shares of Pere Marquette common stock that it held in its treasury.

Toward the early part of 1911 these 110,000 shares were accordingly offered for sale by the Cincinnati, Hamilton and Dayton Railroad. They were not of great money value due to the financial difficulties that the Pere Marquette was having, and which prevented any possibility of dividends for some time to come. But the acquisition of them meant the virtual control of the Pere Marquette, and in this respect they would be of great value; for the holder of them could nominate a majority of the board of directors who in turn would determine what loans should be made, where they should be made, what commissions would be paid on them, the general policies of the railroad, the relation of the Pere Marquette to other roads, etc. In short, it meant that whoever bought this stock became the new master of the Pere Marquette. As has already been seen, the Pere Marquette had experienced some hard masters in previous years; and because this block of stock had resided in certain hands, the board of directors of the Pere Marquette had been made up of the nominees of the masters, who had followed their masters' bidding even to buying worthless stock with Pere Marquette bonds, increasing fixed charges to an unwarranted extent, and in general causing financial difficulties that could lead to only one result—receivership.[9]

9. *Ibid*, 126.

CHAPTER X

THE new master of the Pere Marquette was J. P. Morgan and Company which purchased the 110,000 shares of common stock for the sum of $2,530,000, or $23 per share. At the time this purchase was effected, an agreement between the Baltimore and Ohio and J. P. Morgan and Company was made, (supplemental to the agreement made between them in 1909) whereby the Baltimore and Ohio agreed that whatever the award of· the arbitrators might be in 1916, the Baltimore and Ohio would pay a minimum price for the Cincinnati, Hamilton and Dayton stock at that time of $2,530,000. In other words, J. P. Morgan and Company sold the control of the Cincinnati, Hamilton and Dayton to the Baltimore and Ohio for the same price at which they bought the control of the Pere Marquette. It was an exchange of Cincinnati, Hamilton and Dayton control for Pere Marquette control, at a price fixed in advance and not affected by fluctuations that might take place in the market price of the former stock before 1916. If the Cincinnati, Hamilton and Dayton stock had a market price below the contract price, J. P. Morgan and Company would be the winners; if it had a market price above the price contracted for, there would be a chance for J. P. Morgan and Company to gain more than the contract price (although, perhaps not so much as the market price), since the arbitrators might fix the purchase price above the minimum of $2,530,000.[1]

It was a proposition that bore little risk for J. P. Morgan and Company and at the same time secured control of a system that, detached from the Cincinnati, Hamilton and Dayton, might be financially strengthened and prove to be a profitable investment. However, too much emphasis must not be laid on the motive to secure a good speculative stock, because the Pere Marquette had showed continual deficits each month for the preceding half year and prospects for the future were not flattering.

No sooner had J. P. Morgan and Company taken control of the Pere Marquette than it was evident that large sums would be needed immediately to take care of equipment notes and taxes falling due, and also to meet a crying need for new equipment all over the line. Whether these needs, amounting to several million of dollars, could be financed, seemed to depend upon the ability of the Pere Marquette to offer security suitable as the basis for a loan. This was difficult to do. The refunding mortgage had been practically exhausted, and at first sight it seemed impossible to put a new mortgage on the system as there were already prior liens amounting at that time to over $60,000,000. Bonds sold under such circumstances would not bring a price on the market that would justify the liability incurred. A situation existed where no one would lend money on such security unless he had other interests which ultimately might be of value if the company were financed.[2]

---

1. *Ibid*, 126-7.
2. *Ibid*, 129.

The Pere Marquette needed about $8,000,000 to meet its maturing debts of various kinds and to pay interest on its funded debt, since it was not being earned. In this emergency J. P. Morgan and Company offered to take $8,000,000 five year 6 per cent notes at a five per cent commission, provided they were secured by twice that amount in new bonds. The matter was passed on favorably by the Michigan Railroad Commission and the company received $7,600,000 in cash from J. P. Morgan and Company, giving as security for this amount $16,000,000 of a new issue of general mortgage bonds. It was naturally difficult to give a financial rating to inactive bonds, with so many prior liens on the railroad property, but it was thought that a sale of $16,000,000 of bonds under the hammer would bring in about $8,000,000 cash.[3]

The consent of the Michigan Railroad Commission to this loan in reality meant granting permission to the company to pay interest on the funded debt by means of a loan, since interest on the funded debt was not being earned and had not been earned since receivership, with the possible exception of one year. The floating debt of the Pere Marquette was becoming unmanageable, and the natural tendency of the Commission was to allow some provision to take care of that debt; but in this, as in scores of cases in the past, it proved to be merely the postponing of the end. Inside of this floating debt were items that were not legitimate; and no real service was done, either to the railroad, the security holders or the State, by bolstering up the Pere Marquette for a few extra months. Again,

---

3. *Ibid.*

the unmanageable size of the floating debt merely emphasizes the point made elsewhere, that the funded debt was too large for the earning power of the road, which defect of organization should have been remedied by the reorganization after the receivership in 1907.

The Morgan loan was soon used up, for the most part in the following ways: $2,536,000 to take up the company's notes; $650,000 of equipment principal due March 1st; $100,000 of equipment principal due on another trust; taxes, $720,000; and about $2,800,000 was immediately spent for additions and betterments.[4] Notwithstanding all these funds the road was still in bad financial condition by the end of the year 1911. In the last month of this year the road again began to show a deficit from operations, it being something over $64,000. January 1912 closed with the extraordinary deficit of $456,000, which is to say, that this month's actual expenses of operation exceeded the gross earnings for the month by this sum. February, though a shorter month, showed a still greater deficit than January, amounting to $520,000. For March there was a deficit of $347,000.[5] Part of these deficits were due to reductions in earnings owing to interruptions of traffic because of the extensive improvements being made on the line, and also to the especially severe winter of 1911-1912 which was so extreme for several weeks that practically no freight could be moved on some parts of the line. But by far the larger part of the deficit was due to more fundamental causes and would have existed if other conditions had been more favorable than they were. In other words, there was

---

4. *Ibid*, 131.
5. *Ibid*, 134.

too narrow a margin between net revenues from operation and fixed charges. It was becoming more and more apparent to those conversant with financial affairs as pertaining to the Pere Marquette, that either the former must be increased or the latter decreased. Since the first proposition was daily becoming more obviously an impossibility[6] the latter expedient was looked upon as the only solution of the problem. In other words, another receivership seemed imminent, which of necessity must do what the former receivership failed to do, viz., bring about a contraction of the bonded indebtedness and a resulting reduction in fixed charges.

However, it cannot be said that this view was widespread. Many still held that if the Pere Marquette could be tided over its immediate difficulty it would ultimately earn enough on the average to maintain a safe margin between net revenues and fixed charges, with its then existing bonded debt. Accordingly, new efforts were made to secure requisite capital. About half a million of dollars was borrowed from one of the Detroit banks on short term paper in December 1911, but the problem became acute again in the beginning of 1912; while in July 1912 there came due the $5,000,000 of debentures issued at the time of reorganization. J. P. Morgan and Company were appealed to but they felt that they had done enough in furnishing money the year before. Moreover, a great deal of dissatisfaction was expressed by the stockholders and others regarding the efficiency of the management, and a change was demanded. After a great deal of dis-

---

6. Due to the rapidly increasing operating expenses made necessary by deferred maintenance of former years. See Appendix D.

.cussion, Mr. Newman Erb, a man of extensive railroad experience, was made chairman of the executive committee on February 23, 1912, and it was expected by many that he would bring about better conditions.[7]

Shortly after this date some Boston stockholders were induced to furnish the company $1,200,000 in cash, taking notes therefor, due on June 28, 1912 and secured by the $1,364,000 of Cincinnati, Hamilton and Dayton bonds that the Pere Marquette received as an award from the Toledo Railway and Terminal Company transaction; and also secured by the deposit of $1,200,000 of long term Pere Marquette bonds issued under the new mortgage of March 1, 1911. The extent of the security for this loan shows the attitude of capitalists toward the credit of the Pere Marquette. Also, the notes were made due June 28th because the lenders of this $1,200,000 would not consent to a maturity subsequent to the maturity of the $5,000,000 debentures.[8]

This $1,200,000 was used to pay fixed charges and its expenditure for that purpose was apparently approved by the Michigan Railroad Commission. However, this did not carry the road very far, and it was attempted to make arrangements to secure something over a million of dollars by the issue of 5 year notes under this same collateral indenture of March 1, 1911. This would involve putting up as collateral long term bonds for twice the amount of the face value of the notes, and with the $5,000,000 of debentures coming due the Michigan Railroad Commission believed that this plan would not help out materially, so they refused

----

7. *Ibid*, 135.
8. *Ibid*, 136.

the issue, which of necessity brought on receivership on April 1, 1912.

SUMMARY OF THE FINANCIAL CONDITION OF THE PERE MARQUETTE RAILROAD COMPANY

(January 1, 1900, to June 30, 1914.)

The profit and loss account of the Pere Marquette Railroad started out clean with the consolidation in 1900; that is, there was nothing carried over to either surplus or deficit from previous operations. This fact exists because the excess of liabilities over assets of the three constituent roads was carried into cost of road account.[9]

The profit and loss account shows that on June 30, 1914 a net deficit of $22,559,537.97 had accrued. However, at the end of the year 1907, after the reorganization of the Pere Marquette Railroad Company and the Pere Marquette Railroad Company of Indiana forming the present Pere Marquette Railroad Company, they had a deficit of $2,186,666.16, which according to the reorganization plan was credited to the profit and loss account and charged into their physical property accounts. Therefore this deficit of $22,-559,537.97 would have been larger by this sum of $2,186,666.16 had that remained in the profit and loss account instead of being charged to the cost of road account.[10]

If we take into consideration all the deficits that were dropped in course of reorganization, that is, include them as if they had been shown and accounted

---

9. *Stenographer's Minutes Before the I. C. C.*, Docket No. 6833, 1017.
10. *Ibid*, 1018.

for in the books of the reorganized companies, the deficit on June 30, 1914, instead of being $24,786,-204.13, would have been $31,807,615.41.

CHAPTER XI

THE PRESENT PERE MARQUETTE RAILROAD SYSTEM

THE Pere Marquette extends from Chicago on the west to Buffalo and Suspension Bridge on the east. Chicago is reached by leasing about 40 miles of trackage from other roads beyond Porter, Indiana, which is the end of the Pere Marquette rails. The rails of the Lake Shore are used from Porter to Pine, Indiana, a distance of 17 miles, from which point the Pere Marquette passenger trains run for 22 miles over the Pittsburg, Fort Wayne and Chicago Railroad (Pennsylvania Lines) to 16th Street, Chicago; and from there over the Baltimore and Ohio Chicago Terminal line to this company's Harrison Street, or Fifth Avenue Station. The freight trains go from Porter to Pine over the Lake Shore rails, then over the rails of the Baltimore and Ohio Chicago Terminal line to a freight yard owned by the Pere Marquette located at Tracy, which is about 15 miles from the passenger station.[1]

It will be remembered that two routes had been contracted for in order to gain satisfactory entrance into Chicago. The first was for a distance of 34 miles, from Pine to the Grand Central Station at Chicago, over the rails of the Chicago Terminal Transfer Railroad Company, which route was leased for a period of 99 years. This route was frought with so much delay for passenger trains that the Pere Marquette could not successfully compete for through Chicago passenger traf-

---

1. *Stenographer's Minutes Before the I. C. C.*, Docket No. 6833, page 1118 ff.

fic. For this reason a second route for passenger trains was contracted for, as described in the paragraph above, and the Pere Marquette thus found itself with two routes into Chicago for both of which it was paying rentals. Plans have since been made which will give a single entrance into Chicago, thereby reducing the double rent and helping to make this latter terminal a profitable connecting point.

On the eastern end of the Pere Marquette line, the Michigan Central road (from St. Thomas to Welland, a distance of 100 miles, and branching from there, 18 miles to Buffalo and 15 miles to Suspension Bridge) is used by the Pere Marquette under a long term lease. At Suspension Bridge the terminals of the New York Central are used under lease.[2]

The arrangement with the Michigan Central and the New York Central is very advantageous to the Pere Marquette. It provides that the latter railroad can solicit freight anywhere over the New York Central territory as if it owned its own line into that territory; while the costs of operation under the lease are as low as the costs of operation over the Pere Marquette's own rails. The contract with these railroads does not, however, allow the Pere Marquette to solicit business on the line over which trackage rights exists, that is, from St. Thomas to Buffalo. This stretch of track acts as a bridge for the Pere Marquette to obtain entrance into Buffalo; but once there, it is open for all business and in fact gets a large amount of traffic off the rails of the New York Central and the Lackawana bound for Chicago, as well as for the Northwest. From Suspension Bridge, interchange of traffic takes place

----

2. *Ibid.*

with the Erie, the Lehigh Valley, as well as with the New York Central. Of these connecting roads, more interchange of traffic is done with the New York Central than with any of the others, although it is more or less of a competitor of the Pere Marquette for hauls to Chicago and other points west. The only local business done in Buffalo is in carload lots, delivery being made by switching, the switching charges being absorbed by the Pere Marquette.[3]

One important disadvantage with the lease of the Michigan Central road from St. Thomas to Buffalo is that no passenger traffic is allowed between these two points. This precludes the Pere Marquette from entering into competition for a very profitable through passenger traffic from the East to Detroit and Chicago, although to the latter city the Pere Marquette would be at a natural disadvantage as compared with its competitors because of the round about character of the route.

Two other western terminals for Buffalo traffic besides Chicago, are Milwaukee and Manitowoc. In Milwaukee the Pere Marquette owns its terminals, consisting of a ferry slip and track room for some 250 cars. At Manitowoc it uses the terminals of the Northwestern and the Soo lines. The terminals at Ludington are owned by the Pere Marquette. This route from Buffalo via Ludington and the car ferries gives the Pere Marquette a short line from the East to the Northwest thus avoiding freight congestion in Chicago. This line has been in operation for about twenty years but the business profits have not been as great as were anticipated.[4]

3. *Ibid.*
4. *Ibid*, 1122.

One reason for this is the disadvantageous location of the Pere Marquette ferry slip at Milwaukee in relation to the yards of the Chicago, Milwaukee and St. Paul Railway with which road most of the traffic is interchanged. Plans have been formulated to change the location of the slip, putting it further up river near the mouth of these railroad yards. This ought to prove a profitable line to the East, as the Pere Marquette, over this route from Milwaukee to Buffalo, can meet the running time from Milwaukee through Chicago to Buffalo.

Another reason is the extraordinary terminal expense on the Milwaukee traffic. In fact it "would be prohibitive, were it not for the fact that Milwaukee is such a large terminal and supplies such a large tonnage....."[5] A switching charge is absorbed by the Pere Marquette at this terminal on local business, and certain clerical expense at the Chicago, Milwaukee and St. Paul station, which is really a charge for handling less than car-load lots. On all business originating in Michigan and going to Milwaukee, the Chicago, Milwaukee and St. Paul receives 15 per cent of the earnings, which is a charge, instead of a switching charge, on through traffic. On all traffic originating in Wisconsin and going through Milwaukee to the East, the Chicago, Milwaukee and St. Paul receives 60 per cent of what it would have received had the business gone via Chicago. Some more generous plan for the Pere Marquette is being negotiated for at the present time.

At Manitowoc, where an interchange of traffic takes

---

5. *Stenographer's Minutes Before the I. C. C.*, Docket No. 6833, 1126.

place with the Northwestern and Soo lines, a switching charge of $2.50 and $3.00 per car is charged; also an expense for the use of their stations and their clerical help. The arrangements are reasonable and a good deal of valuable traffic from points north and west of Milwaukee is interchanged at this point for transit over the Pere Marquette.[6]

Toledo is the important gateway from the South. Here the Pere Marquette owns its own tracks and has a 99 year lease on yards that belong to the Ann Arbor Railroad Company. The interchange of traffic is made here through the Toledo Terminal and Railway Company, or direct. They also own a terminal at La Crosse on the west side where connections are made with the Chicago and Eastern Illinois, the Pan Handle and the Chesapeake and Ohio of Indiana lines; the latter railroad crossing a number of trunk lines running east from Chicago thus forming a connection with all these lines and also with southern points.[7]

At Detroit the terminals are the property of the Pere Marquette in the sense that entrance to this city is secured over the tracks owned jointly by the Wabash and the Pere Marquette, the Wabash owning one line and the Pere Marquette owning the other, while 51 per cent of the stock of the Fort Street Union Depot Company is owned by the Pere Marquette.

CONCLUSIONS

The business between Chicago and Buffalo is largely competitive and the fact that the Pere Marquette is 50 miles longer than the other trunk lines perhaps makes

6. *Ibid,* 1127.
7. *Ibid,* 1130.

some difference in favor of the other roads, but it is not of such magnitude that it cannot be overcome by better traffic arrangements and a more vigorous endeavor to strengthen the traffic across Lake Michigan from the Northwest.

Again, at both ends of the line the Pere Marquette is forced to use the property of competitors which might indicate a disadvantage, but it has already been indicated that at the Buffalo end the New York Central allows solicitation for traffic, while at Chicago the competition is not more than would ordinarily be expected from roads in the same territory.

The Pere Marquette is an originating road. It originates along the line more business than it receives, or about 64 per cent. This might show that there is a value in the property beyond the competitive traffic spoken of. However, this traffic originating in Michigan has been almost stationary or declining slightly during the last few years, falling off from 69 per cent in 1908 to 64 per cent in 1913. This indicates that more through traffic is being handled. As the traffic originating in Michigan declines, the through traffic will have to take its place, as the development of agriculture in this State has been too slow in the last two decades to fill the gap left by the declining lumber industry. The fact that earnings of the Pere Marquette have doubled since 1900 indicates the growing importance of through traffic.[8]

While forest products have decreased in tonnage, this kind of tonnage received from other roads has materially increased showing the importance that is being recognized of outside connections. Included in

---

8. *Ibid*, 1132.

this.tonnage from other lines is bituminous coal which is an important item. The local tonnage is partly fruit and sugar beets although these two products comprise a very small portion of the total tonnage. Merchandise and manufactured goods are increasing and in the future will form a large part of the Pere Marquette's tonnage.

The line north from Grand Rapids has keen competition from the Grand Rapids and Indiana and further north from the Ann Arbor line. East and west, the Michigan Central and the Grand Trunk offer effective competition. From Detroit east, competition is offered by the Michigan Central, the Canadian Pacific, the Wabash and the Grand Trunk railroads.

There has been some talk of again making the Pere Marquette a local road. Indications are that this might be disastrous, since the through traffic is the life-giving element for - the Pere Marquette. The decline of originating traffic would emphasize the necessity of reaching out for larger portions of traffic originating outside of the State. While manufacturing is giving more and more tonnage to the Pere Marquette, and agriculture will some day be an important factor, at the present time neither of them has grown to such an extent that, with the present competition, a large enough share could possibly go to the Pere Marquette to make it a self-supporting tonnage, even with other miscellaneous products produced in the State. There is little doubt that the development of the Pere Marquette has been along the right lines and to go back to the old local units would be to lose all that has been gained in this respect. Perhaps an even quicker development of through lines than actually took place would have been better for the railroad rather than the slow manner in which it has expanded.[9]

Compared with the other Michigan competitor lines the Pere Marquette has more branch lines in proportion to its total mileage. So many branch lines make it necessary to operate a large number of small terminals, which can be done only at a great cost. In comparing the Pere Marquette with the Soo line (which has some 2,800 miles of road or 800 more than the Pere Marquette) as regards the cost of terminal switching, it was found that the Pere Marquette switching was much in excess of the Soo although the earnings of the Pere Marquette were smaller; and the station forces on the latter road cost about $1,000,000 per year while on the Soo line the station expenses cost them about $600,000 per year. This fact serves as a handicap to the Pere Marquette by making necessary unprofitable operations in some cases, but being of inestimable advantage to the people of the communities served and to the State of Michigan.[10]

Usually the earnings of a particular branch are not kept separate from other earnings because it is too expensive. However, shortly after receivers were appointed in 1912 they wanted to know what some of the small branches were doing, so for the months of May, June and July of 1912 a record was kept of the earnings per passenger mile of some of the branch lines, as follows:

> Buchanan to Benton Harbor, five cents.
> Freeport to Elmdale, fourteen cents.
> Weidman to Remus, fifteen cents.
> Leota to Clare, nineteen cents.

9. *Ibid*, 1136.
10. *Ibid*, 1105.

Allegan to Holland, fifty cents.
Beaverton to Coleman, twenty-five cents.
Mt. Pleasant to Coleman, thirty-seven cents.
Barrytown to Mecosta, nineteen cents.
Stanton to Haynor, forty-eight cents.
Elk Rapids to Williamsburg, seventeen cents.
Stratford to Rapid City, nineteen cents.
Almont to Tappan, twenty-five cents.
Sandusky to Poland, forty-two cents.
Port Hope to Palms, thirty-one cents.
Fostoria to McGrew, fifty-four cents.

The average earnings of all these branches was 29 cents per train mile during these three summer months. In the winter months perhaps they would be less. For the Pere Marquette Railroad as a whole, the passenger earnings per mile average about one dollar, which under ordinary circumstances ought to pay expenses.[11]

Some of the branches showing a loss through operation as regards freight traffic, are as follows for the year 1913:[12]

Fostoria to Flint, 20 miles; 190 carloads a month.
Beaverton to Coleman, 11 miles; 172 a month.
Clare to Leota, 27 miles; 247 a month.
Port Huron to Almont, 30 miles; 304 a month.
Edmore to Big Rapids, 35 miles; 102 a month.
Mecosta to Barrytown, 12 miles; 30 a month.
Remus to Mt. Pleasant, 13 miles; 44 a month.
Stanton to Haynor, 20 miles: 285 a month.
Elmdale to Freeport, 6 miles; 44 a month.
Buchanan branch, 26 miles; 192 a month.
White Cloud to Big Rapids, 20 miles; 364 a month.

From what has been given it is seen that a great

---

11. Before a Committee of the Michigan Legislature, Testimony by Frederick W. Stevens, page 89
12. The number of car loads is an average per month. Also, all these figures cover loads in both directions. For the year 1915 these branches showed improved traffic conditions.

many miles of the Pere Marquette Railroad are unproductive and will continue to remain so for a good many years to come, thereby making it imperative that outside traffic be secured. This is being done, but there are certain difficulties that are encountered in reaching out for through traffic chief of which is the fact that most of the Pere Marquette's competitors are parts of larger systems, or have intimate relations with larger railroad systems; such as the relation of the Grand Rapids and Indiana with the Pennsylvania, and the fact that the Wabash is an eastern and western system running through to Kansas City, likewise, that the Michigan Central is a New York Central line. Nevertheless, whatever the impediments, the only logical course for the Pere Marquette to follow is to become more and more a through line, by this policy making itself somewhat independent of the peculiar traffic conditions that exist along a great many miles of its branch lines. Sooner or later the unprofitable districts of Michigan must change their character for the better, especially as the competition of more fertile lands in western states loses its force, and then some of the branches that are not now paying operating expenses will no doubt carry a profitable traffic. But it must be remembered that this development is a matter of the future, not the present, and in the meantine the through character of the Pere Marquette must be developed.[13]

---

13. *Stenographer's Minutes Before the I. C. C.*, Docket No. 6833, 1138.

CHAPTER XII

The Plan of Reorganization of the Pere Marquette Railroad Company

THE plan of reorganization expects to accomplish, among other things, the following results:

"The preservation of the Pere Marquette Railroad as a System, and such control for the reorganized property as shall safeguard the rights of security holders.

"Reduction of the fixed charges to a limit believed under all conditions to be safely within the net earning capacity of the reorganized property.

"Adequate provision for present and future requirements.

"Payment or adjustment of all debts and provision for existing equipment trust obligations."[1]

The capitalization of the new company, according to this plan of reorganization, is approximately $105,000,000 as compared with a capitalization of the old company of $113,340,129. The mortgage which secures the bond issues of the new company is for the face amount of $75,000,000 and is a first mortgage on the entire property, interests and franchises of the Pere Marquette Railroad Company, bearing date of July 1, 1916 and maturing July 10, 1956.

There are issued under this mortgage the following securities:

---

1. Reorganization of the Pere Marquette Railroad Company, Plan and Agreement, dated October 30, 1916; page 1 ff.

Series "A" bonds to the par amount of.	$21,782,501.00
Additional issue, Series "A" bonds, par amount of......................	5,870,000.00
Series "B" bonds to the par amount of.	8,479,000.00
Five Per Cent Cumulative Prior Adjustment stock, par value of..........	11,200,011.50
Five Per Cent Preferred stock.......	12,449,244.00
Common stock....................	45,219,255.00
Total capitalization...........	$104,991,011.50

Of this total capitalization, about $88,000,000 will be used to retire capital stock and various note issues and bonds, and about $17,000,000 of stock and securities are expected to yield.$16,000,000 of cash to be used for the immediate purposes of the company. Of this latter sum, approximately $11,500,000 will be used to satisfy obligations already incurred and $4,500,000 for working capital and for additions, betterments and improvements.

What is termed by the Michigan Railroad Commission as "the most important achievement of the proposed plan of reorganization," is the reduction of the bonded indebtedness from $79,638,826 to $36,131,501 and a resulting lessening of the annual interest charges by the amount of $2,481,105. This is a reduction in the fixed charges upon the Pere Marquette property of the equivalent of nearly five per cent on $50,000,000 annually.[2]

The Culminative Prior Adjustment stock of the reorganized company will be entitled to a five per cent dividend each year, provided it is earned, before any

<hr>

2.   Orders and Opinions of the Michigan Railroad Commission of the State of Michigan, Vol. 5; No. 2, page 119 ff.

dividend is paid upon other stock of the company. It is redeemable at par plus accrued dividends, and in the event of liquidation of the company the stock and accumulated dividends has preference over other stock.

The Cumulative Preferred stock will be entitled to a five per cent dividend if it is earned, and is cumulative at 1, 2, 3, 4, and 5 per cent annually and progressively on and after July 1, 1917. This stock is given preference both as to assets and accrued dividends, subject to the Cumulative Prior Adjustment stock.

The issue of common stock to the par value of $45,219,000 for the new company, is as much an increase over the issue of common stock in the old company, as the bonded indebtedness of the new company is a decrease over the bonded indebtedness of the old company. But the new company will have a great advantage over the old company in that it need not face receivership in case it fails to pay dividends on this common stock, while the old company of necessity had to pay interest on its bonds or go into the hands of a receiver.

Some objections against this plan were lodged with the Michigan Railroad Commission, urging that this body refuse to give its approval to the plan, on the grounds that the total proposed capitalization was in excess of the fair value of the physical property of the company. The physical property of the Pere Marquette Railroad Company, as appraised by Dean Mortimer E. Cooley in 1914 under the direction of the Michigan Railroad Commission, showed an estimated reproduction cost of $96,962,771, and a cost of reproduction less depreciation of $78,545,241; and on this evidence it was urged that the new capitalization ought not to be more than $75,000,000. The Commission was also strongly requested to withhold its decision until the receipt of estimates of value that were then being prepared under the direction of the Interstate Commerce Commission.

As regards these objections, the Michigan Railroad Commission in giving its sanction to the plan of reorganization, says, "In our opinion the engineering estimate of the reproduction cost of a railroad property, while a most valuable aid in determining the question of just capitalization of the company, it is not a positive and determining factor. It must be considered in connection with many other factors, among which the particular conditions under which the property was created and developed is most important, for even a state should not be a party to the repudiation of that which has been created in accordance with its laws, and the average judgment of the time. It may establish a new order for the future, but it should be just to the past. In our view, any disparity that may develop between the appraisement now being projected by the federal government, if any such disparity shall be found, would be of small value in solution of the problem involved."[3]

The Commission then goes on to say it will recognize "practical adjustments" in the capitalization of corporations and will not seek to enforce an unvarying rule. The reason for this view is, that "with no class of corporations is the recognition of the practical problems involved more necessary than with railroad corporations with extensive mileage, the sum of many

3. Orders and Opinions of the Michigan Railroad Commission of the State of Michigan, Vol. 5, No. 2, page 120.

consolidations and gradual growth. The Pere Marquette Railroad, ... is a property of this character. At least eighty-six distinct corporate entities have had to do with its creation and more than fifty have been employed in the actual construction of the various parts of the system. The capital stock, not only of the constituent parts, but of the present company, has been issued in accordance with the forms of law that existed at the time of issue. On no less than seven occasions the financial affairs of companies controlling considerable portions of the system have been before the courts in receivership and other proceedings, and been given the Court's tacit or express approval. Today the stock of the company is widely distributed and owned by more than one thousand seven hundred stockholders, the integrity of whose ownership no one questions. At the time of the consolidation of the properties of the present Pere Marquette Railroad the details of the stock and bond issues were fully stated to the state authority which passed upon the consolidation, and received its tacit approval. These facts must be considered by the agency of the State that now gives its approval or disapproval to the readjustment of the company's finances, or the State accept the charge that it does not recognize the moral obligations in force among men."[4]

The Commission continues and shows that a refusal to recognize the equities of the less valuable interests in the property would invite foreclosure of one or more of the divisional mortgages, and hence cause a breaking up of the larger system into others less capable of

____

4.   *Ibid.*

serving the public and with less prospects for successful operation.

Still further, the Commission shows that the credit of the Pere Marquette is such that it cannot borrow from the ordinary sources and hence must rely upon its security holders to keep it supplied with the necessary capital for its successful operation. It says, "Action by this Commission that would result in the forced reduction of the capitalization of the company so as to either wholly or materially eliminate the holdings of those who have contributed the $14,000,000 in the recent past, or who may under any plan of reorganization be called upon to contribute towards the $16,000,000 for the immediate future, would result in most effectually closing the only sources from which, under present conditions, contributions of material amount may be reasonably expected, which at the same time supply the capital necessary for the immediate needs of the company without a corresponding increase in the fixed charges."[5]

For the reasons stated, the Commission gave its approval to the plan of reorganization, and after the necessary negotiations with the holders of the different securities an agreement was effected similar to that outlined in the plan referred to, and on April 11, 1917 the Pere Marquette Railroad Company emerged from receivership (where it had been since April 12, 1912) under the name of the Pere Marquette Railway Company.

---

5. *Ibid.*

CHAPTER XIII

SUMMARY AND CONCLUSION

FROM the preceding pages it has been seen that the Pere Marquette Railroad has had a long and arduous development, fraught with traffic and financial difficulties without, and subject to greedy and unscrupulous foes within. The remaining tasks to be accomplished are two in number, first, to present a brief summary and characterization of the most important outstanding events in the history of the Pere Marquette Railroad System, and second, to suggest such conclusions as may properly be drawn from this experience.

The outstanding events in the historic development of the Pere Marquette, described in detail in the preceding pages, may now be divided into five periods. Though these periods are not always distinct, they serve to differentiate the main currents in this complex development, and may be stated as follows: The Period of Construction, 1857 to 1900; the Period of Exploitation, 1900 to 1906; The Period of Financial Difficulties, 1906 to 1908; The Period of Financial Collapse and Physical Deterioration, 1908 to 1912; The Period of Rehabilitation, 1912 to 1917.

THE PERIOD OF CONSTRUCTION (1857-1900)

The Pere Marquette Railroad System for the most part, was built up by slow, piece-meal methods prior to the year 1900. The conceiving and projecting of its various parts has enlisted the services of over one hundred corporations, half of which have played an active part in the construction of the line as it stands today. Practically all of these railroads started out as lumber roads, sixty to ninety per cent of their total tonnage consisting of lumber and forest products. Because of this fact, their prosperity varied directly as the prosperity of the lumber industry; and during periods of depression they were more acutely and more quickly affected than other roads with a greater variety of traffic. This was true, because at the first intimation of business depression the demand for construction materials fell off more than did other products, and in those days lumber figured as the chief material for construction purposes.

With traffic of a negligible quantity during these periods of business depression after the panics of 1873, 1884 and 1893, several of the roads were forced into receivership. The reorganizations in most cases succeeded in cutting down the fixed charges by an exchange of common and preferred stock for bonds. The deficits that had accrued up to the time of the receiverships were usually put into the cost of road account of the newly reorganized companies, which meant, of course, the capitalization of deficits. Often the books of the reorganized company showed an inflation in value of the property of the old company, for which there was no justification. On the whole, however, the different reorganizations were effectual in putting the railroads on a fairly profitable running basis by a forced reduction of fixed charges.

It had been supposed that when the timber was stripped from the land penetrated by these different railroads, a profitable traffic would spring up from agricultural products. Unfortunately, this was not to be the case in most parts of the State, for the reason that the settler was not attracted by the pine stump lands of Michigan so long as he could have the abundantly fertile lands of the West almost for the asking. Hence, in the late eighties and in the nineties the railroads that now form the constituent parts of the Pere Marquette Railroad found themselves in a critical financial position. Most of them had relied on one commodity for traffic and this mainstay was fast ebbing away with no prospects of anything adequately taking its place.

With this situation existing, the only remedy that appeared to be practicable was to increase through traffic. With the State of Michigan bounded on three sides with water this was indeed a problem. One of the railroads (the Flint and Pere Marquette) partially solved the difficulty by practically extending its tracks to make connections with the great railroad systems of Wisconsin by means of car-ferries across Lake Michigan. For the other roads, however, the problem was still unsolved.

The only remaining way to get through traffic seemed to be through consolidation of those railroads which were thus hampered by local conditions. Accordingly, in the middle nineties a movement was set on foot to consolidate three railroads, viz., the Flint and Pere Marquette Railroad, the Chicago and West Michigan Railway, and the Detroit, Grand Rapids and Western Railroad. These lines roughly aggregated 1,800 miles, and combined would form a through east and west, and north and south system across the State. On January 1, 1900 the Pere Marquette Railroad Company came into being as a consolidation of these roads, but the new company was unduly burdened by the fact that outstanding capital stock in the hands of the public was inflated by $1,461,250 and the book value of the property by $4,290,230.41.

This watering of the property account and the stock outstanding was indeed a great handicap on the financial progress and success of the Pere Marquette, but even with these impediments this railroad might have been fairly successful if certain men had not secured control during the early period of its existence. With the passing of majority control into the hands of these men the doom of the Pere Marquette was sealed; it was destined in the space of a few short months to be transformed from a financially prosperous and physically well-kept railroad, to a financial and physical wreck.

THE PERIOD OF EXPLOITATION (1900 TO 1906)

The history of the wrecking of the Pere Marquette naturally falls into two divisions: that of the F. H. Prince control, from January 1, 1903 to July 1, 1904; and that of Syndicate control, from July 1, 1904 to October 20, 1905. While unfair and unjustifiable practices have transpired in the history of the Pere Marquette and its constituents prior to 1903, it was most certainly within the dates of these two periods that this railroad was sold out by its directors who were nominees of the real forces at work.

F. H. Prince and his associates who succeeded in securing control of the Pere Marquette by the purchase of enough stock to elect their nominees on the board of directors, immediately inaugurated a policy of expansion. This policy consisted of making the Pere Marquette a through line from Chicago to Buffalo, by means of the purchase or lease of nearly 400 miles of main and branch lines most of which had a history of failure. The bonded indebtedness of the Pere Marquette was increased by $7,500,000 on account of this procedure, while the returns anticipated did not materialize, due largely to the fact that strong competitors were met at both of these terminals, and the Pere Marquette being somewhat of a roundabout line between these points suffered accordingly.

The chief reason for this undue expansion seems to lie in the fact that F. H. Prince and Company, bankers, were given very substantial commissions on the Pere Marquette bonds that they sold, in order to make some of these purchases, and further, they were materially rewarded for their services in consummating and carrying out the terms of the contracts for the purchase and sale of the different properties involved.

Besides this policy of costly expansion the Prince interests reversed the other policies of the former administration, which, under the leadership of W. W. Crapo, consisted of maintaining the road in good physical condition, the accumulation of a small surplus for improvements, and the payment of no dividends on common stock. Under the Prince control the road and equipment was undermaintained, unearned dividends were paid on common stock, and in 18 months of this management $2,500,000 net was added to current liabilities. They also added more than $14,500,000 to the outstanding long time debt, and finally formed a

47

syndicate of the Cincinnati, Hamilton and Dayton Railway, selling to this syndicate their "control" of the Pere Marquette for the extraordinary price of $125 per share, which control had been purchased on the market 18 months before this time at $85 per share.

This syndicate, formed by the Prince interests in order to create an extraordinary profitable market for the Pere Marquette common stock that they held, was composed of 29 separate individuals and companies. All of these had something to unload on either the Pere Marquette or the Cincinnati, Hamilton and Dayton railroads, and membership in the syndicate insured a good price for their goods. Besides express contracts, car and locomotive orders and bankers services, the bulk of the goods that the syndicate members sold the Pere Marquette in return for that company's bonds, consisted of worthless railroad stock. Millions of dollars of this worthless stock was forced onto the Pere Marquette by the unscrupulous members of the syndicate, who either owned this stock directly or represented those who did own it. And since bonds were issued as the purchase price for this stock, fixed charges rose out of all proportion to the net operating revenue and thereby made receivership inevitable. Some of the money lost through the syndicate manipulations was subsequently recovered by action against the Cincinnati, Hamilton and Dayton Railway, but for the most part the losses were real, and not only meant the financial failure of the Pere Marquette and the Cincinnati, Hamilton and Dayton railroads, but loss to innocent bondholders who were unaware of the nature of the security behind their bonds.

After having made enormous profits at the expense

of the railroads of which they had secured control, the syndicate now sought to rid itself of the Cincinnati, Hamilton and Dayton stock by selling it to the Erie Railroad through the medium of J. P. Morgan and Company. The true state of affairs of the controlled railroads was obscured as much as possible and the contract of sale was carried out, the Erie Railroad taking the Cincinnati, Hamilton and Dayton stock at the price of $160 per share. This was obviously an attempt to throw an illegitimate burden on the Erie by those who would interest thereby, but the attempt was unsuccessful. Influential stockholders of this road made such strenuous objections to the purchase of this worthless stock, that the stock, and hence the loss, was forced back onto J. P. Morgan and Company. The syndicate had rid itself of the tool with which it had done so much damage, but not in the direction that had been planned.

J. P. Morgan and Company now had control of the Cincinnati, Hamilton and Dayton Railway and through that control also had the governing power over the Pere Marquette. Both roads were in a hopeless financial condition as a result of the syndicate manipulations, being unable to meet their current liabilities much less the interest on their funded debt. Under these conditions the only course open was receivership, which took place on December 5, 1905.

THE PERIOD OF FINANCIAL DIFFICULTIES (1906-1908)

Receivership indicated to outsiders that the Pere Marquette was having financial difficulties, but no one except those on the "inside" ever imagined the far-reaching injury that had been inflicted on this road.

Its credit was very low; it was physically deteriorated; it had an extraordinary funded debt created on which it was obvious it could not pay interest; and finally, gross revenues were nearly stationary, so that no relief could be expected from this quarter.

Under these conditions it would seem to have been quite clear that a reorganization could be successful only on one condition, viz., that the fraudulent nature of certain bond issues be recognized and that they be exchanged for common or preferred stock. Such action would have materially reduced the fixed charges, but on the other hand it would have amounted to a transference of control into new hands, which result the Morgan interests were loath to accomplish. Accordingly, the bonded indebtedness was not contracted, and the sole aim of the reorganization process under the Morgan supervision seems to have been a return of the road to its owners and not the rehabilitation of its affairs and the construction of a solid financial program for the future. Not only were the fixed charges not reduced, but the reorganization served as a further function of being the pretext for additional stock inflation, for an issue of $5,000,000 of 6 per cent debentures, and for writing up as "cost of road and equipment" direct losses aggregating almost $5,000,000 of the former administrations. Besides this, no provision was made for extensive betterments and improvements demanded of the company by a rapidly growing state.

It is a most striking fact that such a plan of reorganization succeeded in securing the endorsement of the Michigan Railroad Commission. Unlike most reorganizations there was an increase in capitalization rather than a decrease. The results of the criminal transactions of the syndicate were not cleared away, and for this neglect the Pere Marquette was immediately to suffer. Large amounts would have to be spent for maintenance of road and equipment, since it was obvious to everyone that the entire road was in an exceedingly deteriorated condition having been under-maintained since the beginning of the Prince administration in 1903. Not only this, but the prospects of a falling gross revenue seemed a certainty because of the new two-cent law that went into effect in 1907, while operating expenses would tend to become larger every year on account of the new demands of the workmen for higher wages and because of the increasing cost of supplies and materials. All of these facts, unfavorable for the future welfare of the Pere Marquette Railroad, seemed to have been overlooked both by the Michigan Railroad Commission and by the courts.

THE PERIOD OF FINANCIAL COLLAPSE AND PHYSICAL DETERIORATION (1908-1912)

Because the reorganization of 1907 failed to bring relief to the Pere Marquette, this road in the next four years was to reach the lowest depths of physical inefficiency that it is possible for a road to reach and still operate; and likewise it was to suffer an absolute obliteration of its borrowing power. Those whose business it was to see that the Pere Marquette was thoroughly rehabilitated both financially and physically, performed no service, either for the railroad, the investor or the public, by sanctioning a reorganization that merely postponed the evil day, and which obviously could not prevent it. By such action, all three parties concerned were wronged and in the end had to pay more heavily for rehabilitation when it did come.

During these four years of postponed over-hauling, the Pere Marquette was in deep financial water practically all of the time. Its 5 per cent refunding bonds would not bring more than 75 on the market, at which price large amounts of equipment had to be purchased. Borrowing at the banks at very disadvantageous rates with the refunding bonds as collateral, was often resorted to in order to pay interest on their funded debt and meet taxes. In other words, during the period between the first and second receiverships the Pere Marquette was financially insolvent. Nevertheless, various schemes for securing cash or credit to continue its existence were formulated by the Morgan interests and were approved by the Michigan Railroad Commission, although it must have been apparent that such expedients were merely palliatives —not remedies.

In 1911 there was a deficit of $1,800,000, due mainly to increased operating expenses as a result of over $1,000,000 for increased wages and nearly $500,000 for increased cost of materials and supplies. The floating debt, created largely to pay interest and taxes, was becoming unmanageable, with the road practically at the end of its borrowing power. Further permission was asked of the Michigan Railroad Commission to issue over one million dollars of 5 per cent notes with refunding bonds as collateral; but by this time the Commission saw, what should have been obvious to it in the reorganization of 1907, viz., that the bonded indebtedness of the Pere Marquette was out of all proportion to its net operating revenue, and of necessity would have to be cut down if the road was to exist in a healthy financial condition and maintain solvency. The refusal of the Michigan Railroad Commsision to sanction any further loans necessarily brought on receivership in 1912, which was to last for the next five years.

Parallel with financial collapse went physical collapse. Under-maintenance had been going on ever since the Prince administration in 1903, and for most of this time the Pere Marquette was expending less for maintenance of way and structures, locomotives, passenger-train cars, and freight-train cars than other roads in the State of Michigan.[1] It was only in this period, however, that the results of such a short-sighted policy proved cumulative and made the Pere Marquette helpless in its efforts to compete successfully with neighboring railroads and hopelessly inadequate as a servant of the public.

Nor was this the only result of an under-maintenance policy. The neglect of repairs usually causes two effects in most enterprises, and in these respects the Pere Marquette was no exception. In the first place, the right of way, structures, and labor force, being fairly fixed in their nature, the absence and inefficiency of equipment caused a loss in the efficiency of the railroad as a whole, disproportionate to the missing equipment. And in the second place, neglect of repairs increased the expense of repairs when they were made, thereby unduly increasing the operating expenses and reducing the net revenue out of which must come

---

1. Appendix D.

fixed charges. From whatever viewpoint it may be considered, under-maintenance of the Pere Marquette was absolutely unjustifiable and resulted disastrously for the carrier, the investor and the public, and in 1912 all three interests were willing to have the road put into the hands of a receiver with the expectation that it would accomplish what the former one had failed to bring about, viz., a complete rehabilitation of the property.

THE PERIOD OF REHABILITATION (1912-1917)

From the very start the conflicting interests under the second receivership seemed to show a unity of purpose that was entirely lacking in the receivership of 1905. This situation existed because there were no more palliatives at hand. The application of remedies was now a necessity no matter what the pain. The first action for which there was a crying need was the substantial improvement of the physical condition of the road, regardless of the fact that such a policy increased the operating ratio in 1914 to over 100. Long needed equipment was purchased which rendered the train service more efficient and served to utilize the unused utilities in the railroad plant viewed as a whole. Likewise, more vigorous and effective management tended to cut down the operating expenses wherever this was possible, as well as maintain an aggressive policy as to the securing of additional traffic. By the end of the receivership in April 1917, it may be said, to the credit of the receivers, that the entire road and equipment had been carefully and thoroughly overhauled and the whole physical structure placed in first class condition. In other words, this receivership effected a complete and satisfactory rehabilitation of the physical property of the Pere Marquette.

Likewise, the reorganization of April 1917, that brought into being the Pere Marquette Railway Company as the successor of the old Pere Marquette Railroad Company, has accomplished a comprehensive and wise rehabilitation of this railroad's financial affairs. It cut down the capitalization by about $8,000,000 and the bonded debt by approximately $36,000,000. Thus the fixed charges were cut in two and the prospects of profitable operation in the future were materially improved.

It is not to be supposed that the drastic measures here described, being deemed necessary to place the Pere Marquette on a solid financial foundation, were received by all security holders without objection. Even though some Pere Marquette bonds, issued during the syndicate control in return for worthless stock, were, like the stock for which they were issued, without value, the holders of the bonds only reluctantly brought themselves to admit that fact, and to receive in return for these bonds common stock of the reorganized company. Such a process of exchanging common stock for bonds was not in reality taking value away from the holders of the bonds, since no value of any magnitude ever attached to these bonds. It would have been an impossibility for the Pere Marquette to meet these obligations at maturity for the simple reason that they did not represent either property or liquid assets. These bonds were issued in a fraudulent manner, and in so far as innocent parties suffered, the public must bear its part of the responsibility for laxity in supervision over security issues. Of course a large portion of these fraudulent bonds were held by the vendors of the worthless stock, and in this case the exchange of common stock for these bonds worked no hardship and therefore is not to be regretted. The only regrettable fact is, that any value at all could accrue to those whose interest it was to unload the worthless secutities on the Pere Marquette.

Besides the accomplishments of the reorganization already stated, the plan provides for the raising of sufficient moneys to take care of the future needs of the company as well as the necessities of the past. So far as can be seen, the Pere Marquette, rehabilitated as it is and under efficient management, ought to be increasingly prosperous as industries grow up in Michigan and as more through traffic is assured. But as we have already observed, a prosperous system can, in only a few short months, be brought to the verge of bankruptcy; and because of this fact certain lessons learned from the history of the Pere Marquette Railroad ought to be suggestive of the character of future public action in respect to railroads.

CONCLUSIONS

While numerous inferences and conclusions have been drawn from the facts throughout this study, the task still remains to classify and here present the most prominent of them. Perhaps none of them are entirely new, but the purpose of presenting them will have been accomplished if they stimulate and emphasize the necessity of having more adequate laws and more intimate and thorough-going control over our public carriers.

In the first place, private exploitation of our railroads would be more difficult if issuance and marketing of their securities were subject to federal regulation. Such central control would insure uniformity of action and more comprehensive and intelligent supervision of railroad affairs.

In the second place, the minority stockholders must be more watchful of their interests and the bondholders must assert their rights before their securities fade away, neglected purposely in order to pay unearned interest and dividends.

In the third place, it is imperative that the stockholders of financial institutions be more alive to the kind of men chosen as directors, and the nature of the securities in which their money is lodged. Nothing disclosed in this study is of more serious consequence than the readiness of great banking institutions to loan enormous sums of money on exceedingly precarious security, in aid of such schemes as have been devised in the wrecking of the Pere Marquette and the Cincinnati, Hamilton and Dayton railroads.

In the fourth place, the people must be vigilant as to their trustees and careful to whom they give their trusts; but on the other hand, the responsibility rests on the government to a large extent, to make breaches of trust as nearly impossible as is attainable. This can be done by more vigorous prosecution of officials of corporations who have been connected with such violations of trust; and the providing of imprisonment as well as fine in such cases of fraud as wrecked the Pere Marquette and the Cincinnati, Hamilton and Dayton railroads. That such vigorous action is necessary seems to be a logical conclusion from this study, since high officials of both the financial institutions and the railroads have been little more than tools and dummies of the promoters. The trustees of other people's money have shown no compunction about violations of their trusts for the benefit and at the demand of the promoters.

In the fifth place, this history proves conclusively that the property investment accounts of the railroads cannot be taken as evidence either of the actual cost or the present value of their properties. This study abounds in situations productive of improper charges to property accounts, whereby, with a few strokes of the pen, worthless accounts became "cost of road and equipment."

In the sixth place, railroad commissions must be more reluctant in approving plans of reorganization without first having throroughly investigated the complete significance of the reorganization plan from the standpoint of the carrier, the public and the investor. If the underlying ramifications of interests were completely understood in the Pere Marquette reorganization, for instance, it is doubtful whether the bodies having the matter under advisement would have given approval to a plan of reorganization, characterized by the funding of defaulted interest and heavy expenses in order to avoid foreclosure and loss to the principal stockholder.

In the seventh place, we must conclude that neither excessive competition, low rates, undue regulations, nor all combined (testimony brought before a committee of the Michigan Legislature by the representative of J. P. Morgan and Company, to the contrary notwithstanding) can be found to have contributed to any appreciable degree to the disaster that has befallen the Pere Marquette. This catastrophy, with its far reaching and deplorable consequences, is due for the most part, to betrayal and breach of trust by corporate officials, usually for personal gain, and not to compulsions from without.[1]

In the eighth place, it may be said that investigations by those who are not close students of the railroad problem or experts in railroad affairs, are, for the most part, of little value in disclosing the real underlying forces at work. Such an investigation was that by the Michigan Legislature in 1913. For the most part, the testimony taken in this investigation was of a very superficial character and failed of the purpose for which it was intended, that is, a disclosure of the real forces at work, which in this case consisted of criminal attempts by officials of the company and others to rob the railroad for their own benefit. And in so far as some of the Orders and Opinions of the Michigan Railroad Commission exhibit a tendency to overlook or ignore the underlying motive forces, they render themselves open to the same criticism.

And finally, praise must be given to the Interstate Commerce Commission for the careful and untiring manner in which they have sought the facts, against almost insurmountable difficulties, and the courage

---

1. The causes for the disaster befalling the Pere Marquette likewise appear as reasons for the ruin of other railroads developed in the following investigations: Consolidations and Combinations of Carriers, 12 I. C. C., 277; The New England Investigation, 27 I. C. C., 560; St. Louis and San Francisco Railroad Investigation, 29 I. C. C., 139; Financial Investigation of N. Y., N. H. & H. R. R. Co., 31 I. C. C., 32; Financial Transactions C., R. I. & P. Ry. Co., 36, I. C. C., 43.

with which they have made known their findings. With such men of broad vision as well as technical knowledge in charge of our railroads, much is being accomplished, and future progress is certain in materially aiding the solution of the railroad problem.

APPENDIX

APPENDIX A

Analysis of the Capital Stock Account

It is believed that a study of this kind would be incomplete without a history of the securities issued by the Pere Marquette and an interpretation of the transactions connected with them. Throughout this financial narrative, one is struck with the inconsistencies in accounting methods—often designedly made, but more often because of ignorance of correct methods—which have failed to exhibit the true status of the corporation. This has resulted in misunderstandings, not only among the investors and creditors of the Pere Marquette, but among the officers as well. It is a sad commentary on this railroad (and many other railroads are equally guilty) that more intelligent methods of accounting were not made use of, and that officials of the company, often directors, determined the accounting policies to suit their own caprice. Uniformity of methods and standard rules for entries are being enforced upon our railroads by state commissions, as well as by the Interstate Commerce Commission, and in this movement lies the hope for a betterment of many of the practices that have been a source of much trouble in dealing with our public carriers.

It is the purpose of this appendix to trace any changes in status of the capital stock during the period January 1, 1900 to June 30, 1914, indicating the disposition of the entire issue and explaining the accounting entries which should have accurately exhibited the same.

For many of the constituents of the Pere Marquette the stock account is incomplete, but for the Pere Marquette itself a true record exists. The statement of the Readjustment Committee to the Pere Marquette Railroad Company on February 1, 1902, gives the manner in which the capital stock had been disposed of, as follows:

	Preferred Stock	Common Stock
Delivery to the Old Colony Trust Company for distribution among the depositors of stock of the Detroit, Grand Rapids and Western Railroad, and the Chicago and West Michigan Railway, pursuant to consolidation		

	Preferred Stock	Common Stock
plan.....................................	$3,820,200	$9,998,700
Delivered to the State Trust Co., for distribution among the depositors of the stock of the Flint and Pere Marquette Railroad, according to plan.............................	6,338,200	4,108,500
Disposed of in acquiring stock of the old companies not deposited under plan, and for providing for expenses of the Committee, etc.............	350,000	20,000
Totoal disposed of...........	$10,508,400	$14,127,200
Held by W. W. Crapo and M. T. Cox, Trustees, to take up outstanding stock of old companies...........	3,800	38,350
	$10,512,200	$14,165,550
On hand for delivery to Trustees, W. W. Crapo and M. T. Cox.........	1,487,800	1,834,450
Total authorized..............	$12,000,000	$16,000,000

Strange to say, there is no record of the $350,000, as to how much of it was used up in acquiring stock of the old companies, the amount spent in providing for expense of the committee and the amount otherwise used. The same is true of the $20,000 of common stock.

The treasury stock, viz., $1,487,800 of preferred stock and $1,834,450 of common, was carried on the books of the company as a part of the "cost of road" and not as capital stock "authorized but unissued" in the hands of the company, as it should have been carried. Such a proceeding increased unduly the asset side of the balance sheet, thereby showing a more favorable financial condition than in reality existed.

The report of the committee showing the disposition of the new stock, came out on February 1, 1902 or two years after the union of the three roads, and yet it does not show whether the $3,800 of preferred and $38,350 of common stock that was set aside to take up stock of the old companies ever performed that function or what became of them.

In accordance with the terms of the lease of the Pere Marquette to the Cincinnati, Hamilton and Dayton Railroad, dated March

1, 1905, the Pere Marquette delivered this treasury stock to the Cincinnati, Hamilton and Dayton.

The Cincinnati, Hamilton and Dayton held this stock until December 5, 1905 when it was turned over to the receivers of this road. It rested with the receivers until August 12, 1907 when it was turned over to the shareholders' protective committee, and used by them to assist in the sale of the five year 6 per cent debentures issued in accordance with the plan of reorganization of the Pere Marquette.

The committee disposed of this stock in the following manner:

Preferred stock to the amount of 14,256.36 shares was converted into first preferred stock at par of the reorganized company and delivered as a bonus of 15 per cent to holders of 95,042.40 shares of preferred stock in the former Pere Marquette Railroad Company who had subscribed for debentures.

Preferred stock to the amount of .24 share was combined with .76 share of first preferred stock of the reorganized company which was acquired by the company and made convertible into a whole share of common stock.

The balance of the preferred stock to the amount of 631.40 shares was converted into preferred stock of the reorganized company at par and returned to the Pere Marquette.

This makes a total of 14,878 shares of preferred stock.

Common stock to the amount of 2,478.80 shares was converted into the common stock of the reorganized company and delivered as a bonus of 20 per cent to holders of 12,394 shares of common stock in the former Pere Marquette Railroad Company who subscribed for debentures.

Common stock to the amount of 395 shares was converted into common stock of the reorganized company and delivered to F. H. Prince and Company as a bonus, on account of a reduction of subscription to the debentures.

The balance of the common stock amounting to 15,470.70 shares was converted into the common stock of the reorganized company and returned to the Pere Marquette.

The total common stock thus treated amounted to 18,344.50 shares.[1]

On August 12, 1907 an agreement of consolidation was entered into between the Pere Marquette Railroad Company and the Pere Marquette Railroad Company of Indiana, and the capital stock of both companies consolidated. Under the provisions of this agreement, 2,400 shares of first preferred stock of the reorganized company were issued in exchange for a like number of

---

1. *Stenographer's Minutes Before the I. C. C.*, Docket No. 6833,
        75 ff.

preferred shares of the Pere Marquette Railroad Company of Indiana, and 2,600 shares of common stock of the reorganized company were issued in exchange for a like number of common shares of this Indiana corporation.   The stock of the Pere Marquette Railroad Company of Indiana was owned by the former Pere Marquette Railroad Company and was turned over to the reorganized company at the time of reorganization.   The 5,000 shares of the Pere Marquette Railroad Company stock mentioned above, therefore, were retained in the treasury of this company.

In addition to this, there was acquired by the Pere Marquette Railroad Company, 620.20 shares of second preferred stock which was issued in exchange for preferred stock of the old company owned at the time of reorganization.

Also, there was issued 15,470.70 shares of common stock in exchange for a like number of shares of common stock of the old company which was owned at time of reorganization; 636 shares of common stock issued in exchange for a like number of shares of common stock of the old company standing in the name of W. W. Crapo and Mark T. Cox, trustees; one share of common stock acquired in accord with resolution adopted by the board of directors on August 18, 1908, authorizing the purchase of outstanding scrip of fractional shares of each class of stock necessary to make total amount outstanding of each class a multiple of $100.

Recapitulation of Pere Marquette Railroad Company stock owned on June 30, 1914:

	No. Shares	Par and Book Values
First Preferred	2,400	$240,000
Second Preferred	620.20	62,020
Common	18,707.70	1,870,770
Total	21,727.90	$2,172,790

On June 30, 1910 this owned stock was shown as a liability at par and held in the treasury at a nominal value.   It was carried on the books as follows:

	Par Value	Book Value
Pere Marquette Common	$1,870,770	$1.00
Pere Marquette Preferred	240,000	193,995.58
Pere Marquette Second Preferred	62,140	1.00
Total	$2,172,910	$193,997.56

This statement was reported to H. C. Adams, in charge of Statistics and Accounts for the Interstate Commerce Commission. In commenting on this, under date of November 23, 1910, he advises as follows: "Page 85, We note under Account B 8, 'Securities issued or assumed—held in treasury,' there is shown against (a) stocks, page 21, \$193,997.56, while returns on page 21 show \$2,172,910, as 'In Treasury.'   In this connection would call attention to instructions on page 18 and 19 of the Form of General Balance Sheet Statement, First Revised Issue, which provides that 'this account should indicate the par value of securities issued by the respondent company that are held unpledged in the company's treasury.   The difference between the par value and the amount paid in re-acquiring such securities should be debited (or credited, as the case may be) to profit and loss.'"[2]

From these instructions it is evident that the Commission had not ascertained the true history of this stock and was never informed that this capital stock that was held in the treasury was anything other than what it purported to be in the annual reports; that is, that it had been issued and was represented as a liability at par, and held in the treasury at a nominal value.

In fact, of course, the stock had never been issued and therefore did not come under the classification of 'treasury stock' but rather under that of 'stock authorized but unissued.'   Therefore, the Pere Marquette never should have written that stock up to par and credited surplus with \$2,172,790.   Such action made the balance sheet misleading, since it was well known that, while this stock had some value, it was not worth anything like its par value, or \$2,172,790.

The Pere Marquette officials made some show of resistance to writing up this stock to par, realizing all the time that such action would misrepresent the facts of the case; but finally they did so, giving as their reason the opinion of the Interstate Commerce Commission.   But it would seem that if the letter from H. C. Adams was the basis for their action that letter would also be the basis for contrary action, because it states specifically that "this account should indicate the par value of securities *issued....*"   If this means anything it would seem to indicate that the letter had reference *only* to securities that had been issued; and therefore the securities in question would not be affected. In other words, it would hardly be asking too much of those concerned to see from the letter referred to, that the Commission was unaware of the true nature of these securities and had given an order that was inapplicable to them.   If such insight had been possible at that time, instead of a protest against the action of the Commission there would have been an explanation to the Commission of the true history of these stocks.   As it was, the balance sheet showed a surplus that in reality did not exist.

---

2.   *Ibid.*

Mr. Gutheim, of the Interstate Commerce Commission, referring to this matter says that "there isn't any doubt in the minds of the Accountants of the Commission who have been through this transaction that there was a great deal of ignorance on the part of all who were connected with the fixing up of those entries, that is, the Pere Marquette people had never checked it out and were actually ignorant of the fact that that was in Cost of Road, and the Commission was not advised of that fact because the Pere Marquette people themselves did not know it. There wasn't any attempt on the part of anybody to put anything over; it was genuine ignorance."[3]

In this connection, it is further interesting to note that the balance sheet showed an unjustifiable duplication of items. It will be remembered that the first entry at the time of consolidation in 1900 indicates that the $28,000,000 which was charged to the cost of road account included the $3,692,250 of 'authorized but unissued' stock held in the treasury, minus the sum of $370,000 to be spent for various purposes specified in the plan of consolidation, or an amount of $3,322,250. Now a portion of this latter sum, amounting to $1,673,516, was subsequently used as a bonus to the subscribers of the debentures that were issued at the termination of the receivership of 1905-1907. This leaves a balance of $1,648,734 which was shown on the balance sheet at a nominal value of $1, and yet this same sum existed on the balance sheet in another form, viz., *in* the cost of road account, amounting to $28,000,000.[4]

If this matter had been checked out as it should have been, it would have been found that the amount of stock on hand which the Interstate Commerce Commission wished to raise to par on the assets side of the balance sheet, was, in fact, in the cost of road account. Then the only way that this could be corrected would have been to take the $1,519,460 (difference between total in hands of trustees, or $3,692,250, and amount of stock in the treasury after consolidation, or $2,172,790) out of the cost of road account and put it where it belonged, that is, in the capital stock of the company held in the treasury, and credit surplus. The Pere Marquette accounting methods would have put this amount in the capital stock of the company held in the treasury, and credited cost of road, thereby creating a fictitious value on the asset side of the balance sheet.

---

3. *Stenographer's Minutes Before the I. C. C.*, Docket No. 6833, 104.
4. *Ibid.*

APPENDIX B

ANALYSIS OF THE BOND ACCOUNT

Besides showing the funded debt at the time of consolidation (TableI), it is intended, in this section, to show the funded obligations issued subsequent to consolidation, indicating how much has been realized on the various issues in the form of cash or property, and showing what was actually outstanding in the hands of the public on January 30, 1914, and how much was matured and remained unpaid on that date.[1]

The funded obligations issued subsequent to consolidation, are as follows:

In the first place, there is an entry in August 1900 which sets up $250,000 of Flint and Pere Marquette First Consolidated 5 per cent bonds, on which there was a premium of $6,250 which was charged up to cost of road.

In December of the same year, an entry charges to cost of road an expense of $30,000 that was incurred in the process of refunding $1,000,000 of Holly, Wayne and Monroe bonds.

Next, there was a series of entries from April 1901 to October 1903 having reference to the issue of the Pere Marquette Consolidated 4 per cent gold bonds, in which it appears that $8,382,000 of these bonds were issued and set up as a liability with various charges. In the debits that appear in that entry there is $4,349,375 on account of the Boston cash account. The Boston cash book does not show how much of this was spent for capital property or in fact how it was expended. The remaining amount which is accounted for .was spent as follows:

TABLE I.—BONDED LIABILITY OF THE PERE MARQUETTE

(January 1, 1900)

Holly, Wayne and Monroe Railway 8% bonds... $1,000,000.00
F. & P. M. R. R. 6% bonds.................... 4,000,000.00
F. & P. M. R. R. First Consolidated 5% Mort-
 gage bonds................................. 2,600,000.00
F. & P. M. R. R. Port Huron Division 5% bonds. 3,325,000.00
F. & P. M. R. R. Toledo Division 5% bonds.... 400,000.00
Pere Marquette Transportation Company, Car
 ferry steamer 6% bonds..................... 140,000.00

---

1. *Stenographer's Minutes Before the I. C. C.*, Docket No. 6833, Vol. I.

Chicago and West Michigan Railway 5% bonds.	5,758,000.00
Grand Rapids, Newaygo and Lake Shore Railroad, Second Division First Mortgage 7% bonds....	19,000.00
Chicago and North Michigan Railroad 5% bonds.	1,667,000.00
Michigan Equipment Company, Ltd., 6% bonds.	205,000.00
Western Equipment Company, Ltd., 6% bonds..	128,000.00
Chicago and West Michigan Railway coupon scrip.....................................	663,622.50
Detroit, Grand Rapids and Western Railroad, First Consolidated Mortgage 5% bonds.......	5,379,168.13
Ionia and Lansing Railroad 5% bonds.........	1,000.00

The bond account of the three companies stood as follows:

Flint and Pere Marquette Railroad...........	11,465,000.00
Chicago and West Michigan Railway.........	8,440,622.50
Detroit, Grand Rapids and Western Railroad..	5,380,168.13
Total bonds issued.....................	$25,285,790.63

$735,625 charged to cost of road, as the discount on $7,275,000 of bonds sold for cash.

$2,190,000 charged out to Robert Winthrop and Company, but there is no information how this sum was spent.

$500,000 went as the purchase price for the Steele roads, comprising the South Haven and Eastern Railroad, the Milwaukee, Benton Harbor and Columbus Railroad, and the Benton Harbor, Coloma and Paw Paw Lake Train Railway.

$107,000 charged out on account of the Grand Rapids, Kalkaska and South Eastern Railroad, this sum being used for the purchase of the capital stock of this company.

$500,000 went as part purchase price of 1,500 freight cars bought of the American Car and Foundry Company.

For the retirement of bonds, there were issues as follows:

Pere Marquette Transportation Company, First Mortgage 6 per cent gold bonds, $60,000.

Marquette Equipment Company, Ltd., First Mortgage 5 per cent bonds, $304,000.

Western Equipment Company, Ltd., First Mortgage registered 6 per cent bonds, $36,000.

Michigan Equipment Company, Ltd., First Mortgage 6 per cent bonds, $181,000.

Chicago and West Michigan coupon scrip, issued in 1894 and 1898, in part payment of annual interest on bonds of the Chicago and West Michigan, and the Chicago and North Michigan railroads, $661,000.

For construction, additions and improvements, new car-ferries, locomotives and other equipment, $6,033,000. There is no itemized statement regarding this last item of $6,033,000, so it is difficult to say exactly, or any where near accurately, just what it does cover.

This makes a total of $8,382,000 of Pere Marquette Consolidated 4 per cent gold bonds issued.

Next are entries showing the issues of miscellaneous bonds as follows:

February 1903 there is an entry setting up as a liability, $2,870,000 of Pere Marquette Collateral Trust 4 per cent bonds, and charging Lake Erie and Detroit River Railroad stock with the same amount. These bonds are collateral for the entire capital stock of the Lake Erie road.

Another entry in March 1903 sets up as a liability, $260,000 of Grand Rapids, Belding and Saginaw Railroad 5 per cent First Mortgage bonds, the liability being balanced by a charge of the same amount to cost of road.

December 1903 an entry sets up a liability on account of the Pere Marquette Railroad of Indiana, First Mortgage 4 per cent bonds, $675,000, and the contra entry is shown to cost of road for the same amount.

An entry of July 1903 charges cost of road, Lake Erie and Detroit River Railroad Company, with $3,000,000 and sets contra a liability on account of the Pere Marquette Railroad Company, 4½ per cent bonds. This issue was discounted to the extent of $105,000. The outstanding 5 per cent bonds of the Lake Erie and Detroit River Railroad were deposited as collateral for the issue of 4½ per cent bonds of the Pere Marquette.

In October 1903 an entry charges up Grand Rapids, Kalkaska and South Eastern stock account with $142,000 and sets up a liability of the same amount on account of this road's 5 per cent bonds.

An entry of November 1903 charges $58,000 to the International Trust Company, trustee, and sets up the same amount in the bond account just mentioned.

An entry whereby the Pere Marquette takes into its books the accounts outstanding against the Lake Erie and Detroit River Railroad, and charges up cost of road account with $5,562,810.60.

Numerous entries of the Pere Marquette Eastern Equipment Company 5 per cent bonds showing the total of $3,201,000 set up as a liability.

Haskell and Barker Equipment 5 per cent notes on which there was authorized $561,633.33, and the same amount issued.

In March 1904 there was an issue of $112,000 of Lake Erie and

Detroit River Railroad Company Equipment 5 per cent bonds, and liability set up for the same amount.

There was issued in June 1904, $301,880.40 of Pullman Company 5 per cent Equipment notes, equipment being charged.

A final issue in November 1904 of $1,520,000 of Robert Winthrop and Company 4½ per cent Equipment notes, crediting equipment note account.

From the above enumeration of entries it is seen that discount on bonds is often charged to cost of road account, contrary to good accounting practice. Also, the incomplete nature of some of the entries makes it impossible to ascertain just what all these sums were expended for. No doubt the greater part of them were used to increase the capital investment; yet, that some moneys derived from these bonds were spent to meet current liabilities is undoubtedly true, but what sum or per cent of the total issue this is, it is impossible to say.

REFUNDING 4 PER CENT BOND ISSUE OF $60,000,000

(January 1905 to January 1912)

On January 1, 1905 there was an issue of $6,000,000 worth of Refunding Bonds which sold at 87½, suffering a discount of $750,000 which was charged to cost of road account. Bond interest was credited with $19,266.33.

This sum was used for general corporate purposes (including payment of bank loans) purchase of new equipment, *payment of dividends, coupon interest*, and other current liabilities. These bonds paid off notes that were due, but these floating debts were originally contracted to pay for current expenses. In other words, the above issue of bonds was authorized with the immediate purpose in view of applying the money from their sale to the payment of notes that were due, but the more important thing to be noted is that the money originally derived from these notes was spent for items, expenditure for which ought to have come from yearly gross revenues and not from an issue of bonds.

Included among the bond issues used for illegitimate purposes would come $210,000 borrowed from Robert Winthrop and Company and used to pay a dividend on Pere Marquette preferred stock, February 1905; and $150,000 for coupons due March 1, 1903. There may be other items of this sort but no one seems to know what this $6,000,000 of bonds was spent for. Of course it paid off certain tangible notes, but the question as to what the money was spent for goes deeper than that. This more vital question has not been answered as yet to any complete extent. The money was all used by the corporation, there seems to be little doubt of that assertion; but whether for capital expenses or current expenses, and in what amounts for each, is not shown on the books of the corporation and seems to be a question that remains unsolved as regards the officials themselves. That the above $360,000 of interest and dividends was paid by creating a funded debt is beyond doubt.

In June 1905 there was a further issue of Pere Marquette Refunding 4 per cent bonds, amounting to $2,361,000, which suffered a discount of 10 per cent, or $236,100. Accrued interest of $44,594.58 should be added to the face value of these bonds.

This issue was sold to the Cincinnati, Hamilton and Dayton Railroad Company, pursuant to resolutions passed by the board of directors of both this road and the Pere Marquette Railroad Company under date of April 27, 1905, which authorized the former road to buy bonds of the Pere Marquette Refunding Mortgage up to the amount of $4,000,000 at 90 and accrued interest.

This $2,361,000 minus the discount of $236,100, plus accrued interest of $44,594.58, was spent as follows:

$1,645,000 of bonds issued in payment of 35,000 shares of the Toledo Railway and Terminal Company stock at $47 per share, as authorized by resolution of the board of directors, April 27, 1905.

$457,000 of bonds issued for equipment, under the provision of the mortgage which authorized the company to issue in any one year $500,000 of these bonds for equipment.

$259,000 bonds issued to pay miscellaneous expenses, viz., $161,000 Eastern Equipment Company bonds; $8,000 Lake Erie International Equipment Company bonds; $14,000 Western Equipment Company bonds; $76,000 Robert Winthrop and Company bonds.

It turned out that this issue of $2,361,000 of bonds was sold to a syndicate, represented by the Central Trust Company of New York, at a net price of 85½ and interest from January 1st; so that the Cincinnati, Hamilton and Dayton netted only $2,063,249.58 from this sale of Pere Marquette bonds. This was an unexpected loss for the Cincinnati, Hamilton and Dayton since by its agreement with the Pere Marquette the latter was to receive 90 for its bonds. However, it was an easy matter to transfer this loss to the Pere Marquette, for it must be remembered that the controlling shares of common stock were held by the Cincinnati, Hamilton and Dayton at this time. This was done, and the loss of 4½ per cent of discount was borne by the Pere Marquette. The discount of $236,100 was charged to cost of road thereby indicating a surplus on the liability side of the balance sheet which in fact did not exist.

In September and October 1905 two batches of bonds amounting to $197,000 and $649,000 were issued respectively, and sold to the

Cincinnati, Hamilton and Dayton under the agreement already referred to. The Cincinnati, Hamilton and Dayton was again unfortunate in the resale of these bonds, selling them at a price of 89 less $3\frac{1}{2}$ per cent commission, thereby losing $4\frac{1}{2}$ per cent on the transaction, which amounted to $37,577.50. The books show this as a loss to the Cincinnati, Hamilton and Dayton, but a later entry, in January 1906, charged discount of $37,577.50 on Pere Marquette bonds sold and credited Cincinnati, Hamilton and Dayton current accounts for the same sum. This amounted to nothing but an assumption by the Pere Marquette of the amount of money which the Cincinnati, Hamilton and Dayton had lost in the sale of these two batches of bonds. The $37,577.50, like the previous discounts, was charged to cost of road account on the books of the Pere Marquette.

On March 1, 1911 there was an issue of $16,000,000 of these bonds which were pledged with the Guaranty Trust Company of New York as collateral for $8,000,000 five year 6 per cent gold notes issued under collateral identure of the same date.

Provision was made in this identure that in case of default of any payment of interest on the notes, the principal should become due and the trustee should have the right to sell the collateral. The interest payments amounting to $480,000 and maturing on September 1, 1912 and March 1, 1913, were not paid. Therefore, the trustee sold these $16,000,000 of bonds at public auction in New York City on March 20, 1913, to a committee representing the holders of the 6 per cent collateral trust notes, for the sum of $6,400,000. After deducting $4,763.96 for expenses in connection with the sale of this collateral, there remained $6,395,235.04 which was applied by the trustee in payment of the notes.

This left $2,125,883 of the notes still outstanding as unpaid. The balance of the notes amounting to $6,395,236.04 were retired on the books of the Pere Marquette but they have never been turned over to the Company by the committee so in reality are outstanding as a liability. What became of the collateral after it was purchased by the committee is not known but it is believed that they were unable to sell it.

The $8,000,000 five year 6 per cent Collateral Trust notes, for which the general mortgage bonds had been issued as collateral, had been sold through J. P. Morgan and Company for a commission of 5 per cent, thereby netting the Pere Marquette $7,600,000. Against the actual acquisition of this last named amount, there was outstanding $16,000,000 of the Refunding Bonds and a liability on account of the notes of $2,125,883.96. In short, it took a liability of $18,125,883.96 in order to acquire $7,600,000 cash. Interest has been accruing all the time on these obligations since the sale of collateral on March 25, 1913.

This $7,600,000 was used for miscellaneous purposes. $2,-536,639.88 was used to retire short term notes, the exact items of which are not known. To retire equipment notes required $650,000; taxes, $630,612.98; additions and betterments, $2,815,110.51; interest on funded debt, $991,528.28; legal expenses, $5,178.42.

Here again we see that large amounts have been borrowed in order to pay interest on funded debt instead of meeting this expense out of current income. Also, taxes should have been paid out of income instead of by creation of new debts. When a road cannot pay its taxes and interest on its funded debt out of yearly net revenues, it is insolvent from a business standpoint, although it may keep out of the courts for some time by the temporary expedients of borrowing on its notes, paying its current expenses and fixed charges out of the amounts realized on these notes, and then issuing bonds to secure funds with which to meet the notes when they come due. Such was the policy followed by the Pere Marquette for several years, the cumulative effect of which was to aggravate the difficulties that already beset the road on every side. A structure built on such a foundation could do nothing but collapse eventually.

AMOUNT OF FUNDED DEBT DISPOSED OF

(January 1, 1900 and June 30, 1914)

The total funded debt that accrued during this period amounts to a par value of $40,167,000. This includes mortgage bonds to the amount of $19,117,000; collateral trust bonds and notes of $11,000,000; equipment obligations of $6,783,000; receiver's certificates amounting to $3,267,000.

The amount realized from the above issue was $37,145,085.59. Of this sum, $16,879,352.50 was mortgage bonds; $10,495,000 collateral trust bonds and notes; $6,579,477.31 equipment obligations; $3,195,235.78 receiver's certificates.[3]

The total discounts suffered on this issue of $40,167,000 of securities, amounted to $3,017,934.41, of which $2,067,341.35 was charged to cost of road and $950,593.06 was charged to profit and loss. Discounts on bonds have been charged to profit and loss since July 1, 1907 in accordance with the Interstate Commerce Classification.

The above figures of discounts do not contain any expenses in

---

3.   This does not include receiver's certificates issued under the first receivership because there was no discount on these.

connection with those bonds other than actual discount. However, it includes $400,000 commission to J. P. Morgan and Company, but this might be considered a discount. Also, $6,250 of premiums and $21,120 commission on Pullman Equipment notes.

If the $9,604,763.96[4] charged to profit and loss after the sale of the $16,000,000 Refunding Bonds, is added to the discounts above referred to ($3,017,934.41), there is a total of $12,622,718.37 discounts.

It is quite legitimate to call this $9,604,763.96 a discount because it represents the difference between the par value of the outstanding securities and the amount that was actually realized by the Pere Marquette from those securities.

No part of this $16,000,000 is carried on the books as an asset because the bonds represented by this amount are in the hands of the public. Perhaps those bonds never went any further than J. P. Morgan and Company but their whereabouts seems to be unknown. At any rate, there would appear to be a legal liability of the Pere Marquette on these bonds although the latter could take measures to prevent their sale to innocent purchasers.

---

4.   The difference between the collateral ($16,000,000) and the amount derived from its sale ($6,395,236.04).

APPENDIX C

ANALYSIS OF MISCELLANEOUS TRANSACTIONS

Many transactions appear on the books of the Pere Marquette that startle the investigator by their crudity and often bizarre character. Some of these have already been described in connection with bond and stock accounts, but the transactions included in this analysis are even more peculiar in their nature than those already enumerated. Especially is this true of the entry indicated by the following excerpt from the minutes of the Pere Marquette. This transaction is the more unusual because it was the direct result of the deliberations of the board of directors and was not made because of an oversight as was the case of some already considered.

PUTTING WORTHLESS ITEMS INTO THE PROPERTY ACCOUNT

"This is to certify that the adjourned regular meeting of the Board of Directors of this company, held at New York City, August 18, 1908, a quorum being present, the following action was taken:

"The attention of the board was called to the following asset or debit accounts appearing on the books of the Pere Marquette Railroad Company, viz.:

"Toledo Railway and Terminal Co., stock	$1,645,000.00
"Advances to Toledo Railway and Terminal Company	70,000.00
"Advances to the Chicago, Cincinnati and Louisville Railroad Company	423,009.34
"Chicago, Cincinnati and Louisville Railroad Company settlement	400,000.00
"Sarnia, Petrolia and St. Thomas Railway stock	9,884.52
"Discount and expenses in connection with the issue of the 4 per cent Refunding Bonds	128,047.00
"Profit and Loss Debit, June 30, 1907	2,186,066.16
	$4,862,007.02

and also the following credit or liability accounts appearing on the said books, viz.:

Inventory, Overages, prior to receivership	117,335.56
Steel rail Suspense Account, prior to receivership	33,201.02
	$150,536.58

"The president requested authority to write off or cancel the above accounts on the books of the Company, stating that the debit accounts did not represent existing assets of any value, and explaining that the carrying of said items in the accounts would make our balance sheet misleading as to the true assets and operations of the new Company. On motion the President was authorized to have the necessary entries made on the books, charging the amount of the loss to Property Account."[1]

The necessary entries to effect the will of the board of directors were accordingly made, and received the O. K. of F. W. Stevens who was general solicitor for the company; also certified to as correct by Mr. J. O. Talbott who was chief clerk to the comptroller; approved by Mr. William Cotter, president of the board; and approved for entry by Mr. J. L. Cramer, comptroller.

Such a peculiar system of accounting and the reason given for it would appear humorous if the results coming therefrom were not misleading and productive of disaster. By action of the board of directors, the accountants of the Pere Marquette took a worthless item out of one asset account (individual account) and put it into another asset account (cost of road). It is exceedingly difficult for anyone to see how the latter method of writing up this loss would be any less misleading than the former method. This amount should have been written off the books as a loss and the reorganized company started off with a deficit. Otherwise, if the assets were made larger than they really were, there would sooner or later become the necessity of earning on this amount, or in other words, demanding higher rates to get earnings on a liability or deficit rather than on an asset.

Mr. J. L. Cramer, comptroller for the Pere Marquette, explains the above entry as follows: "That entry merely carries out the plan that was adopted by the Board in the purchase of the two properties. The new company necessarily could not start with a Profit and Loss deficit without having any operations, and that was to enable the new company to start with a clean sheet."[2]

From this it appears that Mr. Cramer believed the new company could not start out with a deficit. So, presto, with miraculous Alladin-like power, the deficit is turned into an asset, the loss into a gain; and the new company can now start out with greater equanimity simply because what was formerly called a liability is now called an asset. Alas, such fairy-tale transformations do not exist in every-day life; no matter what the deficit is called it is still a deficit, and the company is starting out with a deficit

---

1. *Stenographer's Minutes Before the I. C. C.*, Docket No. 6833, 285.
2. *Ibid.*

regardless of whether it puts the loss into the profit and loss account or into the cost of road account.

INCONSISTENCY IN ACCOUNTING METHODS

The arbitrators in the controversy between the Cincinnati, Hamilton and Dayton and the Pere Marquette, awarded the latter railroad the sum of $1,364,387 par value of Cincinnati, Hamilton and Dayton General Mortgage 4 per cent bonds. These were put on the books of the Pere Marquette at a nominal value of $1.00, on August 3, 1909, and their value remained at this figure until the directors met in New York City, April 14, 1910, and passed upon the value of these bonds, which they declared were worth 60 per cent of their par value, or $818,400. This value was then placed upon these bonds instead of the nominal value of $1.00, and $818,400 was credited to the profit and loss account.

Here again is evident another peculiar accounting transaction. If the loss suffered by the Pere Marquette because of the transactions of the syndicate was taken as a proper charge to cost of road account at the time of reorganization on August 12, 1907, why was not this $818,400 *credited to cost of road account?*

In answer to this question, Mr. C. L. Sikes, accountant for the Pere Marquette replied: "It is not credited to Cost of Road, as I understand it, because the Board of Directors or the President instructed that it should be credited to Profit and Loss."[3]

It seems that the board of directors determined the accounting theories for the Pere Marquette and as a result there was an accounting practice unique in character to say the least. If such a policy was followed by railroads in general, it would come to pass that the general balance sheet of each road would have no value from the standpoint of the investor or stockholder as an indicator of the real status of each corporation; which condition would necessitate a laborious independent investigation of each railroad as regards its financial situation, by each prospective investor and creditor as well as by administrative bodies.

In other words, the accounting policies followed by the Pere Marquette destroyed the function of the general balance sheet, at least to a great extent, and instead of it truly representing the company's financial condition, it tended to confuse different accounts and make difficult a correct conception of the company's affairs.

THE PERE MARQUETTE RAILROAD COMPANY OF INDIANA

In accordance with the agreement of consolidation between the

---

3. *Ibid.*

Pere Marquette Railroad Company of Indiana and the Pere Marquette Railroad Company, dated August 12, 1907, the capital stock, bonded debt, cost of road and all other accounts of the former company were transferred to the books of the latter. To the cost of road account was charged the entire capital stock and bonded debt of the Pere Marquette Railroad Company of Indiana, as follows:

Charge:

Cost of Road, P. M. R. R. of Indiana.......... $1,175,000

Credit:

P. M. R. R. of Indiana, 1st Mtge. 5% Bonds... $675,000
Capital Stock, Pref. of P. M. R. R. of Indiana..   240,000
Capital Stock, Com. of P. M. R. R. of Indiana..   260,000

Total.................................... $1,175,000

It may be recalled that the actual work of constructing the road and property held by the Pere Marquette Railroad Company of Indiana had been done by a separate corporation, the Marquette Construction Company. The agreement between these two companies specified that in consideration of the construction of the line from New Buffalo, Michigan, to Pine, Indiana, a distance of 22 miles, the Construction Company was to receive the First Mortgage 4 per cent thirty year gold bonds of the Railroad Company, to an amount at par equal to $25,000 per mile of single track and $35,000 per mile of double track line, exclusive of switches and sidings; and also the Construction Company was to receive certificates for the total capital stock of the Railroad Company amounting at par to $500,000 full paid non-assessable.

The accounts of the Pere Marquette Railroad Company of Indiana were especially in bad shape, making it exceedingly difficult to find the true state of affairs. Journal entries were written up several years after the transactions had taken place and suffered more or less in consequence. Mr. J. L. Cramer, solicitor for the Pere Marquette Railroad Company, says that when he came to the property of the Indiana corporation they had neither a journal nor a ledger; in fact they had no books that could be found. The accounts had to be made up from the results of a search among correspondence.

From the information that does exist, however, it is found that the Marquette Construction Company did not comply with the terms of the contract with the Pere Marquette Railroad Company of Indiana. The Construction Company began work but did not finish it. The work was really done in charge of the Pere Marquette Railroad Company which advanced $237,000 of labor and supplies to the Construction Company.

The Construction Company commenced work with the sum of $464,618.80 which resulted from the sale of $575,000 of bonds given to it by the Pere Marquette Railroad Company of Indiana, these bonds suffering a discount of 18 per cent. An additional bond issue of $100,000 which sold at 15 per cent discount was given to the Construction Company. Only $44,992.47 of this last issue was used in construction, the balance being turned over to the Knickerbocker Trust Company to the credit of the Pere Marquette Railroad Company as a partial offset to the supplies that this latter company had advanced to the Construction Company. The balance of $40,842.10, subtracted from the $237,000 advanced to the Construction Company by the Pere Marquette Railroad Company, leaves approximately the sum of $193,995.56 that the latter company actually expended on construction work. For this advance the Pere Marquette Railroad Company was paid nothing by the Marquette Construction Company or the Pere Marquette Railroad Company of Indiana.

Although the Construction Company had not fulfilled the agreement as to the completion of construction work, the Pere Marquette Railroad Company of Indiana turned over to it, its entire capital stock amounting to par value of $500,000; and the Construction Company in turn gave it to the Pere Marquette Railroad Company in exchange for a guarantee by the latter company of the bonds of the Pere Marquette Railroad Company of Indiana. Thus the control of this latter company, through its stock, came into the hands of the Pere Marquette Railroad Company. The Pere Marquette Railroad Company carried this stock on its books at a value of $193,995.56, or the amount that .it had advanced for construction purposes. That is, this stock amounted to a settlement by the Pere Marquette Railroad Company of Indiana and the Marquette Construction Company for the amount that had been advanced to them by the Pere Marquette Railroad Company.

From what has been given it will be seen that the actual cost of the 22 miles of road in Indiana must have been the sum of three figures. First, the $193,995.56 advanced by the Pere Marquette Railroad Company; second, $44,992.47 used out of the $100,000 of bonds; and third, $464,618.80 realized from the $575,000 issue of bonds. This total, plus about $10,000 for miscellaneous expenses, makes the entire cost of the road amount to about $713,606.83. Outstanding against this cost is a total of $1,175,000 of securities ($675,000 in bonds and $500,000 in stock), or an excessive issue of securities above the property value amounting to $461,392.17.[4]

---

4. *Ibid.*

There were several reasons for building this stretch of road by means of companies other than the Pere Marquette Railroad Company. The first that is often prominent in cases of this kind, is the desire of those interested to make an illegitimate profit off the transaction. In the case under consideration the officers of the subsidiary companies were substantially the same persons as those of the parent company, but the stock issued in excess of property value did not accrue to these persons. This excessive issue, however, went into the books of the consolidated company in 1907 as the cost of road and thereby augmented surplus, which in turn misrepresented the actual status of the reorganized Pere Marquette Railroad Company. To this extent, then, its issue·was a cause of difficulty and was unjustified.

In the second place, the organization of these two subsidiary companies made it possible to keep the accounts separate. However, it has been shown that this was not done, and that the construction accounts were entangled with the accounts of the Pere Marquette Railroad Company.

In the third place, such procedure would make a mortgage on this 22 miles of property more secure, in that the general mortgage over the Pere Marquette Railroad Company property would not operate as a prior lien. It seems that this did not have much effect, for the bonds of the Pere Marquette Railroad Company of Indiana sold at a much lower rate of discount than the bonds of the Pere Marquette Railroad Company were selling for at the same time. It is hard to account for this difference in discount suffered, unless it be that the issue of bonds by the Indiana company had a much smaller market than the Michigan corporation.

A fourth reason, was the fact that a Michigan corporation could not condemn land in Indiana through which state the Pere Marquette Railroad Company wished to operate.

The anticipated functions of the Pere Marquette Railroad Company of Indiana were large, in that it was expected to build the road to Chicago, and in that case the advantages of having a separate corporation would have been material. But the arrangements that were soon made with other railroad companies to run Pere Marquette trains into Chicago made unnecessary any further work on the part of the Indiana corporation, and hence it was consolidated with the Pere Marquette Railroad Company in August 1907.[5]

---

5. As stated elsewhere, this consolidation offered a pretense to the Pere Marquette officials for further stock inflation and manipulation of accounts.

APPENDIX D

Deferred Maintenance

As regards the charges to operating expenses for "ties" and "rails," it will be seen from Plate I that there is not one year from 1900 to 1913, with one exception, when the Pere Marquette spent as much for ties and rails per mile of road as did the Grand Rapids and Indiana, the Ann Arbor or the Michigan Central. This lack of maintenance is woefully evident during this period, especially during the years 1903 and 1904 when the Prince-Zimmerman interests were in control. In the latter year only $75 was expended for ties and rails per mile of road, which low figure is not attained by any of the other roads. There is only one instance where one of these roads under consideration spent less than $200 per mile of road, while with the Pere Marquette only twice during this period did rail and tie maintenance reach this sum. In other words, what was the rule with the other roads was the exception with the Pere Marquette when it came to rail and tie maintenance.

The cause of the especially rapid increase in the charges to rail and tie maintenance in 1913 and 1914 could not be due to the new 90 pound rail programs being carried out over the main line, because that would go into additions and betterments. It is due to only one thing, viz., the taking up of deferred maintenance. That is, the Pere Marquette was spending money in these years to take up expenses that in the usual course should have been taken care of in past years, and this unusual expenditure was to continue for the next three years until reorganization in 1917.

LOCOMOTIVES

Beginning with 1906, expense on locomotives (Plate II) runs between $722,000 and $772,000 annually until 1911 when it is $1,032,000; in 1912, $1,240,000; in 1913, $1,332,000; and in 1914, $1,636,000. Most of the extraordinary expense since 1914 is due to writing in depreciation at a higher rate, and also writing in, in that year, depreciation that had accrued at a higher rate since the beginning of the receivership in 1912. After 1912 approximately $500,000 more was written off yearly for depreciation than had been written off in previous years. This includes all equipment and not merely locomotives.

As compared with other Michigan roads, it will be seen that charges for repairs, renewals and depreciation on locomotives of the Pere Marquette per locomotive mile had almost quadrupled

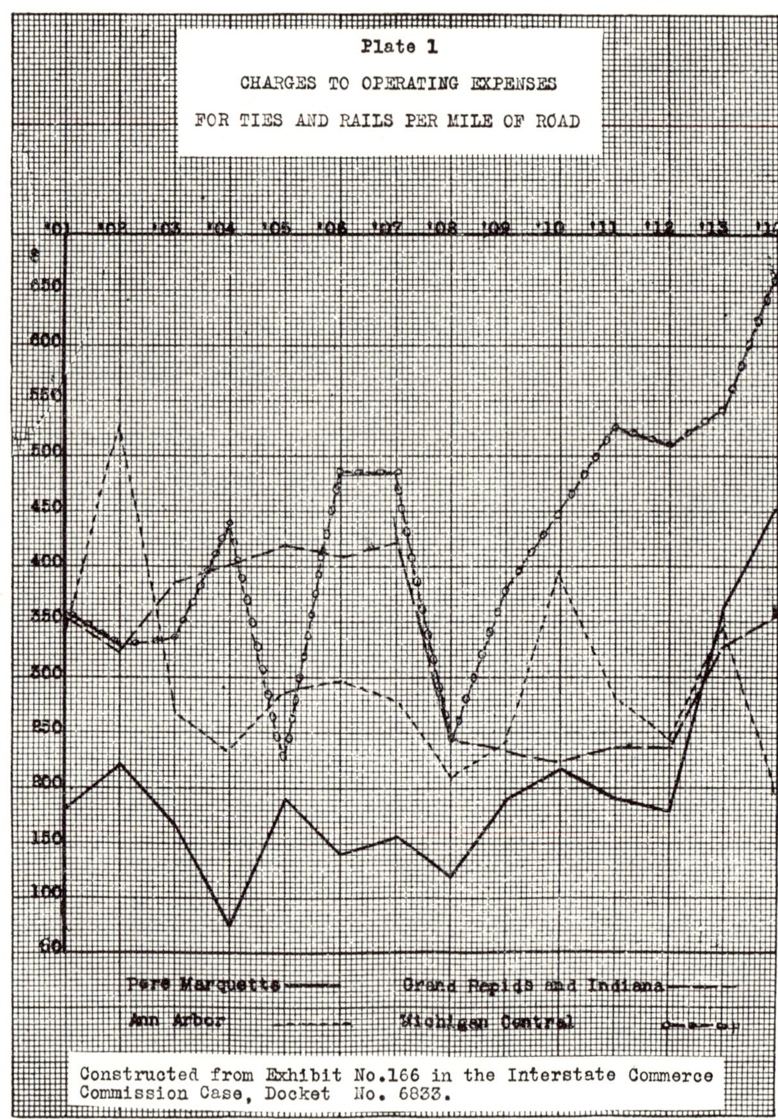
Plate 1
CHARGES TO OPERATING EXPENSES
FOR TIES AND RAILS PER MILE OF ROAD
'01 '02 '03 '04 '05 '06 '07 '08 '09 '10 '11 '12 '13 '14
Pere Marquette
Ann Arbor
Grand Rapids and Indiana
Michigan Central
Constructed from Exhibit No.166 in the Interstate Commerce
Commission Case, Docket No. 6833.

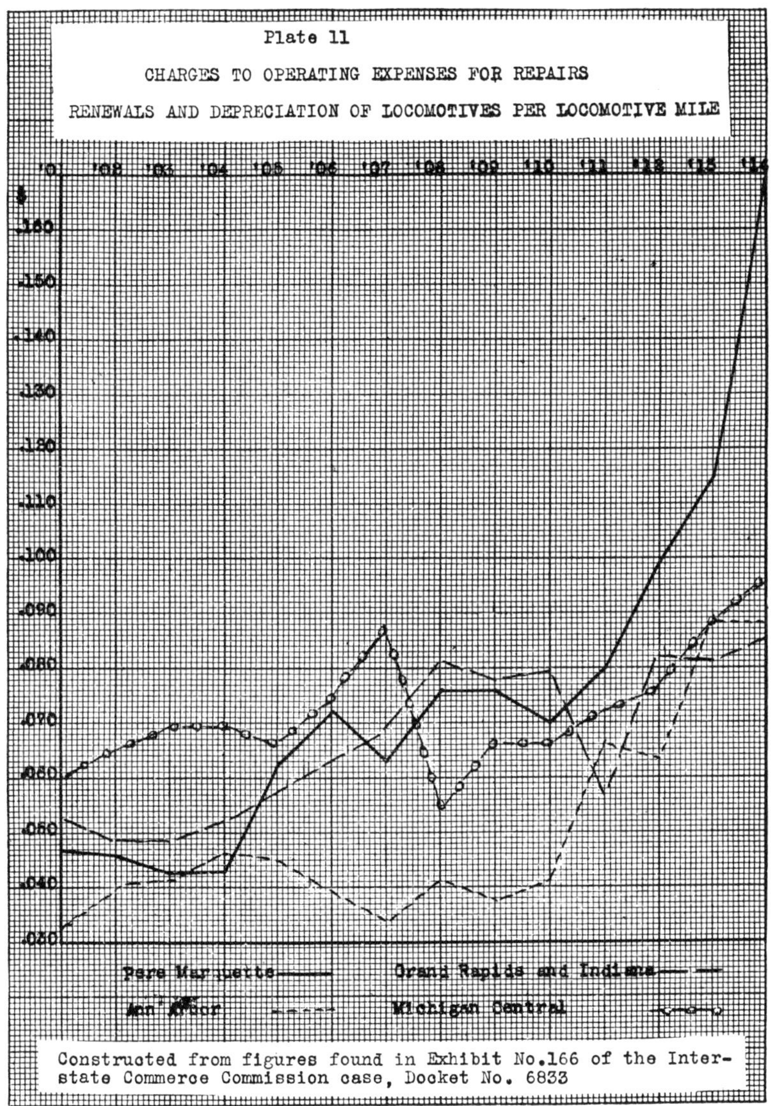

Constructed from figures found in Exhibit No.166 of the Interstate Commerce Commission case, Docket No. 6833

from 1900 to 1914; while on the other three roads these combined charges per locomotive mile had in no instance increased by this amount, having only tripled in the case of the Ann Arbor and not even doubled in the case of the other two roads. Generally speaking, the charges to operating expenses for repairs, renewals and depreciation, whether considered from the standpoint of per mile of road, per locomotive or per locomotive mile, are smaller than for other roads at the beginning of this period, while at the end of it they have become the largest, with the exception of the charge per mile of road for the Michigan Central. It seems quite evident that these charges were too small at the beginning of the period and hence they were unusually large at the end of it. Such charges, if not met when they are due from year to year, become cumulative in their effect and of necessity are paid in the end.

PASSENGER-TRAIN CARS

The repairs for passenger-train cars was more uniform than for locomotives, fluctuating between $130,000 and $190,000 from 1900 to 1911, after the latter date rising to $247,000 around which figure it remained for the next three years. However, between 1913 and 1914 there was a tremendous increase in the total charge to depreciation on passenger cars, rising from $10,000 in the former year to $106,000 in the latter. This was due for the most part to the higher rate of depreciation adopted in that year, but still it must be noted that some of this increase consisted of deferred depreciation of former years.

As compared with the other Michigan roads, the charges to operating expenses for repairs, renewals and depreciation per passenger-train car-mile for the Pere Marquette, had doubled from 1908 to 1914 (Plate III); while with other roads, in no instance had it increased more than 50 per cent, and one case, the Grand Rapids and Indiana, it had not increased even that. The fact that inadequate charges per mile of road and per passenger-train mile had been made during the earlier portion of this period accounts for the abrupt increase in the combined charges made to operation noticed in 1914, but which is not noticeable in the case of the other three roads whose earlier charges were comparatively larger and more uniformly kept up from year to year.

FREIGHT-TRAIN CARS

It is significant that freight-train car repairs, which never exceeded $620,000 up to 1910, rose to about an even million dollars in 1911, 1912 and 1913, and then jumped to $2,333,000 in 1914; while depreciation of freight train cars, which had run about $60,000 in the years from 1908 to 1913, shows $1,003,000 in 1914. Renewals which had never risen higher than $55,000 from 1908 to 1913 inclusive, rose to $326,000 in 1914.

As compared with the other Michigan roads, the Pere Marquette charges to operating expenses for repairs, renewals and depreciation, per mile of road and per freight-train car mile, from 1900 to 1909, were smaller than any of the other roads; and this statement holds true for some years after the date last named, with the exception of the Ann Arbor line. (Plate IV) These combined charges per freight-train car-mile are low during the first part of the period but increase by five fold in 1914, while two of the other roads do not even double their charges and the Michigan Central only doubles its charges by a small amount.

It seems that operating expenses for the greater part of this entire period were lower than they should have been had a proper amount been charged each year for repairs, renewals and depreciation. Because of this fact net revenues were unduly large, and hence there was left a larger amount for the payment of interest on funded debt and for dividends than legitimately existed. It is safe to say, that if operating expenses had borne their just shares of these charges during the first five years of the life of the road, it would have been impossible to have paid dividends on common stock at all, and preferred stock would have had to bear a smaller rate—perhaps none whatever. In other words, the dividends paid by the Pere Marquette during its lifetime have for the most part been paid out of capital. This has been accomplished by a purposeful policy which failed to charge to operating expenses each year an amount sufficient to take care of repairs, renewals and depreciation on rolling stock, ties and rails, way and structures. To state it in a different way, the Pere Marquette even prior to receivership in 1905, presented a far healthier appearance in its yearly balance sheet than it was warranted in doing by the facts. It was a business failure to some extent during these earlier years although not a legal one.

WAY AND STRUCTURES

From 1900-1911, with the exception of the year 1904, the total charge to operating expenses for maintenance of way and structures is quite uniform, ranging from $1,300,000 to $1,500,000. In 1911 it rose to $1,800,000 and remained about the same for 1912, but the following year it rose to the unusual figure of $2,697,000, while in 1914 it went still higher by $100,000. In no year up to 1913, with one exception, did the Pere Marquette charge as much to operating expenses for maintenance of way and structures per mile of road, as did the other three Michigan roads. (Plate V)

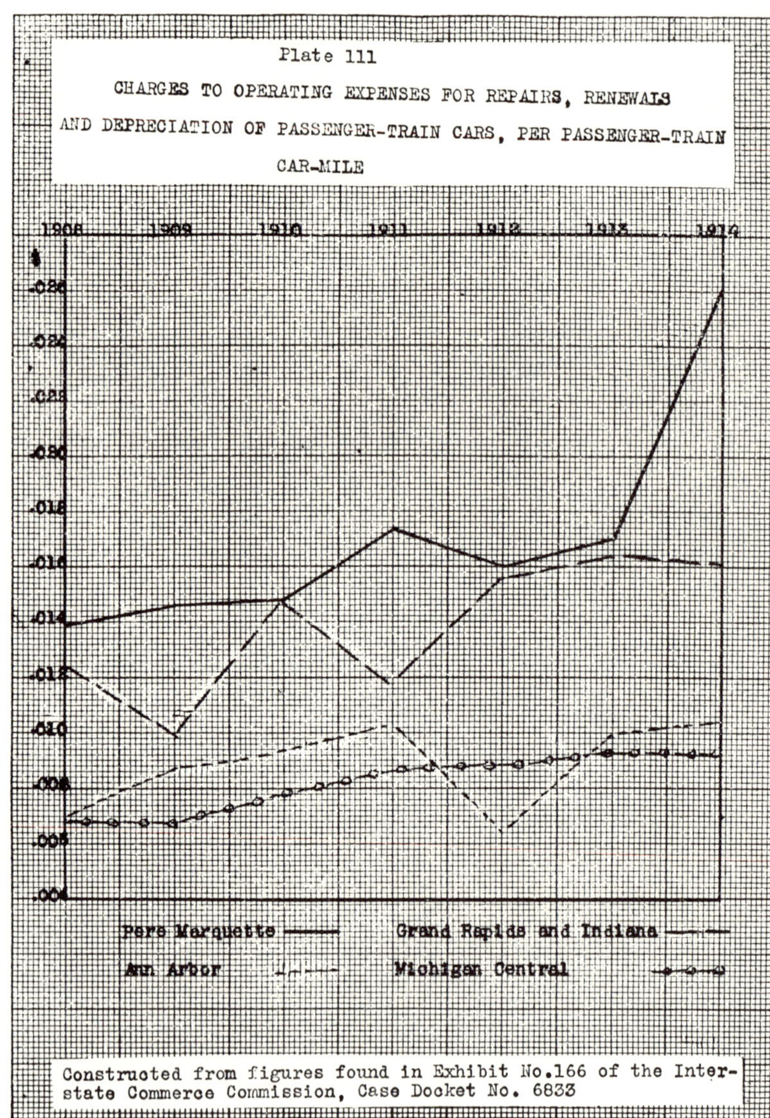

Plate 111
CHARGES TO OPERATING EXPENSES FOR REPAIRS, RENEWALS
AND DEPRECIATION OF PASSENGER-TRAIN CARS, PER PASSENGER-TRAIN
CAR-MILE
1908
1909
1910
1911
1912
1913
1914
.024
.022
.020
.018
.016
.014
.012
.010
.008
.006
.004
Pere Marquette ———   Grand Rapids and Indiana —·—·—
Ann Arbor —··—··—   Michigan Central —o—o—o—
Constructed from figures found in Exhibit No.166 of the Interstate Commerce Commission, Case Docket No. 6833

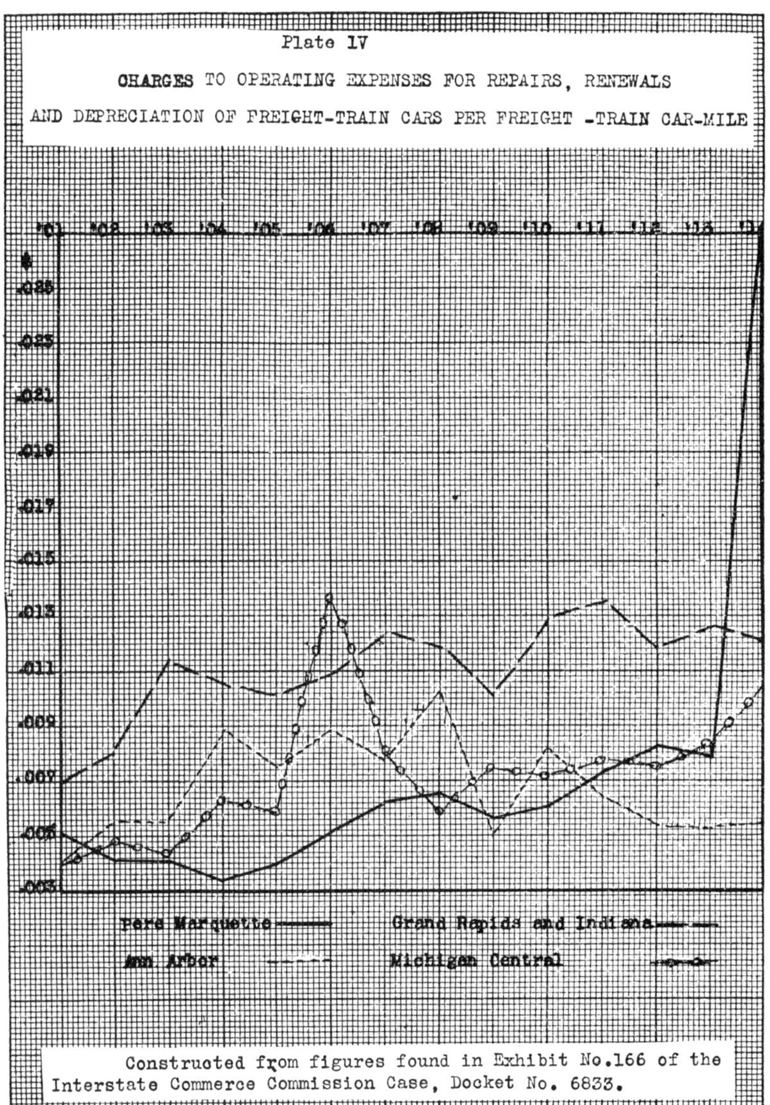
Plate IV
CHARGES TO OPERATING EXPENSES FOR REPAIRS, RENEWALS
AND DEPRECIATION OF FREIGHT-TRAIN CARS PER FREIGHT -TRAIN CAR-MILE
Pere Marquette
Ann Arbor
Grand Rapids and Indiana
Michigan Central
Constructed from figures found in Exhibit No.166 of the
Interstate Commerce Commission Case, Docket No. 6833.

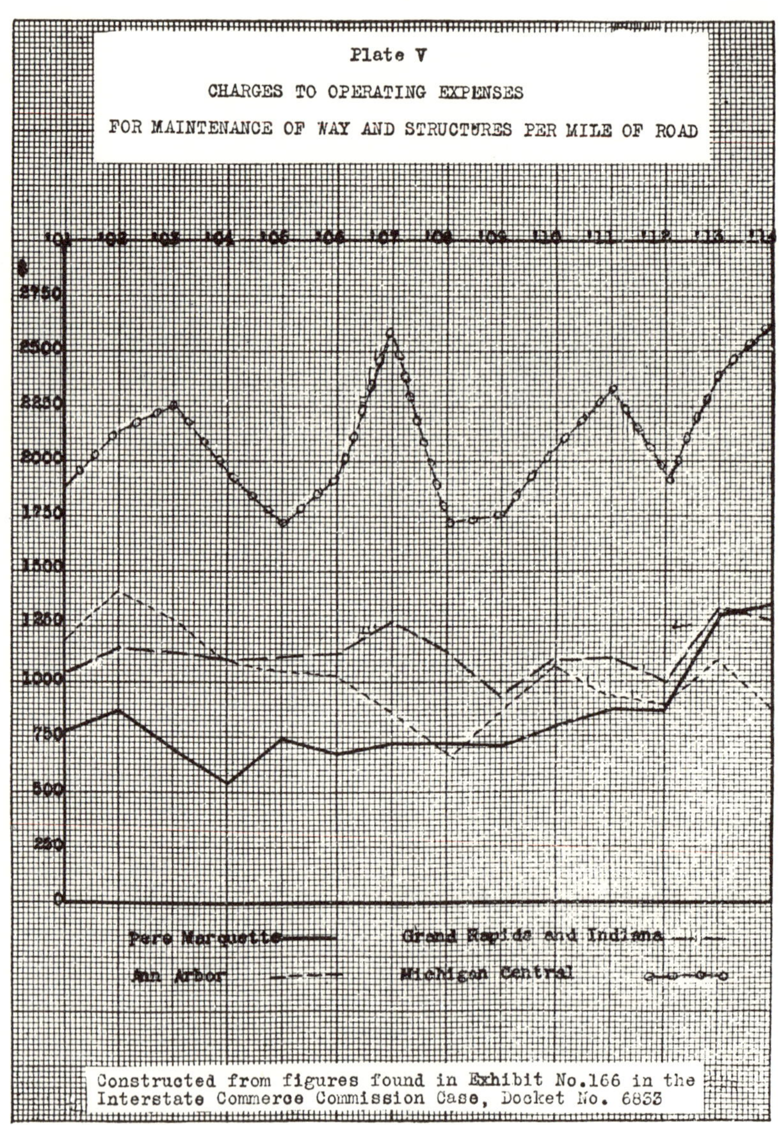
Plate V
CHARGES TO OPERATING EXPENSES
FOR MAINTENANCE OF WAY AND STRUCTURES PER MILE OF ROAD
Pere Marquette
Ann Arbor
Grand Rapids and Indiana
Michigan Central
Constructed from figures found in Exhibit No.166 in the
Interstate Commerce Commission Case, Docket No. 6833

In 1915 there was some deferred maintenance on fences amounting to \$24,600 and it was necessary to build 140 more miles of fence than was normal.

As regards bridges there was not so much deferred maintenance compared with the other items that have been referred to.

Ballasting had not been kept up, making it necessary to do more of this work in 1914 than was done in any other previous year, and as a result of which, traffic was held up and gross revenues diminished.

The conclusion, then, would seem to be, that the large increase in operating expenses during the latter part of this period was due to deferred maintenance over all parts of the road, but especially on freight-car equipment. For the year 1914 operating expenses were larger than in 1913, not only because of deferred repairs but because of the strike in the shops; while in 1913 it also became apparent that prices of materials and labor were advancing rapidly.

Mr. Frank Hooker Alfred, the general manager of the Pere Marquette, testified before the Interstate Commerce Commission that the road was not in as good condition in 1912 as when he left it in 1905; and on the latter date it cannot be said to have been in first class condition. Mr. Alfred went on to say, "It is the practice on well maintained railroads when business slumps, to decrease their expenditures in maintenance and reduce it over the year, a short period like a year, with a little work, but it has to be made up in the end, and when those times are prolonged, it will result in a condition as was found here in 1912. They must pay the penalty."[1]

Further, in answer to the question whether the lack of material does not cause the necessity for more labor expense, he said, "Material and labor sort of work together. It is a fact that if maintenance is deferred to such an extent that it begins to require more attention and more labor to keep it up, then the labor item becomes more expensive than the labor and material items combined, if the road is well maintained. That is true."[2]

In other words, during the time when the Pere Marquette was allowed to run down, that is, when new ties and new rails and new fastenings were not put in regularly, there was really a greater expenditure in keeping up of the old track, because of the necessity of picking up joints and taking care of increased maintenance due to lack of material.

---

1. *Stenographer's Minutes Before the I. C. C.*, Docket No. 6833, 1166.
2. *Ibid.*

APPENDIX E

Comparison of the Pere Marquette with Other Railroads

As regards the number of passengers carried one mile per mile of road, the Pere Marquette does not compare favorably with the other railroads with the possible exception of the Ann Arbor line. Even in comparison with the latter road it is seen that the Pere Marquette has fallen below this line during the past three years and was at no time much above it.   (Plate VI)

Compared with the railroads in the United States as a whole, the Pere Marquette carries on the average approximately forty thousand less passengers one mile per mile of road; fifty-five thousand less passengers than for Group III or middle western railroads; and in 1914, one hundred and sixty thousand less passengers than the Michigan Central was carrying.

From this it is seen that the Pere Marquette is lacking a very dense passenger traffic, in fact is lacking anywhere near the average density, and hence is at somewhat of a disadvantage compared with some of its competitors.

This sparsity is partly due to the fact that no passengers are carried on the line east of St. Thomas, Ontario, because of the terms under which this stretch of track is leased; and therefore there is no possibility of through passenger traffic to Buffalo over the Pere Marquette lines. It is also partly due to the fact that the Pere Marquette has more miles of branch lines than any of these other roads that are compared with it. Passenger traffic is necessarily light on these branches because of the character of the country in which they are located. That is, the lumbering industry has died out and the agricultural industry has not filled the gap in many counties, and in others only at a very slow rate. Still further, the Detroit-Chicago passenger traffic is light because of the roundabout way of getting there and the consequent longer schedule as compared with their competitors.

From Plate VII it is seen that the Pere Marquette compares very favorably with other Michigan roads and with the roads of the United States as regards the average distance that each passenger is carried.

The Pere Marquette hauls each passenger from five to ten miles further than the roads for the United States as a whole, the Ann Arbor and the Grand Rapids and Indiana. The length of haul is about the same compared with the middle western roads (Group III) but is far below the Michigan Central which has a very large through traffic.

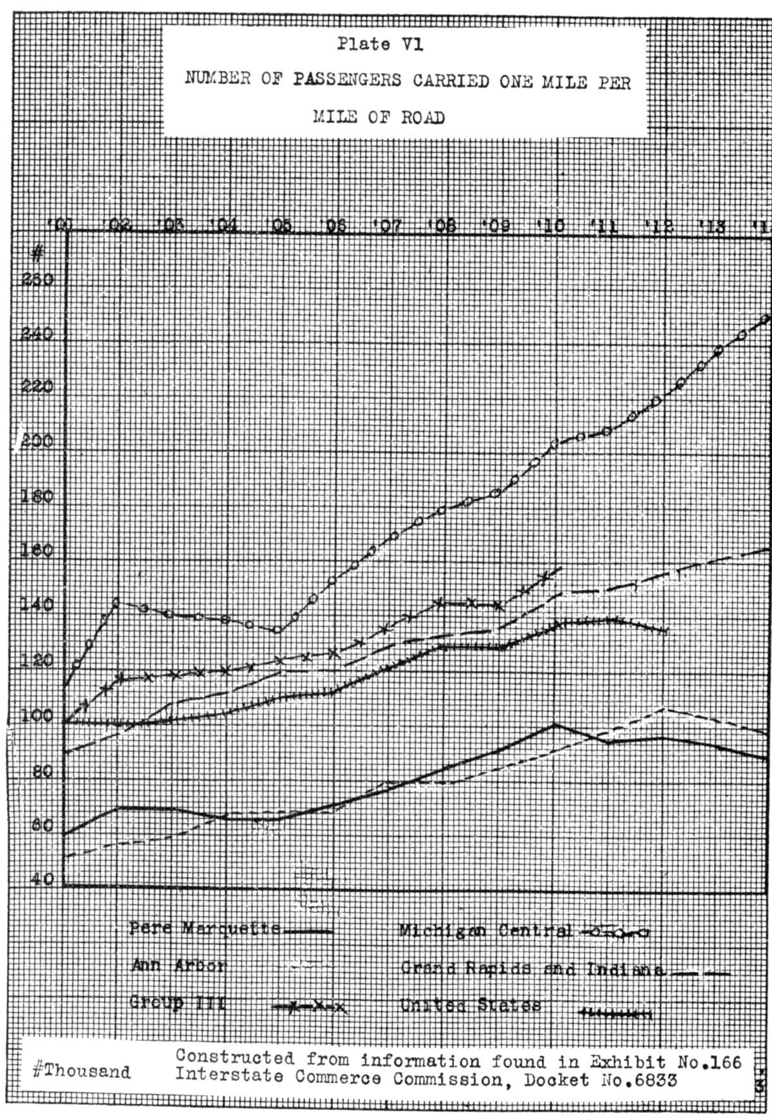
Plate VI
NUMBER OF PASSENGERS CARRIED ONE MILE PER
MILE OF ROAD
'01 '02 '03 '04 '05 '06 '07 '08 '09 '10 '11 '12 '13 '1
#
260
240
220
200
180
160
140
120
100
80
60
40
Pere Marquette
Ann Arbor
Group III
Michigan Central
Grand Rapids and Indiana
United States
#Thousand
Constructed from information found in Exhibit No.166
Interstate Commerce Commission, Docket No.6833

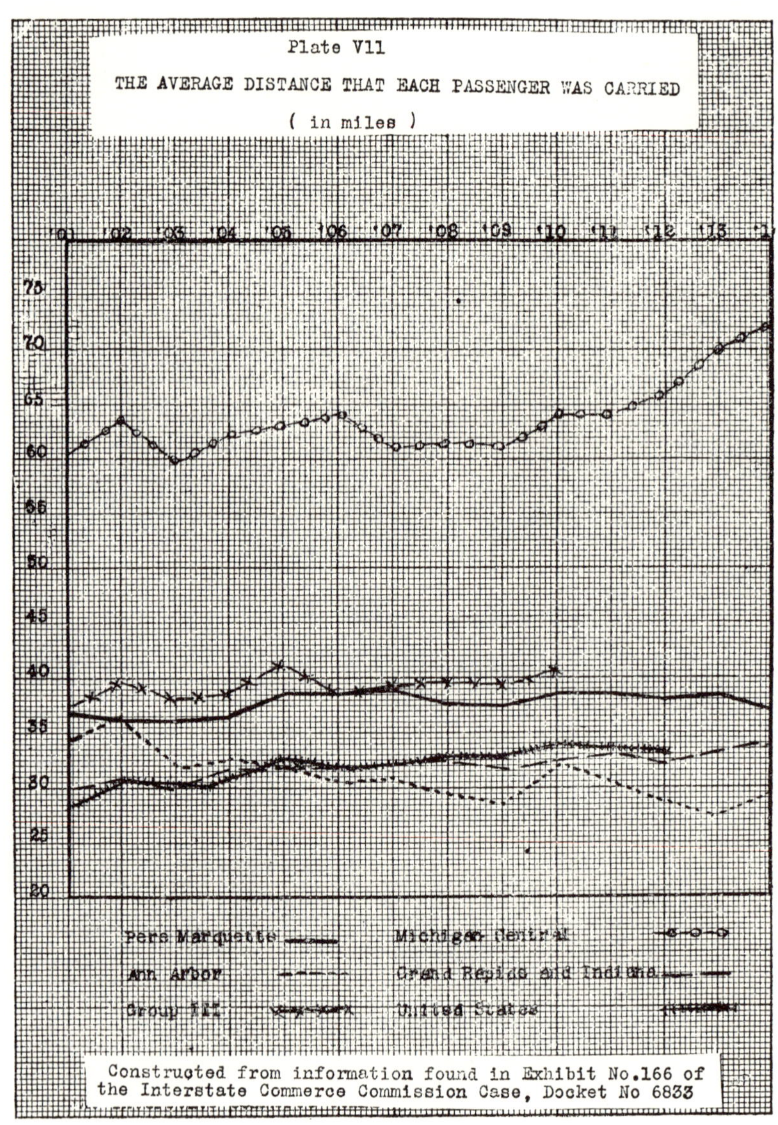
Plate Vll
THE AVERAGE DISTANCE THAT EACH PASSENGER WAS CARRIED
(in miles)
'01 '02 '03 '04 '05 '06 '07 '08 '09 '10 '11 '12 '13
75
70
65
60
55
50
45
40
35
30
25
20
Pere Marquette
Michigan Central
Ann Arbor
Grand Rapids and Indiana
Group III
United States
Constructed from information found in Exhibit No.166 of
the Interstate Commerce Commission Case, Docket No 6833

Plate Vlll
AVERAGE AMOUNT RECEIVED FROM EACH PASSENGER
.500
.400
.300
.200
.100
.000
.900
.800
.700
.600
.500
.400
Pere Marquette
Ann Arbor
Group III
Michigan Central
Grand Rapids and Indiana
United States
Constructed from information found in Exhibit No.166 of
the Interstate Commerce Commission Case, Docket No 6833

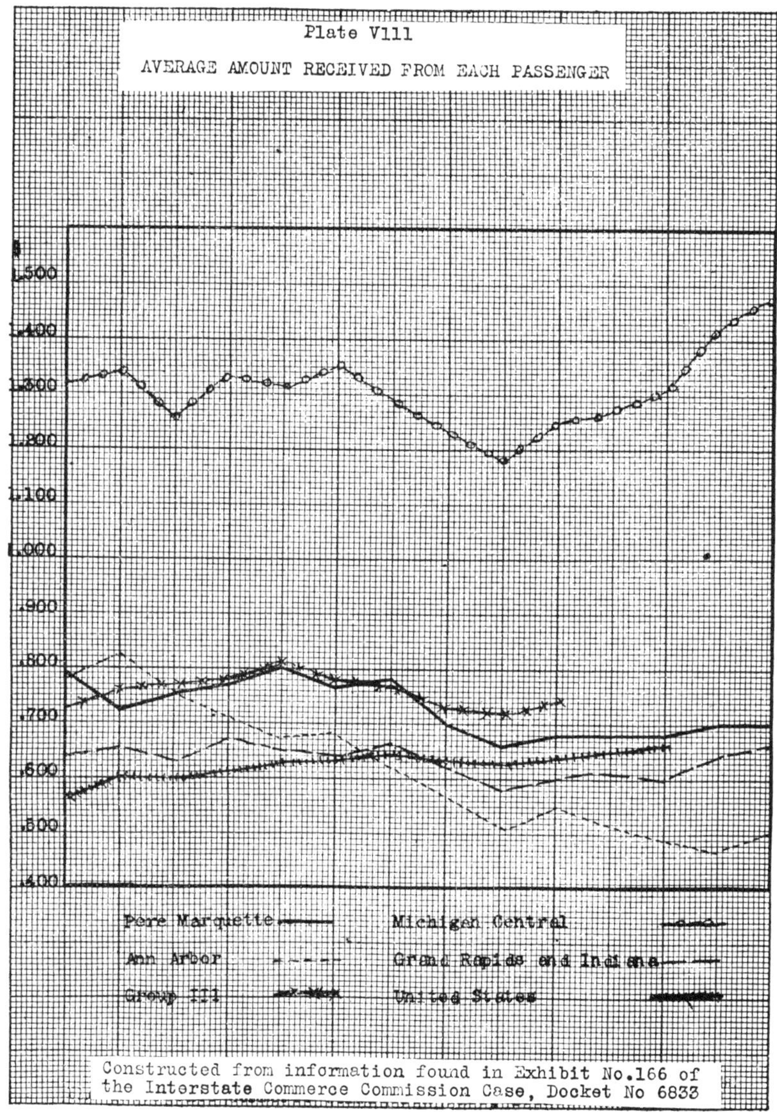

53

It can be said that, for the most part, the Pere Marquette has quite a large through traffic on some of its divisions (like the one from Detroit to Grand Rapids, and Saginaw to Toledo) and a lack of passenger traffic on many of its branch lines, both of which facts makes the average haul somewhat above the average of the roads under consideration.

Since the average passenger haul is fairly large for the Pere Marquette, it should follow that the average amount received from each passenger should be comparatively large. This is shown in Plate VIII. Here it is seen that the Pere Marquette gets from seventy to eighty cents from each passenger while the average for the United States as a whole, the Ann Arbor and the Grand Rapids and Indiana is from two to twenty cents below this amount. The average for Group III is about the same as for the Pere Marquette, perhaps a trifle above, while in 1914 the Michigan Central took in seventy cents more from each passenger than did the Pere Marquette, and for the rest of the period under consideration, about fifty cents more on the average.

With reference to the average receipts per passenger per mile, it will be seen from Plate IX that from 1902 to 1907 the Pere Marquette was getting about two cents per mile, which was about the amount that was being received on the average from the roads in Group III and for the United States as a whole. The other Michigan roads were receiving from one-twentieth to one-third of a cent more than this.

In 1907, due to the two cent law going into effect, the receipts per passenger per mile fell for all the roads in the country, but it fell more for the Pere Marquette than most of the other Michigan railroads. From 1909 to 1914 the Pere Marquette was receiving less per passenger per mile than the other roads, barring the Ann Arbor line. In the last few years the roads doing an inter-state traffic show the largest receipts per passenger per mile, due to the fact that they are allowed to charge two and one-half cents per mile as compared with two cents per mile for intra-state traffic. In 1914 the Pere Marquette was getting within one-twentieth of a cent of what the Grand Rapids and Indiana was receiving, and within one-seventh of the receipts per passenger per mile of the Michigan Central. As the inter-state traffic of the Pere Marquette increases, due to better equipment and more connections, the average receipts per passenger per mile will tend to increase. It is doubtful, however, whether they will be as large as the Michigan Central or the Grand Rapids and Indiana, both of which do a large inter-state traffic and receive important traffic from other roads with which they are affiliated.

Since the number of passengers that the Pere Marquette carried one mile of road is low as compared with the other roads, it is

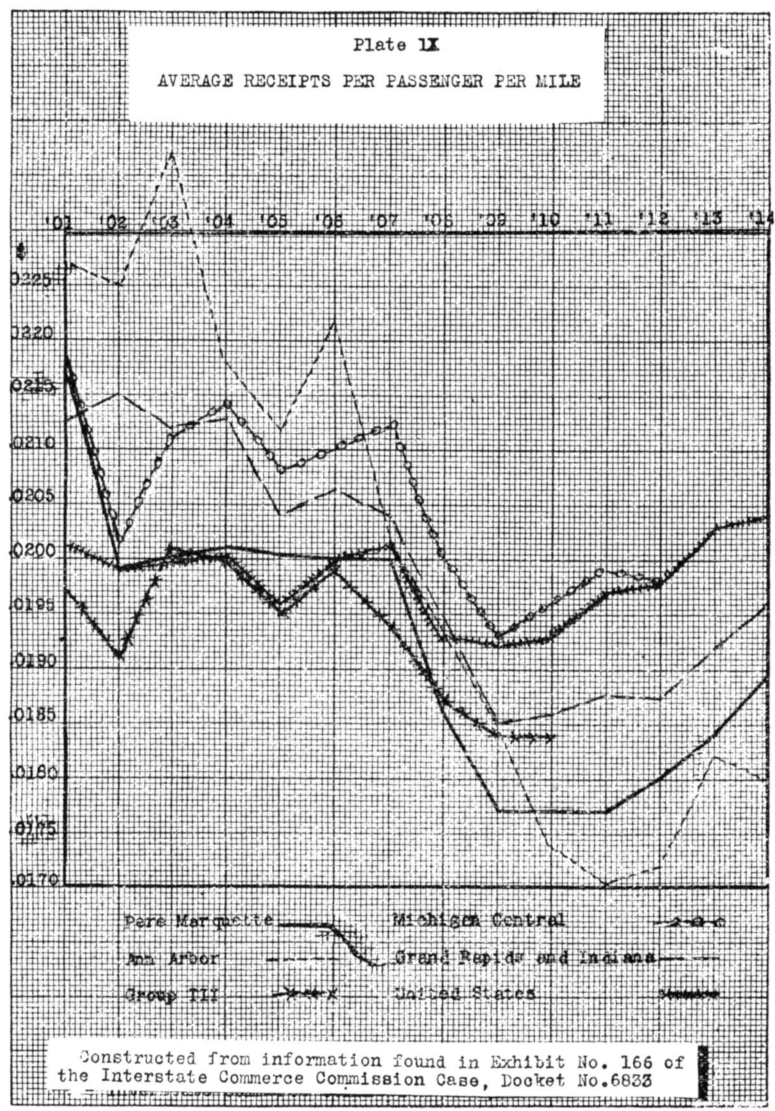

Plate IX
AVERAGE RECEIPTS PER PASSENGER PER MILE
'01 '02 '03 '04 '05 '06 '07 '08 '09 '10 '11 '12 '13 '14
$
.0225
.0220
.0215
.0210
.0205
.0200
.0195
.0190
.0185
.0180
.0175
.0170
Pere Marquette
Michigan Central
Ann Arbor
Grand Rapids and Indiana
Group III
United States
Constructed from information found in Exhibit No. 166 of
the Interstate Commerce Commission Case, Docket No.6833

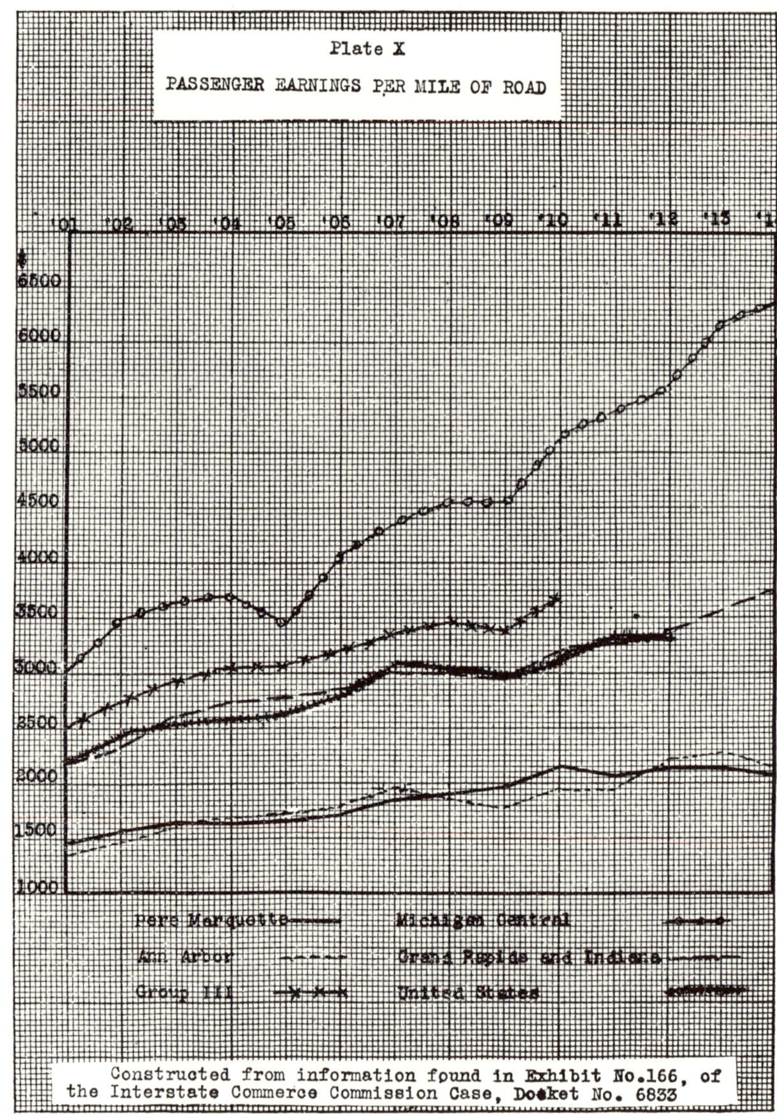
Plate X
PASSENGER EARNINGS PER MILE OF ROAD
'01 '02 '03 '04 '05 '06 '07 '08 '09 '10 '11 '12 '13 '1
$
6500
6000
5500
5000
4500
4000
3500
3000
2500
2000
1500
1000
Pere Marquette
Ann Arbor
Group III
Michigan Central
Grand Rapids and Indiana
United States
Constructed from information found in Exhibit No.166, of
the Interstate Commerce Commission Case, Docket No. 6833

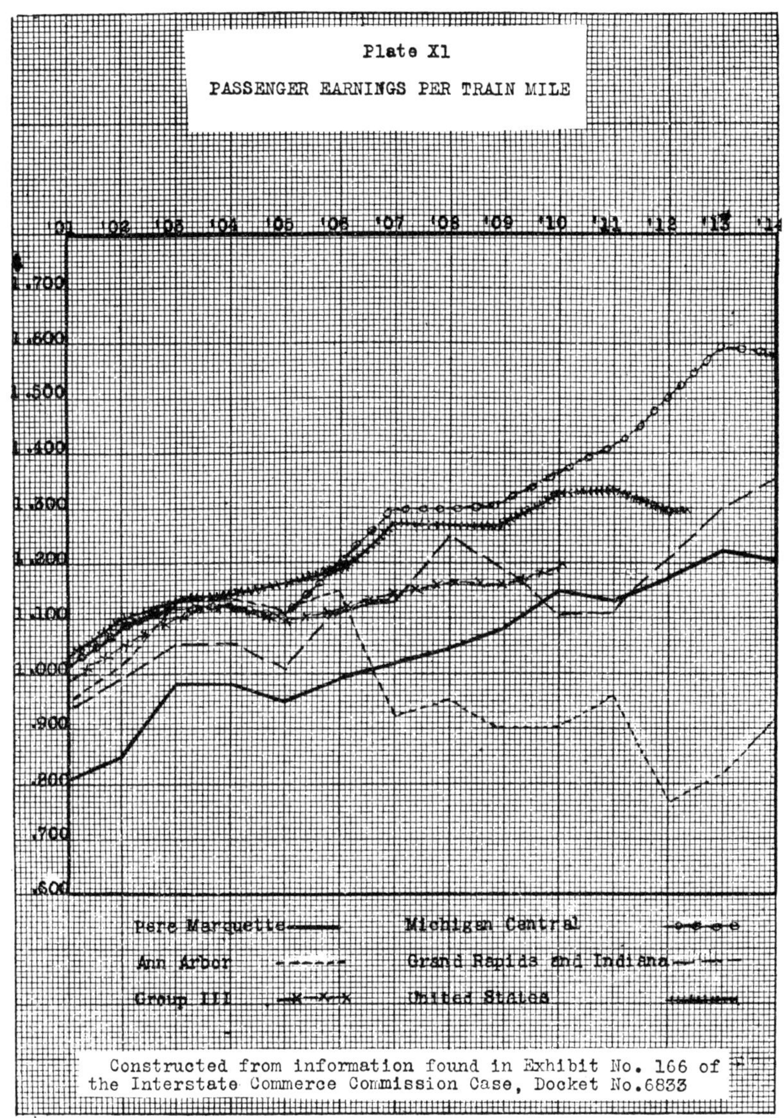

Plate Xl
PASSENGER EARNINGS PER TRAIN MILE
'01 '02 '03 '04 '05 '06 '07 '08 '09 '10 '11 '12 '13 '14
1.700
1.600
1.500
1.400
1.300
1.200
1.100
1.000
.900
.800
.700
.600
Pere Marquette
Michigan Central
Ann Arbor
Grand Rapids and Indiana
Group III
United States
Constructed from information found in Exhibit No. 166 of
the Interstate Commerce Commission Case, Docket No.6833

natural that the passenger earnings per mile of road would be comparatively low also.   In-Plate X it is seen that the average earnings per mile of road from passenger traffic are from $1,500 to $2,100, which are also the approximate figures for the Ann Arbor line; but all the other roads are much above this, the average of the United States ranging from $2,200 to $3,300 and for Group III from $2,500 to $3,700.   The Michigan Central, which has about the same mileage as the Pere Marquette, in 1914 showed earnings of about $6,400 per mile, and for the period under consideration showed higher passenger earnings per mile of road than any of the other roads or groups of roads with which it was compared.

While the passenger earnings per mile of road are very low, the passenger earnings per train mile are also low (Plate XI).   In other words, the sparseness of passenger earnings does not exist merely for the total mileage of the road but also for each train that is run.   With the exception of the Ann Arbor line, the passenger earnings per train mile for the Pere Marquette are lower than for any of the other roads or groups of roads compared. They run from eighty cents to one dollar and twenty cents while for the other roads they run from five to forty cents more.

FREIGHT

As regards the number of tons carried one mile per mile of road' the Pere Marquette stands at the bottom of the list of roads under comparison, with a tonnage ranging from 400 to 800 (Plate XII).   The Michigan Central and Group III average between 1,200 and 2,000 tons while for the United States as a whole the tonnage runs from 750 to 1,050.   The Ann Arbor line averages at least 200 tons more than the Pere Marquette until 1911, after which date it runs somewhat over 100 tons.   The Grand Rapids and Indiana for the most part keeps slightly above the tonnage of the Pere Marquette until the last two or three years.

Looked at for the whole period it would seem that the Pere Marquette has been at a disadvantage with its competitors as to the tonnage carried per mile of road.   That this disadvantage will be lessened, to a small degree at least, seems certain as the Pere Marquette becomes more of a through line.   For it has been an evident fact for some time that the tonnage originating in Michigan was on the decline and of necessity had to be supplemented by through tonnage, or traffic originating on other lines and in other states, if the Pere Marquette was to make operating expenses.   The increase of tonnage in the latter part of the period is due to a large extent to the absorption of traffic originating

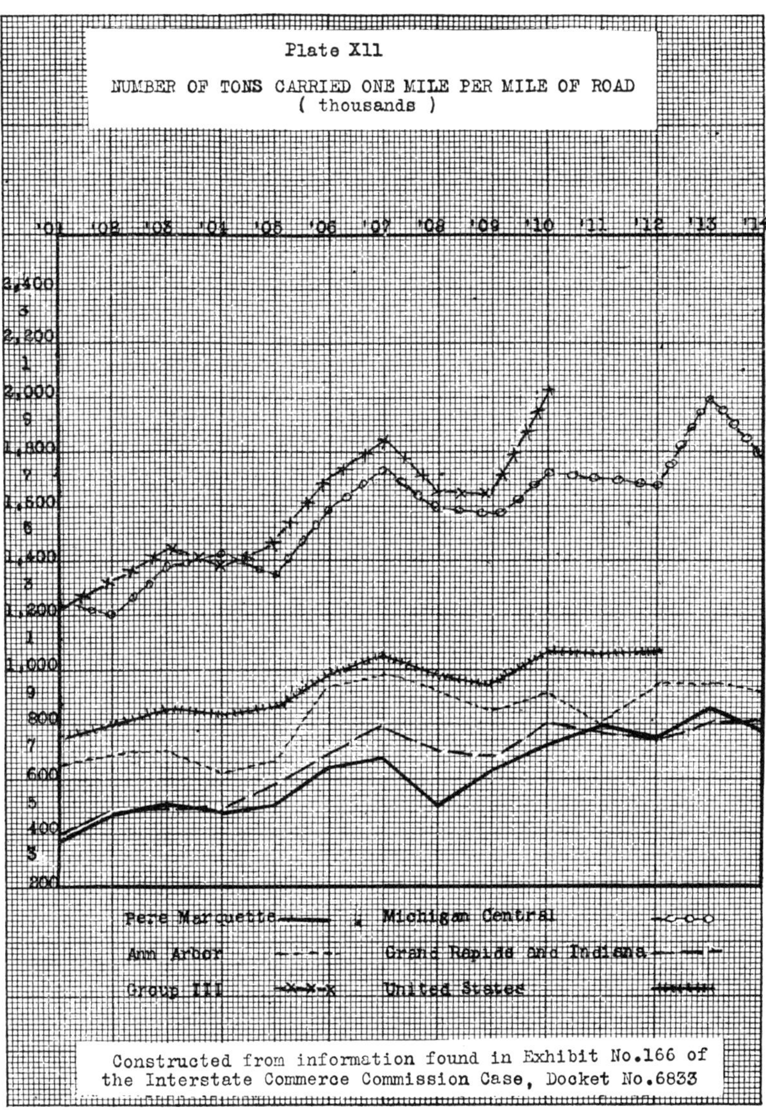

Plate X11
NUMBER OF TONS CARRIED ONE MILE PER MILE OF ROAD
(thousands)
'01 '02 '03 '04 '05 '06 '07 '08 '09 '10 '11 '12 '13 '14
2,400
2,200
2,000
1,800
1,600
1,400
1,200
1,000
900
800
700
600
500
400
300
200
Pere Marquette
Michigan Central
Ann Arbor
Grand Rapids and Indiana
Group III
United States
Constructed from information found in Exhibit No.166 of
the Interstate Commerce Commission Case, Docket No.6833

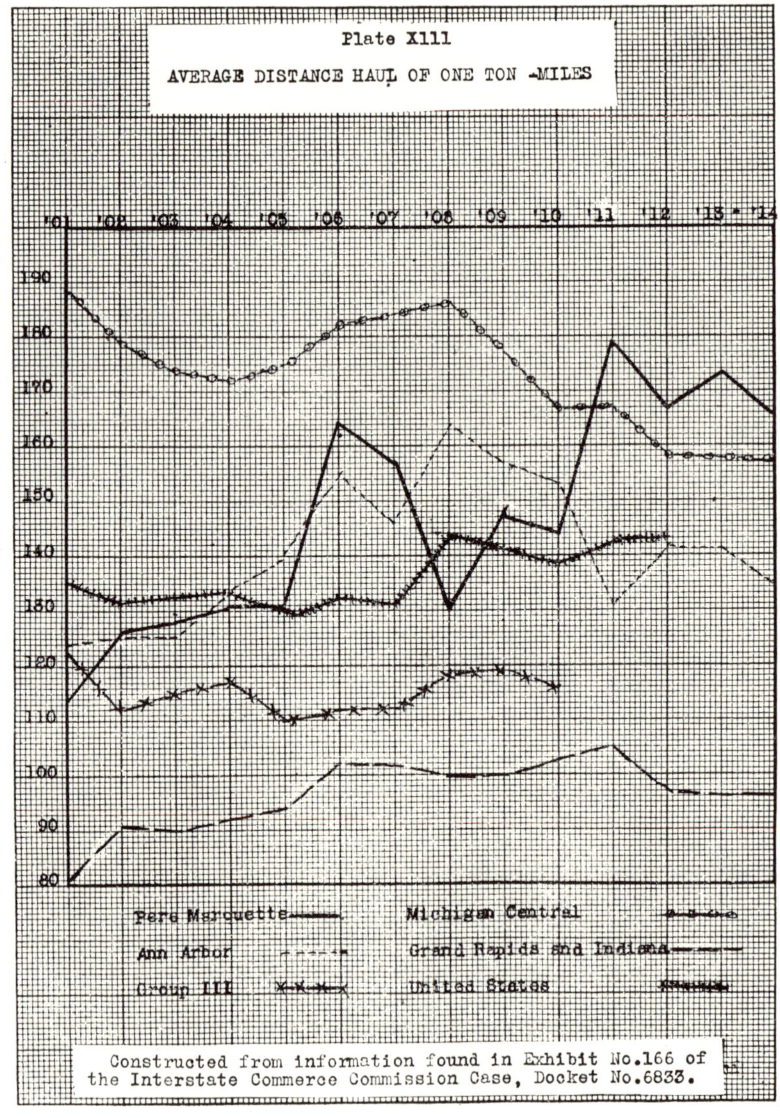
Plate Xl11
AVERAGE DISTANCE HAUL OF ONE TON -MILES
'01 '02 '03 '04 '05 '06 '07 '08 '09 '10 '11 '12 13 - '14
190
180
170
160
150
140
130
120
110
100
90
80
Pere Marquette———   Michigan Central
Ann Arbor   Grand Rapids and Indiana———
Group III   x—x—x—x   United States
Constructed from information found in Exhibit No.166 of
the Interstate Commerce Commission Case, Docket No.6833.

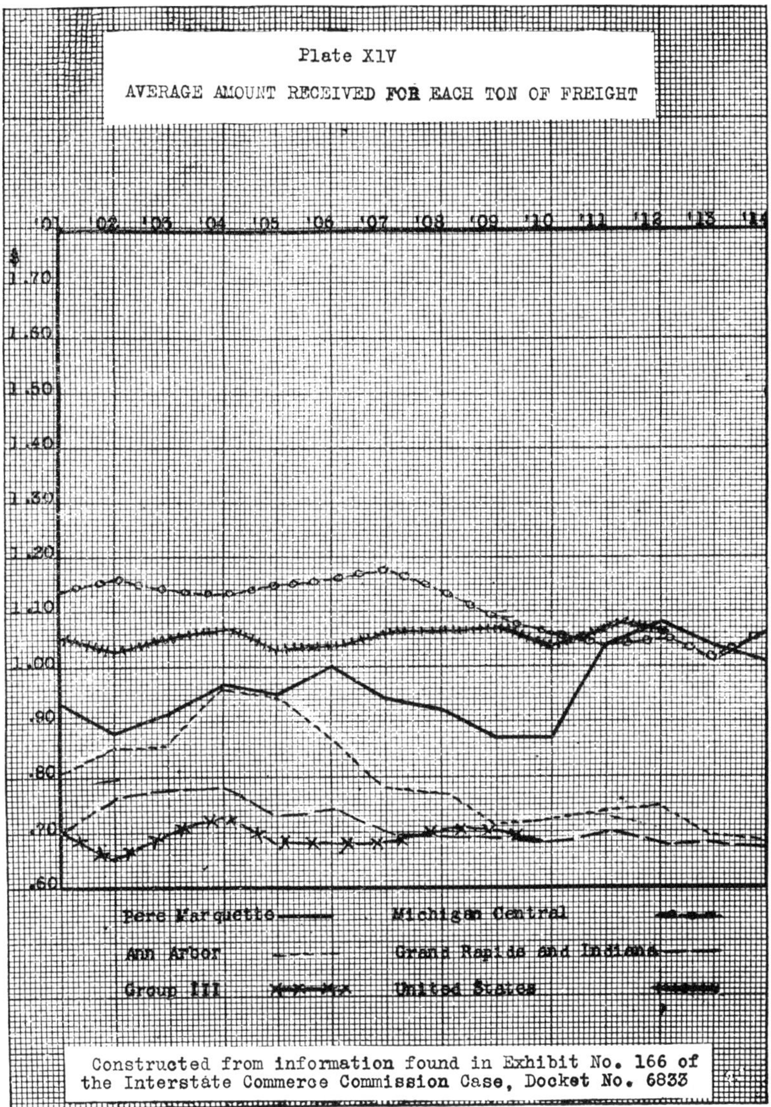

Plate XlV
AVERAGE AMOUNT RECEIVED FOR EACH TON OF FREIGHT
'01 '02 '03 '04 '05 '06 '07 '08 '09 '10 '11 '12 '13 '14
$
1.70
1.60
1.50
1.40
1.30
1.20
1.10
1.00
.90
.80
.70
.60
Pere Marquette
Ann Arbor
Group III
Michigan Central
Grand Rapids and Indiana
United States
Constructed from information found in Exhibit No. 166 of
the Interstate Commerce Commission Case, Docket No. 6833

on other lines and going over the rails of the Pere Marquette by virtue of its through character. This emphasizes again the compelling need of making outside connections and the impossibility of each constituent railroad running its own line with success on the basis of the traffic originating on it.

The Pere Marquette compares very favorably with the other railroads as regards the average number of miles that one ton of freight is hauled (Plate XIII). The average distance haul for this road ranges from 114 to 165 miles, while the average for the roads in the United States as a whole is from 135 to 143, and for the middle western roads from 122 to 116.

During the latter portion of the period under consideration, the average distance haul has materially increased and no doubt will continue to do so as the road loses more and more its local character.

The average amount received from each ton of freight is greater for the Pere Marquette than for any other Michigan road with the exception of the Michigan Central (Plate XIV). It is also greater than the amount received by the roads in Group III, ranging from ninety-three cents at the beginning of the period to one dollar and one cent at the end, which is close to the average for the United States.

The increase of high grade shipments from the Northwest via Lake Michigan ought to increase the amount received for each ton of freight, as low grade timber shipments are being more and more displaced by high grade merchandise traffic. This tendency can likewise be seen on other portions of the road and no doubt will continue to exist.

The average receipts per ton per mile for the Pere Marquette is about the average for the roads under comparison (Plate XV). This indicates that the traffic is fairly high grade for the most part, at least up to the year 1908. After that year, due to the growth in the tonnage of products from mines, the receipts per ton per mile have been lowered and are lower in 1914 than for any other Michigan road under consideration with the exception of the Ann Arbor line.

A large part of the products of mines consists of mineral ores but a larger portion consists of coal. This coal traffic has been built up largely through agreements with Ohio railroads and the organization of car-ferry service across Lake Erie to make connections with the Canadian lines of the Pere Marquette. As Michigan becomes more and more an industrial state, enormous quantities of coal will be needed and it can be expected that a large tonnage of coal will continue to be hauled. Of course lumber and timber products have declined very materially which of itself would ·tend to make the average receipts per ton per mile much greater, but this has been offset by other low grade traffic as already explained. On the whole, the average receipts per ton per mile should increase, although slowly, by reason of the high grade manufactured goods and products that will more and more be in evidence in the State of Michigan as a result of the automobile and other manufacturing industries.

The freight earnings per mile of road are lower than for any of the roads compared (Plate XVI). One of the reasons for this fact is that the Pere Marquette has more branch lines in proportion to its mileage than any other line in the State of Michigan. The country along these branches has been stripped of its timber, and agriculture has not developed quickly enough to take the place of it. That this situation will become more favorable as time goes on, seems to be true for a large portion of the branches, but a railroad cannot wait until the future to pay interest on its bonded indebtedness; and on many miles of the road it would seem that a good many years may elapse before enough tonnage develops to make railroading profitable for these particular districts. One such district is that between Baldwin and Traverse City; also along the Kalkaska branch[1] and the territory in the "Thumb" district.

The freight earnings per train mile for the Pere Marquette were lower than for any of the other roads considered, until the year 1910, since which time they have risen quite rapidly so that in 1914 they were larger than either the Ann Arbor or Grand Rapids and Indiana lines (Plate XVII). However, as compared with the average for the United States, for the Michigan Central and for the railroads in Group III, the Pere Marquette has had much lower freight earnings per train mile during the entire period.

One of the chief reasons for the rapid rise in freight earnings per train mile since 1911, is that a larger amount of low grade traffic has made necessary more heavy trainloads. Not only has low grade traffic on some of the divisions made this necessary but also, heavier locomotives and cars have been required to handle all kinds of increasing traffic over most of the main line. As a contrast to the overtaxed divisions are the undertaxed divisions and branches where less trains are now run than formerly, but those that are run are heavier. This latter class, however, is quite negligible compared with the former. In all probability freight earnings per train mile will continue to increase as heavier

---

1. Part of this line has recently been torn up, permission for such action being received from the Michigan Railroad Commission because of the practical non-existence of traffic originating on it.

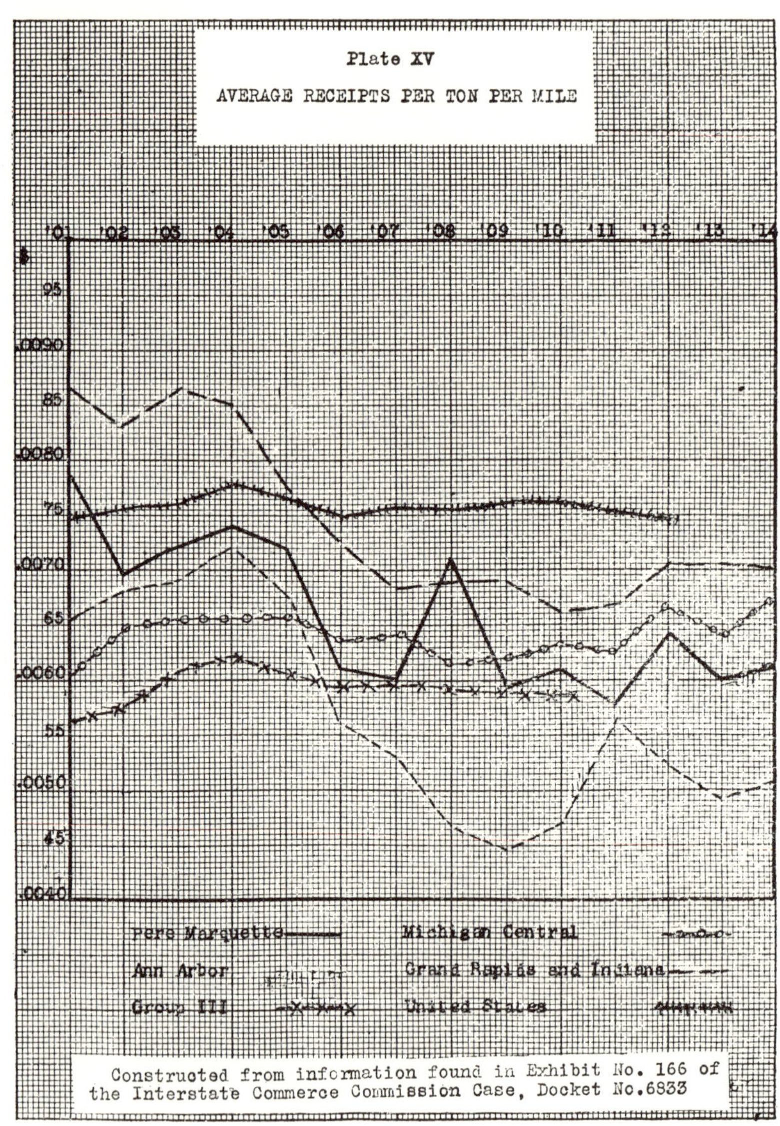

Plate XV
AVERAGE RECEIPTS PER TON PER MILE
'01 '02 '03 '04 '05 '06 '07 '08 '09 '10 '11 '12 '13 '14
$
.0095
.0090
.0085
.0080
.0075
.0070
.0065
.0060
.0055
.0050
.0045
.0040
Pere Marquette
Ann Arbor
Group III
Michigan Central
Grand Rapids and Indiana
United States
Constructed from information found in Exhibit No. 166 of
the Interstate Commerce Commission Case, Docket No.6833

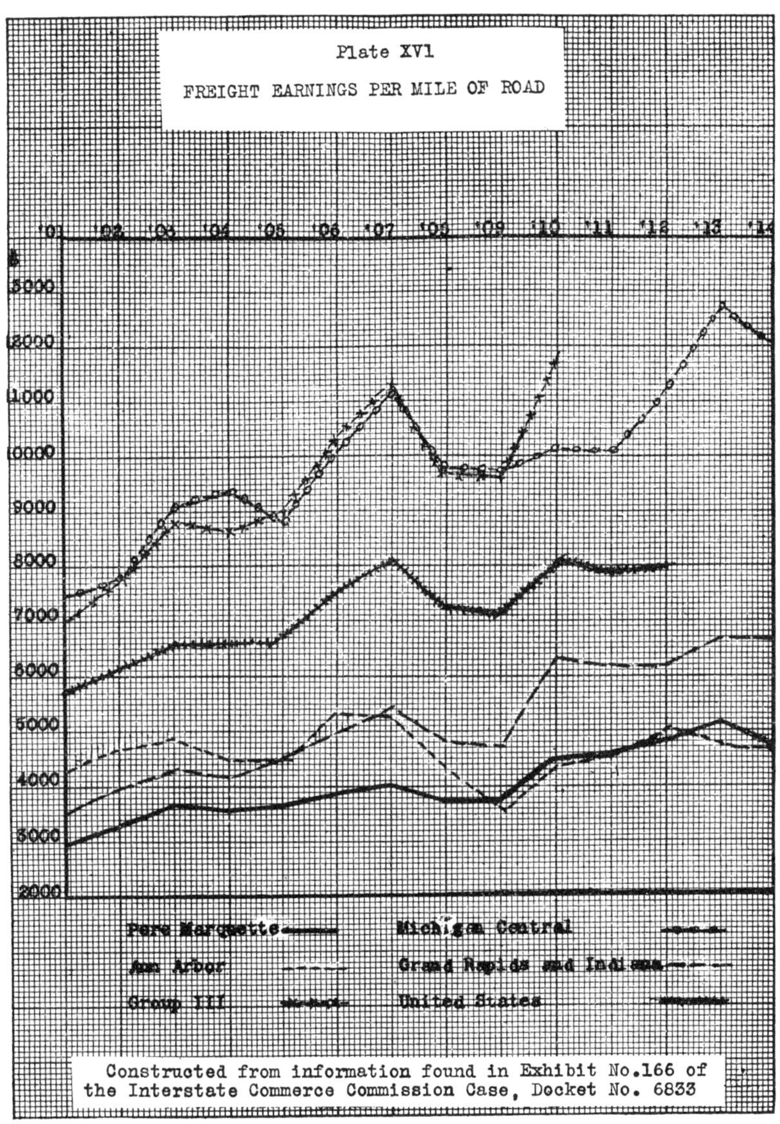
Plate XVl
FREIGHT EARNINGS PER MILE OF ROAD
'01   '02   '03   '04   '05   '06   '07   '08   '09   '10   '11   '12   '13   '14
$
13000
12000
11000
10000
9000
8000
7000
6000
5000
4000
3000
2000
Pere Marquette
Michigan Central
Ann Arbor
Grand Rapids and Indiana
Group III
United States
Constructed from information found in Exhibit No.166 of
the Interstate Commerce Commission Case, Docket No. 6833

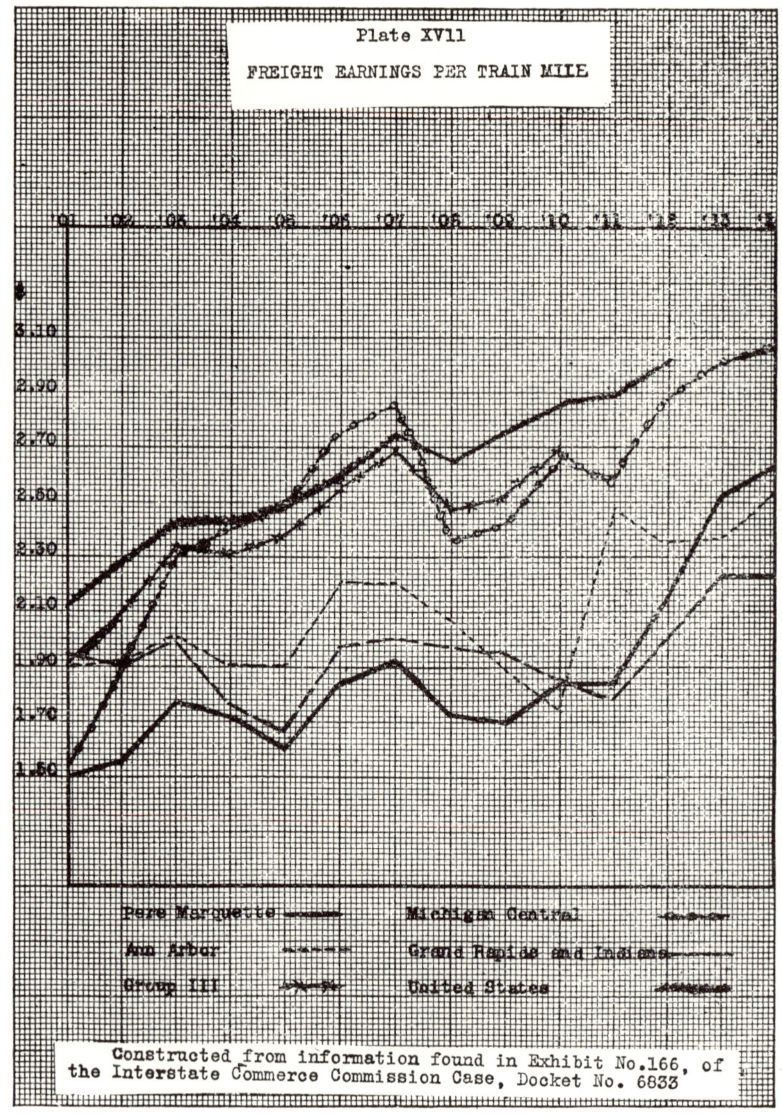

Plate XVll
FREIGHT EARNINGS PER TRAIN MILE
'01 '02 '03 '04 '05 '06 '07 '08 '09 '10 '11 '12 '13
$
3.10
2.90
2.70
2.50
2.30
2.10
1.90
1.70
1.60
Pere Marquette
Ann Arbor
Group III
Michigan Central
Grand Rapids and Indiana
United States
Constructed from information found in Exhibit No.166, of
the Interstate Commerce Commission Case, Docket No. 6833

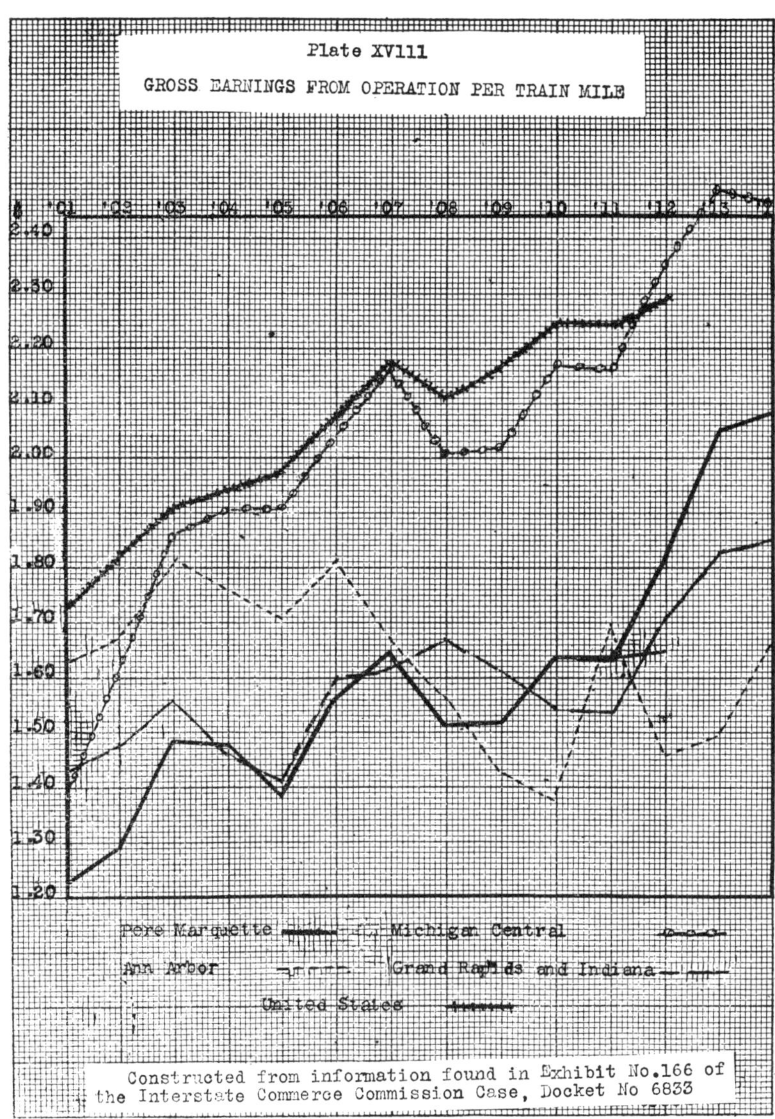
Plate XVlll
GROSS EARNINGS FROM OPERATION PER TRAIN MILE
'01 '02 '03 '04 '05 '06 '07 '08 '09 '10 '11 '12 '13
2.40
2.30
2.20
2.10
2.00
1.90
1.80
1.70
1.60
1.50
1.40
1.30
1.20
Pere Marquette
Michigan Central
Ann Arbor
Grand Rapids and Indiana
United States
Constructed from information found in Exhibit No.166 of
the Interstate Commerce Commission Case, Docket No 6833

trains are being necessitated by changed traffic conditions already indicated.

Gross earnings from operation per train mile for the Pere Marquette were lower than for the other railroads compared with it until the year 1908, from which date they have risen steadily (Plate XVIII).   Considering the whole period, it is seen that the gross earnings per train mile have nearly doubled, which is not the case with any of the other roads with the exception of the Michigan Central.   For the United States as a whole the increase in gross earnings per train mile during this period was about 30 per cent, for the Ann Arbor line no increase, and for the Grand Rapids and Indiana an increase of about 35 per cent. Since 1911 the increase has been especially rapid for the Pere Marquette, due partially to the laying of 90 pound rail and the reballasting of some of the divisions which makes it possible for heavier trains to be used.   There are still some portions of the road to be treated in this manner so it is reasonable to suppose that gross earnings per train mile ought to continue to increase, but perhaps not at such a rapid rate as they have since 1911.

The operating expenses per train mile were lower than any of the other railroads that we are considering, up until the year 1905, from which year until 1910 they remained about the average for the other Michigan roads.   After 1910 they rose more abruptly than for any of the other roads, and reached a higher figure in 1914 than any of them attained   (Plate XIX).

The low figure for the first four years is due to the fact that maintenance of the road and equipment was not kept up.   In other words, the road was allowed to run down and hence operating expenses were not so large as they would have been had more charges been made for maintenance. From 1910 to 1914 the abnormally rapid increase in operating expenses per train mile was due to the taking up of large amounts of deferred maintenance on ties, rails, locomotives, passenger and freight-cars and way and structures. Operating expenses should have been at least 20 cents higher per train mile during the first four years of the life of the Pere Marquette, which would have made unnecessary the extremely high operating expense per train mile in the latter portion of the period.   If this policy had been followed it is certain that the financial condition of the road would not have appeared as healthy as it did directly after consolidation, and dividends could not have been paid. In other words, the payment of dividends during the first five years of the road's existence was not justified because they were not earned; and their payment merely meant the payment of dividends out of capital. This is true because the property was allowed to run down in order to pay dividends and interest on bonds, and later on capital had to be borrowed to make good this depletion of physical condition.

Again it was a case of following an immediate policy instead of laying a sound foundation for the future prosperity of the railroad system. It seems .quite certain that operating expenses will continue to increase for some time since there is much more deferred maintenance that must be charged to this account; also, heavier trains must be run with a correspondingly larger expense.

The situation is summed up in Plate XX where a comparison is made between the operating revenues per train mile and the operating expenses per train mile. Here it is seen that up until 1910 the two lines run fairly parallel to each other, but after that date they converge quite rapidly until they come together in 1914. If there was a widening margin between these two lines it would indicate a gain for heavier trains. That is, the greater operating expense per train mile would be more than offset by the greater operating revenue per train mile and hence the creating of heavier trains would be a profitable policy to follow. However, it is readily seen that this is not true. In fact, just the opposite holds true, viz., that greater expense from operation per train mile seems to mean a comparatively smaller return from operating revenue. Of course it must be remembered that the operating expenses after 1910 are abnormally high because of taking up deferred maintenance, and hence it is not conclusive to say that heavier train loads have not proven profitable. They may prove so in the.future when the physical condition of the road gets back to normal.

Although the Pere Marquette has more mileage than any of the other Michigan roads under consideration, its gross earnings from operation per mile of road are less than any of the other railroads up to the year 1909, and since that year have only been slightly above one of them, viz., the Ann Arbor line   (Plate XXI).

While the Michigan Central has nearly the same mileage as the Pere Marquette, a larger portion of the mileage of the former road is used for through traffic instead of consisting of branch lines as is the case with the latter road. However, the Grand Rapids and Indiana and the Ann Arbor lines, which deal with traffic conditions similar to those of the Pere Marquette, show lower gross earnings per mile of road than do the roads of the middle west (Group III). Since 1910 there has been a slight upward trend to gross earnings per mile of road which ought to continue as more outside connections are made and some of the unprofitable interior lines are abandoned.

While gross earnings per mile of road are lower for the most part than the other roads under comparison, it is equally true that operating expenses per mile of road are lower, at least until recently, than the other roads (Plate XXII). Since 1909 there

55

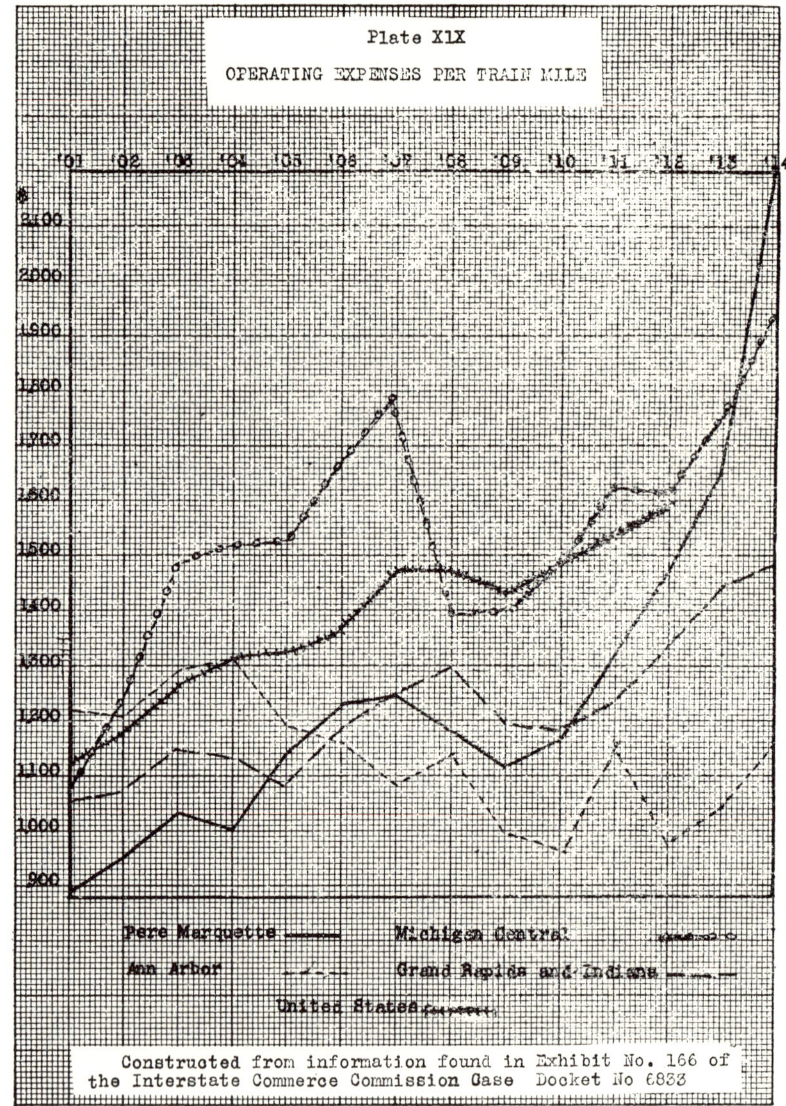
Plate XIX
OPERATING EXPENSES PER TRAIN MILE
'01 '02 '03 '04 '05 '06 '07 '08 '09 '10 '11 '12 '13 '14
$
2100
2000
1900
1800
1700
1600
1500
1400
1300
1200
1100
1000
900
Pere Marquette
Ann Arbor
United States
Michigan Central
Grand Rapids and Indiana
Constructed from information found in Exhibit No. 166 of
the Interstate Commerce Commission Case Docket No 6833

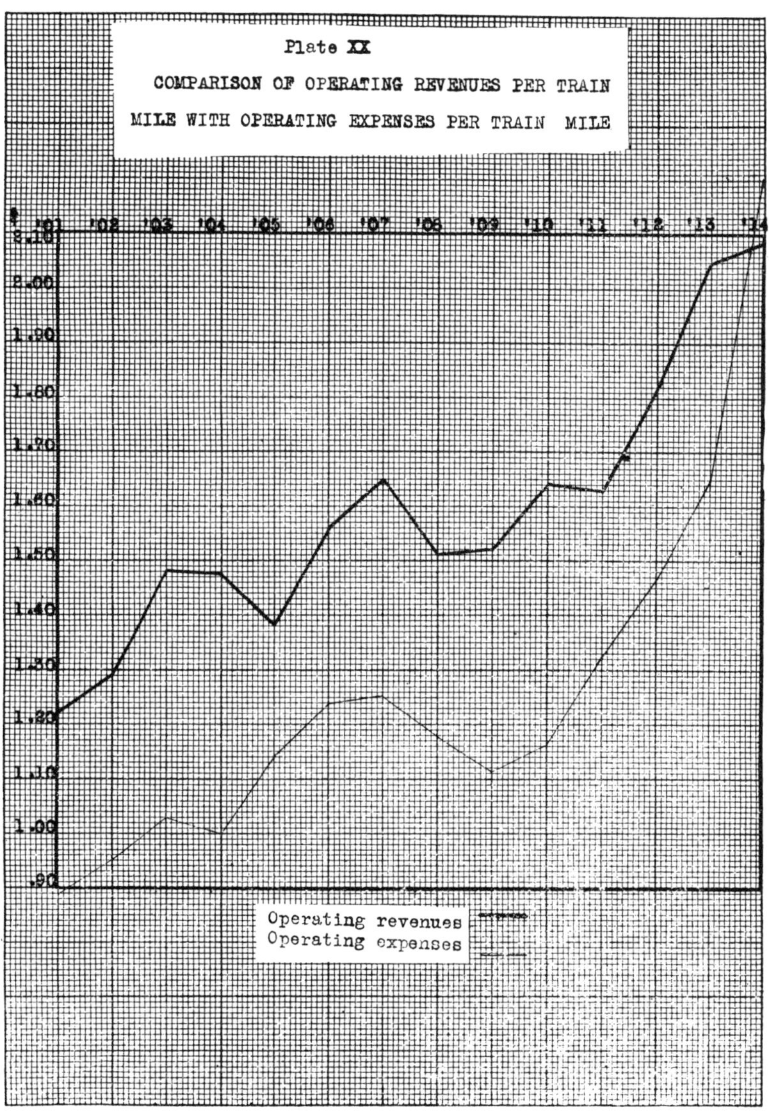

Plate XX
COMPARISON OF OPERATING REVENUES PER TRAIN
MILE WITH OPERATING EXPENSES PER TRAIN MILE
'01 '02 '03 '04 '05 '06 '07 '08 '09 '10 '11 '12 '13 '14
2.10
2.00
1.90
1.80
1.70
1.60
1.50
1.40
1.30
1.20
1.10
1.00
.90
Operating revenues
Operating expenses

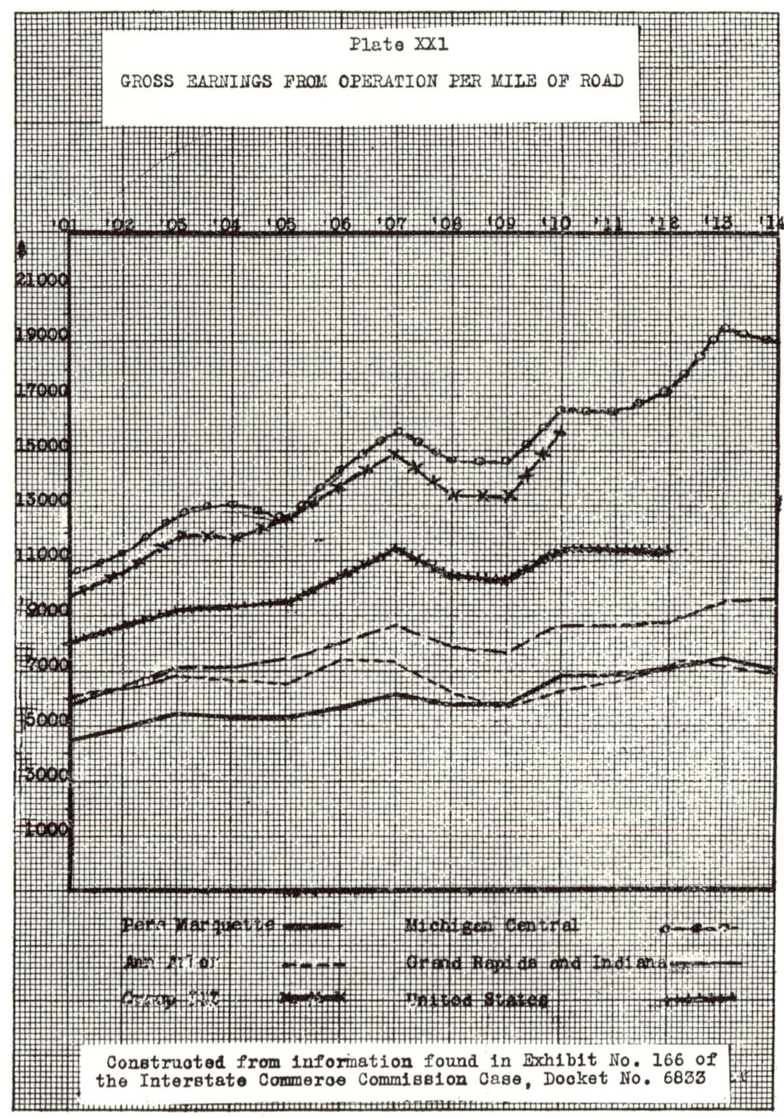

Plate XX1
GROSS EARNINGS FROM OPERATION PER MILE OF ROAD
'01 '02 '03 '04 '05 '06 '07 '08 '09 '10 '11 '12 '13 '14
21000
19000
17000
15000
13000
11000
9000
7000
5000
3000
1000
Pere Marquette
Ann Arbor
Chicago
Michigan Central
Grand Rapids and Indiana
United States
Constructed from information found in Exhibit No. 166 of
the Interstate Commerce Commission Case, Docket No. 6833

has been a rise in operating expenses (especially in 1914) due to the taking up of deferred maintenance, which was not met by an increase in gross earnings but an actual falling off, so that a large deficit accrued in the latter year. It will be noticed that in the years 1900 to 1905 operating expenses are lower than they would have been had road and equipment been fully maintained. Especially is this true in the year 1904 when there was an actual decrease in the operating expenses per mile of road under the Prince-Zimmerman administration.

A summary of the situation just described is found in Plate XXIII. Here it is seen that not only the increase in operating expenses tended to squeeze out net revenues but also the abrupt declining of gross revenues. This can be attributed partly to the depression in business in 1913 and partly to the hindrance to traffic caused by the extensive improvements being made along the roadway and on the structures. From 1913 to 1916 more ties and rails were laid than in any other three-year period, and more ballasting was done than ever before. With these improvements completed this depressive influence on gross revenues will no longer exist, and with business on the upward trend gross revenues can be expected to rise, at least at the former rate, while operating expenses should be lower after a few years.

The ratio of operating expenses to operating revenues is comparatively low for the first four years of operation, but since 1905 it has been higher than the average for the middle western roads and the United States, while from 1911 to 1914 the operating ratio for the Pere Marquette was higher than for any of the roads under consideration (Plate XXIV). From 1911 to 1913 the operating ratio was about 80, and in 1914 reached the exceptionally high figure of 106. The low operating ratio of 1903 and 1904, and 1909 and 1910 made necessary the high ratio later; and it is quite certain that the high ratio of later years would not have existed if the operating ratio had been kept at an average comparable for instance with the Grand Rapids and Indiana Railway which fluctuates between very narrow limits.

Because of the low gross earnings per mile of road it would seem that the operating ratio of the Pere Marquette must continue for some time to be above the average of the roads under consideration, and hence the net income must be comparatively low, at least for some immediate years. For this reason it would be wise to cut down the fixed charges materially in the process of reorganization so that there will not be an undue tax on the net earnings.

The necessity of such action may be seen from the status of the income from operation per mile of road (Plate XXV). Practically without exception the net revenues per mile of road

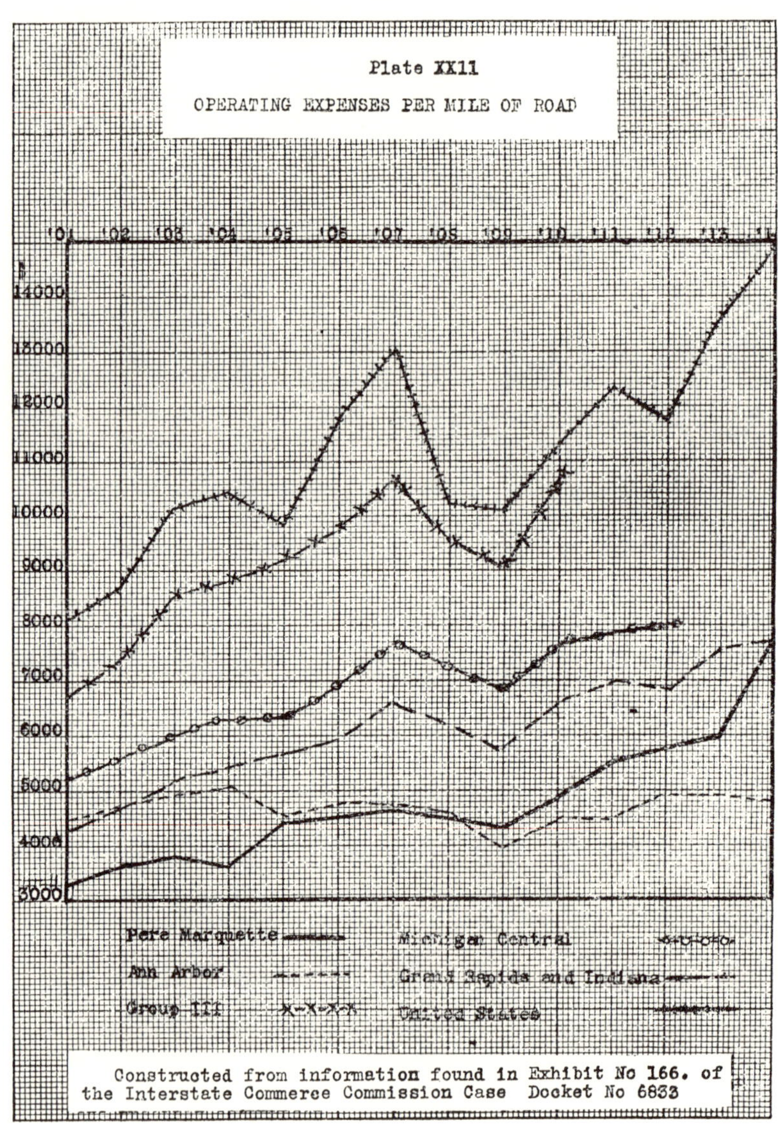

Plate XX11
OPERATING EXPENSES PER MILE OF ROAD
'01 '02 '03 '04 '05 '06 '07 '08 '09 '10 '11 '12 '13 '14
14000
13000
12000
11000
10000
9000
8000
7000
6000
5000
4000
3000
Pere Marquette
Ann Arbor
Group III
Michigan Central
Grand Rapids and Indiana
United States
Constructed from information found in Exhibit No 166. of
the Interstate Commerce Commission Case Docket No 6833

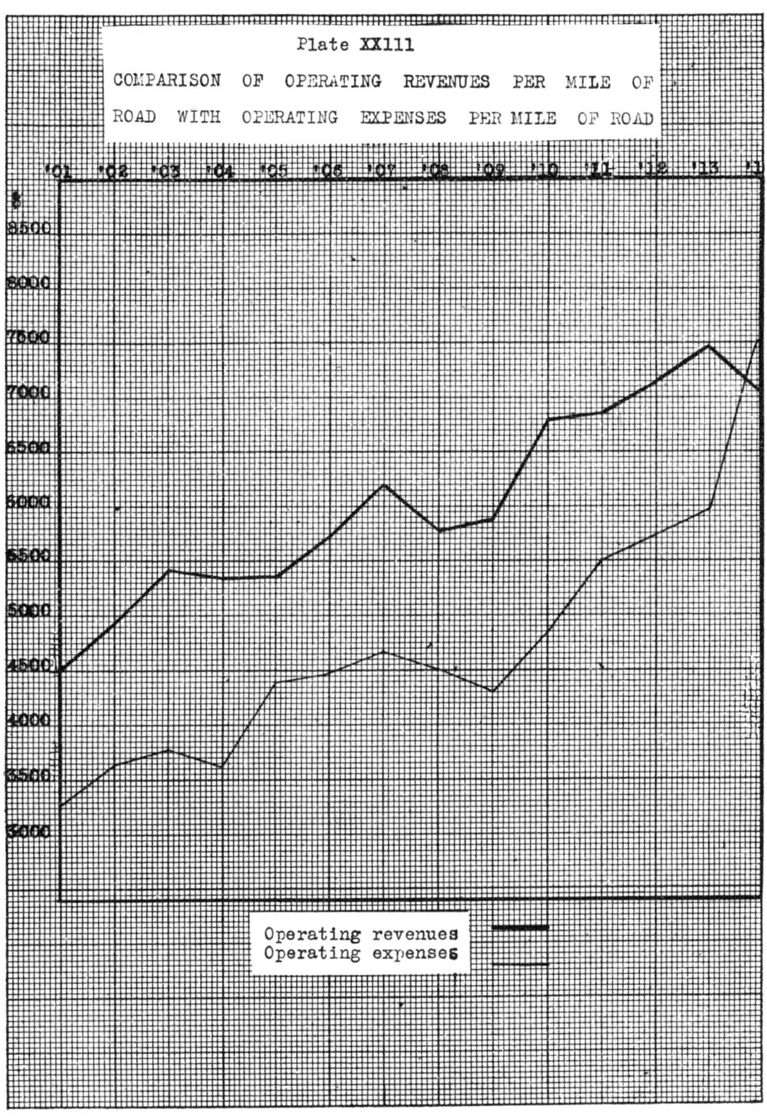
Plate XXlll
COMPARISON OF OPERATING REVENUES PER MILE OF
ROAD WITH OPERATING EXPENSES PER MILE OF ROAD
'01 '02 '03 '04 '05 '06 '07 '08 '09 '10 '11 '12 '13 '1
$
8500
8000
7500
7000
6500
6000
5500
5000
4500
4000
3500
3000
Operating revenues
Operating expenses

for the Pere Marquette are lower than for any of the roads compared with it. All of the roads had some distinct upward trend in net revenues for the period, excepting the Pere Marquette, which showed a widely fluctuating net operating revenue with a distinct downward trend in 1914. During a large part of this time the net revenues for the Pere Marquette should have been lower than they actually were, since operating expenses were not sufficiently large to take care of legitimate maintenance charges. In other words, if the operating expenses had been larger the net revenues would have been smaller; taking for granted that the gross revenues remained unchanged which was practically the case.

All in all, the Pere Marquette has a large unprofitable mileage, and it is doubtful whether this condition will be changed within the near future. As has so often been stated before, without this originating traffic the only hope of the Pere Marquette is to increase its through traffic and wait for the future development of districts which, while not now productive, will no doubt some day lend themselves to some remunerative industry.

Concerning the character of the freight traffic of the Pere Marquette, it may be considered from two aspects: first, the per cent of the total tonnage that each classification of freight comprises (Plate XXVI); and second, each classification of, freight in tons (Plate XXVII).

Taking the first method, we find that products of agriculture were about the same per cent of the total tonnage in 1914 (18 per cent) as they were in 1901 (17 per cent). Looking at products of agriculture from the standpoint of tonnage, however, it is seen that they have almost doubled during this period—increasing from 1,086,796 to 1,857,069.

Products of animals have almost doubled in tonnage, increasing from 107,965 to 204,875; but they have remained about stationary as regards per cent of total tonnage, being 1.86 per cent in 1901 and 1.88 per cent in 1914.

Products of mines have nearly quadrupled in tonnage, increasing from 1,304,260 to 4,456,930; although their per cent of the total tonnage has only about doubled, rising from 22.41 per cent to 41.01 per cent.

Products of forests have fallen off in tonnage, from 1,718,035 to 1,353,966 or over 25 per cent; while their per cent of the total tonnage decreased from 29.53 per cent to 12.46 per cent or over 60 per cent.

Manufactures have increased in tonnage but not in per cent of the total, rising from 774,144 tons in 1901 to 1,372,644 tons in 1914, while the per cent of the total was 13.31 and 12.63 respectively.

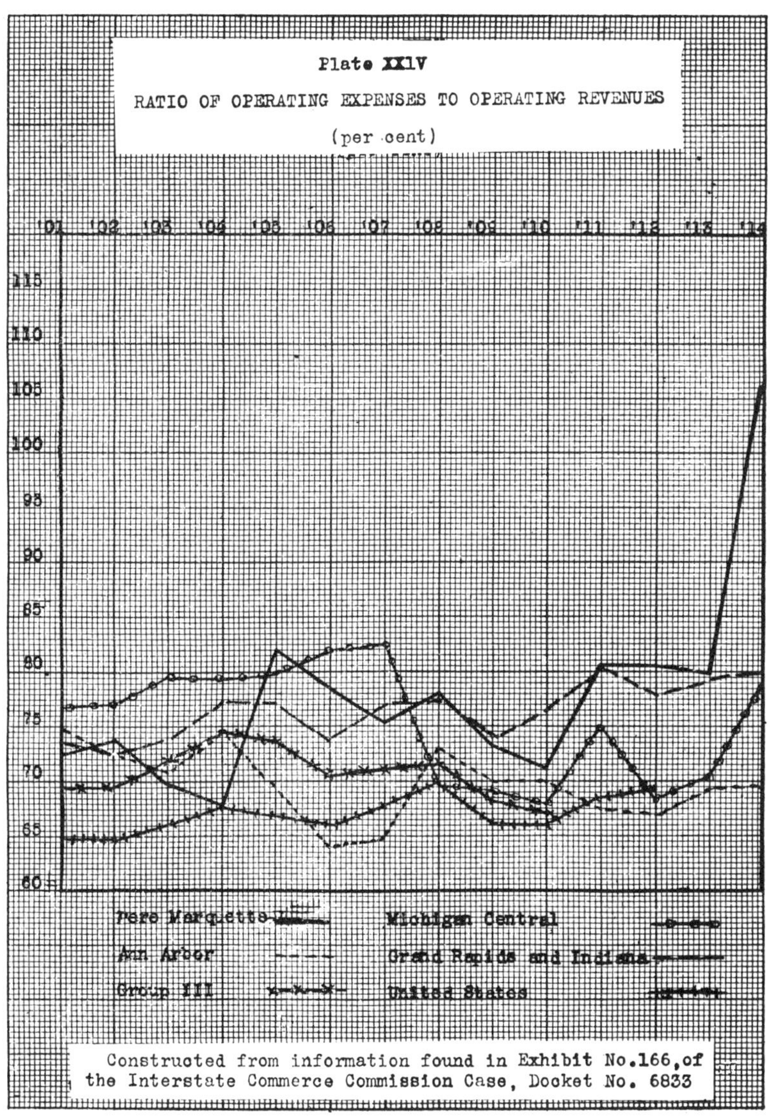

Plate XXlV
RATIO OF OPERATING EXPENSES TO OPERATING REVENUES
(per cent)
'01 '02 '03 '04 '05 '06 '07 '08 '09 '10 '11 '12 '13 '14
115
110
105
100
95
90
85
80
75
70
65
60
Pere Marquette
Ann Arbor
Group III
Michigan Central
Grand Rapids and Indiana
United States
Constructed from information found in Exhibit No.166,of
the Interstate Commerce Commission Case, Docket No. 6833

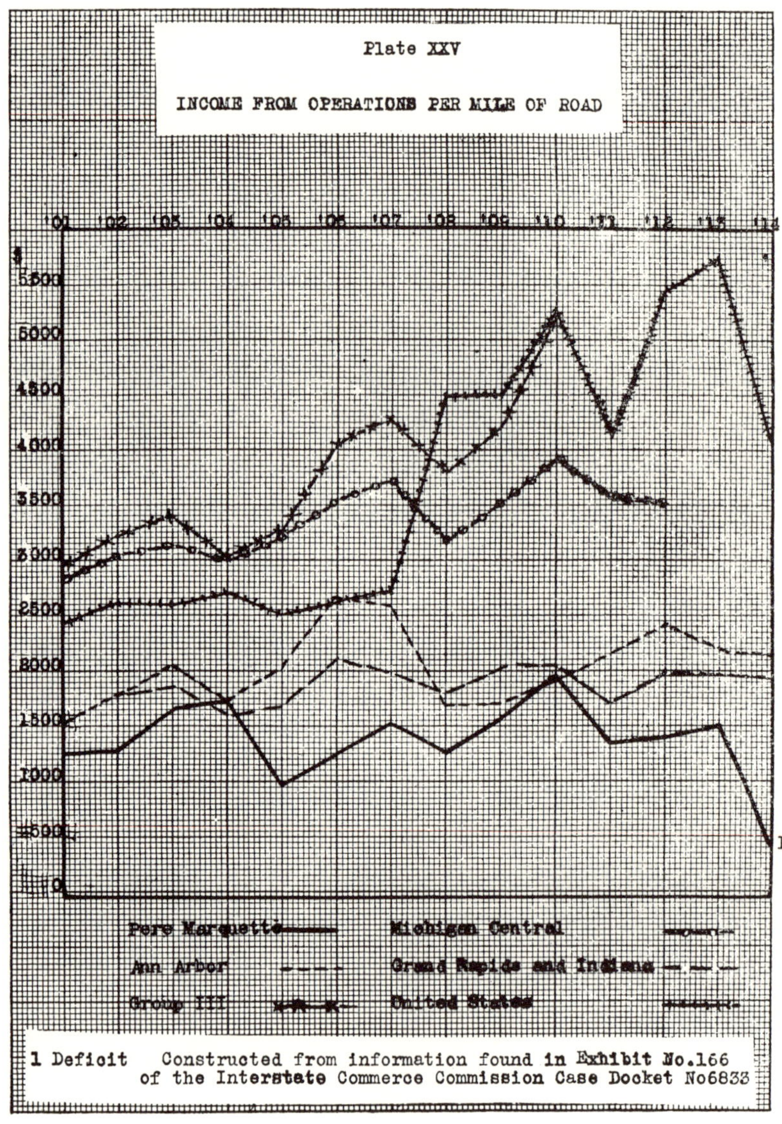

Plate XXV
INCOME FROM OPERATIONS PER MILE OF ROAD
'01 '02 '03 '04 '05 '06 '07 '08 '09 '10 '11 '12 '13 '14
5500
5000
4500
4000
3500
3000
2500
2000
1500
1000
500
0
Pere Marquette
Ann Arbor
Group III
Michigan Central
Grand Rapids and Indiana
United States
1 Deficit   Constructed from information found in Exhibit No.166
of the Interstate Commerce Commission Case Docket No6833

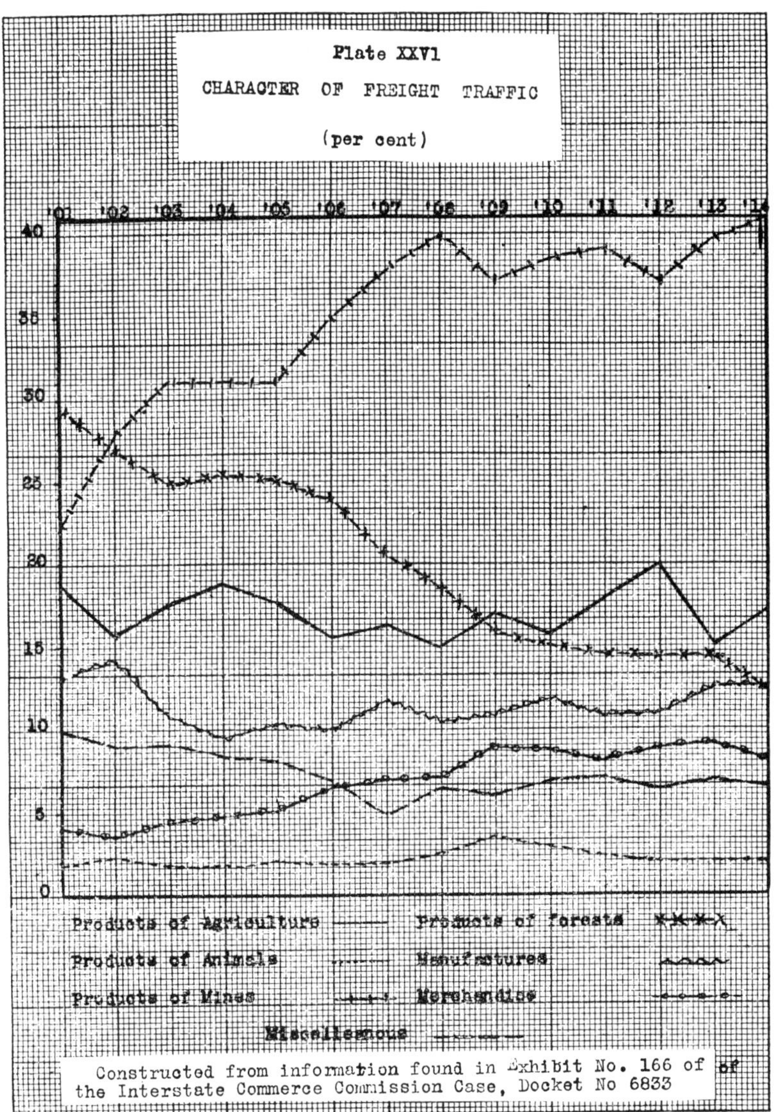
Plate XXVl
CHARACTER OF FREIGHT TRAFFIC
(per cent)
'01 '02 '03 '04 '05 '06 '07 '08 '09 '10 '11 '12 '13 '14
40
35
30
25
20
15
10
5
0
Products of Agriculture
Products of Animals
Products of Mines
Products of Forests
Manufactures
Merchandise
Miscellaneous
Constructed from information found in Exhibit No. 166 of
the Interstate Commerce Commission Case, Docket No 6833

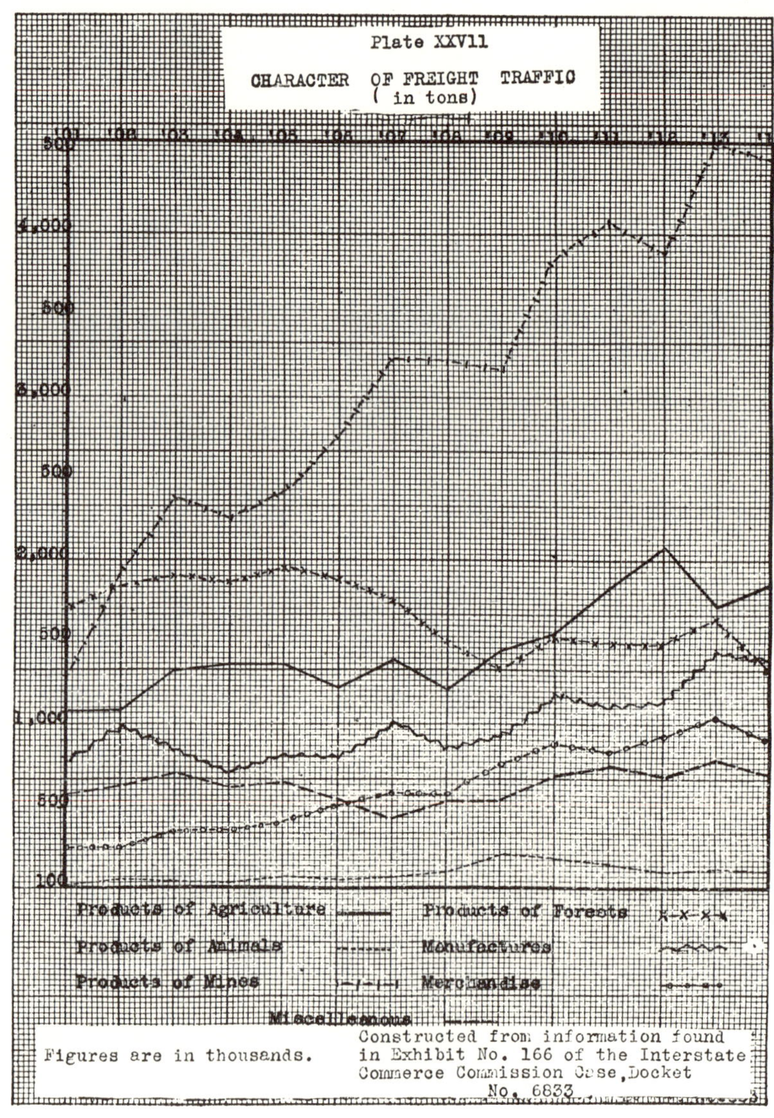
Plate XXVll
CHARACTER OF FREIGHT TRAFFIC
(in tons)
Products of Agriculture
Products of Forests
Products of Animals
Manufactures
Products of Mines
Merchandise
Miscellaneous
Figures are in thousands.
Constructed from information found
in Exhibit No. 166 of the Interstate
Commerce Commission Case, Docket
No. 6833

Merchandise quadrupled in tonnage and doubled in per cent of the total, being 248,178 tons or 4.27 per cent of the total tonnage in 1901 and 906,113 tons or 8.34 per cent of the total tonnage in 1914.

Miscellaneous tonnage increased from 579,072 to 715,831, but per cent of the total tonnage decreased from 9.95 to 6.59.

Taking all the tonnage together, it increased from 5,818,450 to 10,867,428 or practically doubled. Products of mines are seen to be increasingly important as a product of transportation, while forest products are declining, especially forest products originating in the State of Michigan. Traffic in lumber originating on other roads has remained about constant during these fourteen years as regards the per cent it holds to the total tonnage, but as regards the number of tons, it has nearly tripled, increasing from 234,970 to 648,926. This indicates that the Pere Marquette is supplanting its local traffic by traffic originating on other roads, and no doubt will continue to do so even to a greater extent. This statement not only applies to lumber and forest products but also to manufactures and agricultural products.

BIBLIOGRAPHY

GENERAL WORKS ON TRANSPORTATION

BROWN, H. G. *Transportation Rates and Their Regulations.* Macmillan, 1916.

CALLENDER, G. S. *Selections from the Economic History of the United States, 1765-1860.* Ginn, 1909.

Chicago Commercial Association. Deep Waterway Committee. *From the Great Lakes to the Gulf of Mexico.* 1906.

CHISHOLM, G. G. *Inland Waterways.* Smithsonian Institute *Annual Report*, 1907.

CLARK, J. B. *Essentials of Economic Theory as Applied to Modern Problems of Industry and Public Policy.* Macmillan, 1907.

COOKE, F. H. *Commercial Clause of the Federal Constitution.* Baker, 1908.

COOLEY, C. H. *Theory of Transportation.* American Economic Association *Publications*, 1894. Vol. 9, no. 3.

DEWSNUP, E. R. *Railway Organization and Working.* The University of Chicago Press, 1906.

DUNN, S. O. *American Transportation Question.* Appleton, 1912.

FLEMING, R. D. *Railroad and Steel Transportation.* Cleveland Foundation *Publications*, No. 14.

GEPHART, W. F. *Transportation and Industrial Development in the Middle West.* Columbia University *Studies in History, Economics and Public Law*, 1909, Vol. 32, no. 1.

HADLEY, A. T. *Railroad Transportation; Its History and Its Laws.* Putnam, 1895.

HOUGH, B. O. *Ocean Traffic and Trade.* La Salle Extension University, 1914.

JACKMAN, W. J., and RUSSELL, T. H. *Transportation, Interstate Commerce, Foreign Trade.* Whitman, 1916.

JAMES, E. J. *Canal and the Railway.* American Economic Association *Publications*, 1890. Vol. 5, nos. 3-4, pt. 1.

JOHNSON, E. R. *American Railway Transportation.* Appleton, 1903.

JOHNSON, E. R. *Ocean Travel and Inland Water Transportation.* Appleton, 1906.

JOHNSON, E. R. *Panama Canal and Commerce.* Appleton, 1916.

JOHNSON, E. R., and VAN METRE, T. W. *Principles of Railroad Transportation.* Appleton, 1916.

KIRKLADY, A. W. *The History of Economics and Transportation.* Pitman, 1915.

KIRKMAN, M. M. *The Science of Railways.* Phillips, 1894.

KNAPP, M. A. *Address, Transportation and Combinations.* American Association for Advance of Science. *Proceedings,* Vol. 55, p. 459-469. Washington, 1906.

McCAIN, C. C. *Diminished Purchasing Power of Railroad Earnings.* C. C. McCain, 143 Liberty St., N. Y., 1908.

McPHERSON, L. G. *Transportation in Europe.* Holt, 1910.

McPHERSON, L. G. *Working of the Railroads.* Holt, 1907.

MEYER, B. H. *History of .Transportation in the United States before 1860.* Carnegie Institute of Washington, 1917.

MILLS, J. C. *Our Inland Seas.* McClurg, 1910.

MOULTON, H. G. *Waterways versus Railways.* Houghton, 1912.

QUICK, J. .H. *American Inland Waterways.* Putnam, 1909.

ROPER, C. L. *Railroad Transportation.* Putnam, 1912.

SHALER, N. S. *United States of America.* Vol. 2, p. 65-133. Appleton, 1897.

SHARFMAN, I. L. *Railroad Regulation.* La Salle Extension University, 1915.

SPEARS, J. R. *Story of the American Merchant Marine.* Macmillan, 1910.

The Utilities Magazine, Vol. 1, January 1916, no. 3. *Proceedings* of the Conference on Valuation.

U. S. Industrial Commission. *Report on Transportation.* In U. S. Industrial Commission *Reports.* 1900-1902. Vols. 4 and 9.

U. S. Interstate Commerce Senate Committee on *Prompt Furnishing of Transportation Facilities,* 1908.

U. S. Corporation's Bureau. *Report* of Commissioner on Transportation by Water in the United States. Vols. 1-2, 1909.

U. S. Interstate Commerce Commission. *Evidence taken. . . .in the Matter of Proposed Advances in Freight Rates by Carriers,* 1911.

U. S. Senate, Select Committee on Interstate Commerce; *Report* submitted to the Senate, January, 1886. 2 vols.

WELD, L. D. H. *Private Freight Cars and American Railways.* Longman, 1908.

PUBLIC DOCUMENTS AND REPORTS

Annual Reports to Stockholders: Flint and Pere Marquette Railway Co.; Flint and Pere Marquette Railroad Co.; Flint and Holly Railroad Co.; Chicago and West Michigan Railway Co.; Chicago and West Michigan Railroad Co.; Michigan Lake Shore Railroad Co.; Grand Haven Railroad Co.; Chicago and Michigan Lake Shore Railroad Co.; Detroit, Grand Rapids and Western Railroad Co.; Ionia and Lansing Railroad Co.; Detroit, Lansing and Lake Michigan Railroad Co.;

Detroit, Lansing and Northern Railroad Co.; Pere Marquette Railroad Co.

Before a Committee of the Michigan Legislature, Testimony of Frederick W. Stevens. Vols. 1 and 2.

COOLEY, MORTIMER E. *Michigan Railroad Appraisal; Valuation of Physical Property*. Publications of the Michigan Political Science Association, 1900-1902, vol. 4.

Michigan Railroad Commission *Reports*.

Orders and Opinions of the Michigan Railroad Commission of the State of Michigan.

Reorganization of the Pere Marquette Railroad Co., Plan and Agreement, dated October 30, 1916.

Stenographer's Minutes before the Interstate Commerce Commission. Docket No. 6833. Vols. 1, 2 and 3.

INDEX

INDEX

Abridged corporate history chart, Pere Marquette Railroad Company.

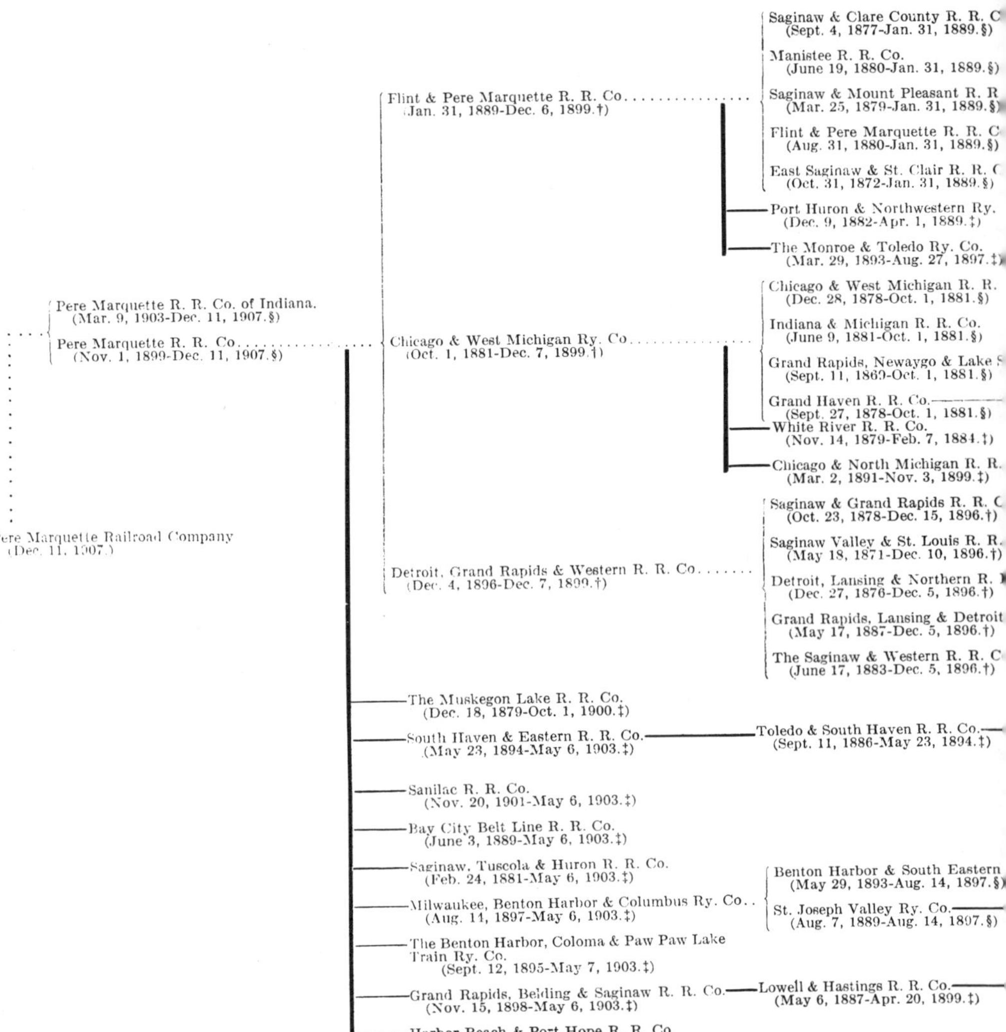

EXPLANATORY NOTES.

The first date shown under the name of each company represents the date of filing incorporation papers or agreements of consolidation, the date of change in name, etc. The second date represents, in general, the conclusion of the corporate activities of the company and is marked in each instance to indicate the nature of such change in corporate identity or ownership as follows:

§Indicates a consolidation, the date shown being that on which the agreement was filed. If filed in more than one state the date of the latest filing is used.

‡Indicates a sale, the date shown being the date of the deed.

*Indicates a foreclosure sale, the date shown being the date of the deed from the court officer. Trusteeships intervening between the sale and the final delivery to the successor company are omitted.

‖Indicates a change in name.

†Indicates a union under an agreement whereby securities of a newly organized company are exchanged for those of the constituent companies, the date shown being the date of deed of property to the new company.

¹ From the Interstate Commerce Commission Report, Docket No. 6833.